# Inviting Reflexivity into the Therapy Room

## *How Therapists Think in Action*



**Fabienne Kuenzli**

**University Press of America,® Inc.**
**Lanham · Boulder · New York · Toronto · Oxford**

**University Press of America,® Inc.**
4501 Forbes Boulevard
Suite 200
Lanham, Maryland 20706
UPA Acquisitions Department (301) 459-3366

PO Box 317
Oxford
OX2 9RU, UK


Printed in the United States of America
British Library Cataloging in Publication Information Available

Library of Congress Control Number: 2005933174
ISBN 0-7618-3334-X (paperback : alk. ppr.)

∞™ The paper used in this publication meets the minimum requirements of American National Standard for Information Sciences—Permanence of Paper for Printed Library Materials, ANSI Z39.48—1984

# Table of Contents

# Acknowledgments

So many conversations have influenced and generated this manuscript. I feel thankful for all the people who allowed me through conversations to move along in my reflections.

I want to thank, Michelle Paris, Jennifer Andrews, David Clark, Mari-José Manidi, Carol Press, Monica Casabella, Cherie Sands, Barbara Wieseman, Jeannette Ward, Lynn Stadler, Linda Gilbert, and Harlene Anderson, for allowing me to start my project, listening to me for hours talking about this project, for reading part of my work, and for providing helpful feedback. I want to thank you J.M. Massi for your helpful comments to assist me in improving the manuscript in its early stages.

I want to thank all of the participants in my research. Thank you other clinicians who thought you could or wanted to and finally were not able to participate in my research: you also helped me a lot.

I want to thank also several clinicians who told me how useful my work on reflexivity could be in our daily practice. These responses have been the fuel allowing me to continue important research in our field.

I want to thank you, my mentor and my professor, Rémy Droz. You have taught me to think on my own. You believed in me, I think more than I ever could. I am forever grateful for your assistance when needed. You have been an extraordinary teacher. This research is also my humble way to say "thank you".

I want to thank Janet Gordon for the careful and attentive correction of a manuscript that is not in my mother tongue, and the untiring work you have put into respecting my deadlines. You are a testimony to an ever-young soul. You were an angel on my path. I want to thank you, Laura Becerra for climbing the last few miles before the summit and helping me with the formatting of the text. I might have lost it, if it were not for you. I want to thank you, Michelle Fischer for assisting me with the last formatting and editing of the text, your availability, gentleness, and reassuring presence made a big difference.

To you, my clients, you allowed me to visit your life at a time of vulnerability, crisis or pain. You, all of you, remain *my best teachers* and *you are the reason of my commitment to create better practice*. I feel grateful to be working in a profession that is so meaningful, humbling, important, and fascinating.

I want to express my deep gratitude to the University Press of America for choosing to publish my manuscript.

Last but not least, I want to express here my infinite gratitude to my best friend, my soul mate, the most intriguing and challenging colleague I have ever had, and also the man of my life, André. If it was not for you and all the joyful sacrifices you did to allow me to complete this research, I do not know if I would have completed the unthinkable " this book". You were there with me in the midst of an immigration process, facing all the adversity that life sometimes has to offer. You accomplished with me the impossible. You believed in me when I could not. You have made this project possible by your ongoing support, love, enjoyment, and incurable passion for life.

To you of course my little Jessie Benjamin, the ultimate gift of my life, and the joy of my every day. Your birth in the midst of this work made it all the more important to complete this long journey through the desert (in the periphery of Los Angeles and the beginning of the Mojave Desert). You, my little boy, are a constant source of inspiration, joy, and learning and a beautiful celebration of life.

Los Angeles, California, March 2005

# Foreword

This is an important book. It will be useful for qualified psychotherapists and graduate students or interns who want to learn how to become a good clinician. It is also useful for well-trained therapists who want to understand what are the core elements of a good practitioner. Fabienne Kuenzli does an admirable deconstructive (but helpful!) work to show how therapists think in the midst of their work. This book is also a great reference for qualitative researcher in the field of "psychotherapy process research".

In the 21st century, it is now about time for clinicians to understand the underlying mechanisms intervening in psychotherapy. Clinicians need to learn to approach what Fabienne Kuenzli defines as reflection-in-action, meaning a *theory of practice* in constant transformation. Fabienne Kuenzli explores in this cutting edge of research: "How do we know what we know -as therapists- and how do we do what we do".

This book is not another treatment modality, not even a meta-model, **what this book offers is a tool to understand and refine the practice of psychotherapy**. Reflection-in-action allows the clinician to evaluate the quality of his treatment and his practice, and to measure and observe his work to potentially gather better outcomes with patients.

The subject of this book is crucial to the field of psychotherapy, but much too rarely discussed, and unfortunately fairly often simply ignored. Ignored by sheer ignorance, by arrogance, and by those annoying beliefs most of us have that scientific dogmas are more important and "more true" than the narratives we construct, than our subjective truths, or than our feelings.

In "Inviting Reflexivity into the therapy room: How therapists think in action?" Fabienne Kuenzli tells us how psychotherapists make sense of the constantly changing reality that is theirs, how they do their work and how they seem to build theory of practice. Fabienne Kuenzli explores the differences and similarities between the expert and the less expert therapists and how they practice psychotherapy. Less experienced psychotherapists seem to have a tendency to adhere too closely to their preferred theories, their allegiance, or their "school of thought", in doing so they may loose track of their client. She also mentions that less expert clinicians may feel challenged to share with their clients their emotional response. Yet, it is often the same therapists who appear to encourage or push their patient for an expression of emotions. This, as the author states, may lead to therapeutic impasses.

More experienced psychotherapists tend to complete their listening and their hearing by a third process: they use *reflexivity*. They try to listen into themselves in order to hear and to feel what reactions and which responses their inner being accepts to give to what came from the outside. These answers may be quite "cognitive", just as they are with less experienced psychotherapists. These answers may be quite different, too. Trying to identify emotional reactions, feelings, trying to detect these micro-emotions that trigger reactions and judgments without really appearing into consciousness, seem to be processes that not only are going on in experienced psychotherapists, but seem to be part of the building blocks of therapeutic attitudes, postures and interventions. The whole process has to do with the acceptance of subjective reactions as co-determinants of a therapeutic gesture, and fundamentally the acceptance of the validity of information emanating from the client. It may not sound terribly scientific, and then, subjectivity has never had such a good reputation among the scientifically minded. One thing is certain. If you want to say anything to your patient that has to do with his or hers feelings, maybe you should know first what you are feeling, your emotions, what your judgments are. It may help.

Most important reminder of this book is also that every good scientific move can only invite doubt. Every decent psychotherapist should be daily able to doubt and to question the quality of his practice. Rather than being threatened or annihilated by the doubt, the use of the postmodern critique, as Fabienne Kuenzli presents it, can be a powerful foundation for a practice that aims to defend a put the notion of ethics-in-practice and respect for clients and development of better practice in a primary position.

The field of psychotherapy has been packed for years with "content knowledge". It happens all too often that many clients may now be more informed than psychotherapists on content. This book transcends these old issues, offering ways to build theories of practices, theories based on process, first and foremost.

This is a courageous and innovative book, one of those where research and science become directly relevant and applicable to your day-to-day contact with clients. It accepts and recognizes this absolute evidence: clients are heroic and they are of the same world we are. I highly recommend this book.

The whole approach presented by Fabienne Kuenzli is objective, scientifically grounded, and labeled with an academic *nihil obstat* of excellent quality: she obtained a doctorate in psychology at the University of Lausanne, Switzerland. She also holds is also a licensed clinical psychologist in Switzerland (Psychologue, Psychothérapeute FSP) and is a licensed Marriage and Family Therapy in Los Angeles, California.

Rémy Droz, Ph.D.
Professor of Psychology, University of Lausanne, Switzerland, author of « Understanding Piaget » .

# Part one:

# Elements of theory

# Introduction

*"It is not necessary to know everything in order to understand something"*
*(Geertz, 1983, p. 120)*

In order to solve the constant and growing problems that we face in our practice, we, psychotherapists, cannot count only on the recipes or formulas learned at the University[1]. We have to improvise, struggle, and create, to gradually build a repertoire of practical knowledge, to finally feel rather comfortable in our practice. Psychotherapists are left to deal with tasks that become increasingly complex, in a field that is now uncontrollable for the human mind. It is impossible nowadays to be aware of everything that arises in our field. Meantime our patients suffer from increasingly complex issues. Multiple diagnoses are our daily bread. Changing contexts, endless psychosocial stressors, substance dependence, social and family violence, and multiple traumas add up to the profound and complete transformation of family structures. The family that we took a few decades ago as the norm has become a bizarre singleton. Our theories are less and less a comprehensive approach to the complexity we face. On a planetary level, the technological changes and the

1 This work and research was first presented and accepted by an international committee of experts for a Doctorate in Psychology for the University of Lausanne, Switzerland in September 2004. A few changes have been made to publish the present book.

growth of information request that each professional master techniques to solve new problems.

In the field of psychotherapy, *content knowledge* is not nearly enough. Content knowledge is more accessible than ever to our patient. A patient may have a more exhaustive knowledge of the existing treatment on his condition than his therapist because he has a strong investment in it. We are losing the control we thought we had over our field.

In a professional field that becomes daily more uncertain, and unstable, we need to know *how* we know. Therapists must seek a different kind of knowing that overarches the content knowing.

The purpose of this book is to explore and enhance the description of a psychotherapist's reflection-in-action (RIA). In other words, I try to approach, understand and clarify how a psychotherapist makes sense of his[2] work. Among many others, Geertz (1983) has inspired me by his reflections on local knowledge. He highlights the importance of approaching a phenomenon through narratives. He validates the attempt to define narratives by looking at the local definitions, and the vernacular. The work I present here is not a comprehensive process that aims toward a final definition. Rather, it is a continually evolving definition based upon a growing repertoire of narratives.

2 The question of using a non-sexist language is in my mind. I will not sacrifice the readability of my text for a pompous use of both gender pronouns.

I shall start with a definition of a concept I constantly refer to: reflexivity. Reflexivity is at the core of this work. It is the constant underlying theme of my thesis. I use reflexivity and reflexive processes also as a methodological tool. Reflexivity carries in its meaning a reflexive loop, a continual process of back and forth. Being reflexive means that I have an awareness of myself while I am interested in the process of the other person. At the same time, I make sense of our interaction. Reflexivity encompasses simultaneously these three movements.

In the field of psychotherapy, reflexivity means staying connected with oneself, while connecting with the patient and at the same time being able to conceptualize the work. Reflexivity is not a linear process. It is constantly inviting other levels of meta-processes.

Few colleagues asked me why I have not used the simpler concept of reflection instead. If I use the less common word of reflexivity, it is neither to confuse the reader, nor to complicate the present issue. On the contrary, by using the term of reflection, the reader can easily misunderstand what I intend to convey. Reflection encompasses a broader and often blurred definition. Reflection can be understood as a thought or an idea. Reflection can be the action of thinking as well as the result of it. It can also be used as a description of the physical phenomenon of reflecting light. The notion of reflexivity is common to the postmodern critique, which inspires me. As opposed to reflection, reflexivity implies an action from the person who wants to use reflexivity, meaning an active participation. I do not want the concept of reflexivity to be eroded. Introspection is another close but not quite similar concept. However, introspection only covers one side of the equation. Reflexivity carries a relational value that is lacking in introspection. Reflexivity demands that the person looks inside and, at the same time, at the other and at the relationship forming between the two. The term of introspection originally refers to an inward movement, where the person aims toward a better awareness of the self. Reflexivity refers to both an inward and outward movement. It is more than the sum of the two. It creates a generative movement.

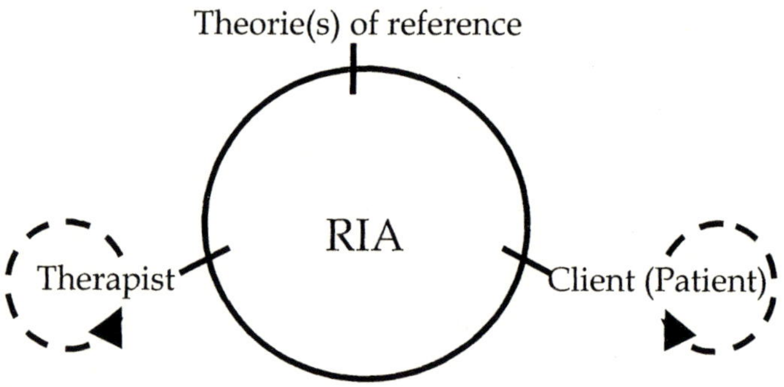


At the core of reflexivity lies the ability of the psychotherapist to put himself in the patient's shoes. By utilizing an "as if position", the psychotherapist can better imagine how it would feel to experience the effect of his interventions, words or attitudes. The "as if position" is not a tool, nor an intervention. Rather, it is a posture guided by an intent to better understand the other *in his context*. If the psychotherapist understands the "as if position" as a tool. He misses the whole point of reflexivity. Putting oneself in the shoes of the other is a reminder that building and maintaining a relationship is a work in progress. It is an attitude that expands and improves through its very use. Instead of creating a linear and unidirectional movement, reflexivity creates a circular movement and a generative loop.

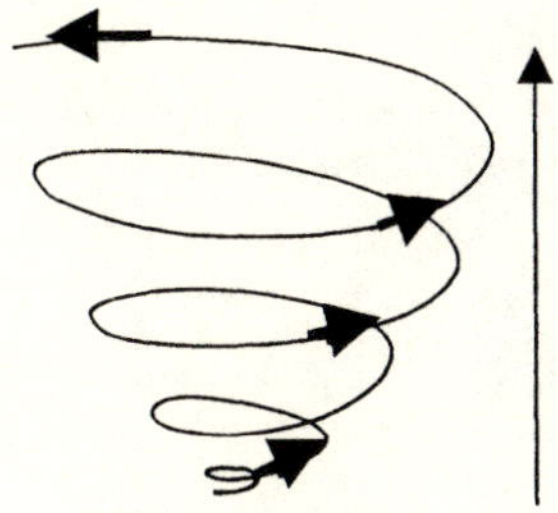

Generative loop

Reflexivity is one of the core concepts of the postmodern critique. It feeds a critique in that it implies a constant change of the point of view and the perspective one takes. The psychotherapist who uses reflexivity and practices RIA is at the heart of the postmodern critique. He remains, uncertain of the certainties. He maintains a posture of curiosity. The original idea of reflexivity lies in this never-ending movement of back and forth. Through its perpetual movement, reflexivity infiltrates doubts in the mind of clinicians. Reflexivity is an essential element of de-centration (Piaget, 1950, 1956, 1970, 1974). It enables the clinician to continually take different perspectives. Reflexivity allows the clinician to stay acutely aware of the fact that perceptions are not the world's perception. Perceptions are singular and original, but certainly not the norm.

Powerful instrument, reflexivity can also impede the psychotherapist's connection with his client[3]. If the psychotherapist pays too much attention to his reflexive processes, he may lose sight of his client. If he puts too much emphasis on articulating what is happening in the moment, he loses sight of what is in the room. Reflexivity can be productive and generative as well as destructive. Reflexivity can become an end in itself, rather than an instrument to connect. In this case, reflexivity brings a sterile self-involvement. If the only purpose of reflexivity is to turn the mirror inward, reflexivity becomes a dangerous seduction (litt. leading away from the path *se-ducare*). This narcissistic process damages the very intent of reflexivity.

Reflexivity is one of the most advanced features of humans. Reflexivity distinguishes humans from animals. It gives us the freedom to choose, rather than to be simply guided by our drive, instinct or need. Without evaluating what he does, a person just does the thing he does almost on automatic pilot. If "doing" is not processed and reflected upon, there is no choice. The sense of freedom and choice is linked to the reflexive ability. If I think while acting (or slightly before or after), then, I have power over my behavior.

---

[3] Throughout the text, I refer to both terms of client and patient. I like the word patient for its reference to what it means etymologically: "a person in a state of pain". I dislike this word because it may place unnecessary distance between the person and me. In research, there is a similarity between the words subject and object. These words add a distance between knower and to be known. The word "patient" carries notions of hierarchy, power, and assumptions of pathology. The word "client" frequently carries a mercantile connotation.

Neither needs, nor instincts, nor drives dictate my life. The choice may be small, but I have options to choose from.

RIA is the conceptualization of the psychotherapist's work. The conceptualization of the work goes far beyond a simple access to existing theories to justify and explain the work. RIA is a theorization in progress of the evolving relationship forming between the psychotherapist and his patients. RIA is a discourse forming through language. It is a thought in process, which grounds itself in the theoretical background of each psychotherapist. Reflection-in-action (RIA) is the result of using reflexivity. One cannot produce RIA without being reflexive. By practicing RIA, a psychotherapist creates a theory in motion. RIA forms a theory that emerges from the practice and that refers constantly back to it. Clinicians construct a theory of practice referring to their preferred theories. They use preexisting theories as guidelines (Cognitive Behavioral Therapy, Gestalt, Family Systems, Psychoanalysis, Object-Relation, Narrative Therapy, etc.) and refer back to them while they construct RIA. Simultaneously, they observe the forming relationship with their patients and their own response and integrate these data to form a reflection-in-action. Throughout my research, I refer to three concepts that create the evolving notion of RIA: the psychotherapist, his theories of reference, and the client (the patient). I study how these three entities interact through RIA. Reflection-in-action (RIA) maintains a difficult equilibrium among these three instances. I am interested in how this discourse can be made public for the purpose of enhancing knowledge. In order to perform RIA, clinicians often refer to an existing repertoire of practical knowledge (their clinical experience). Sort of a data bank of practical knowing, these previous clinical experiences are adapted to the present situation. RIA stays in movement and in construction. RIA is in motion because the relationship between the therapist and the client is, by nature, in movement and in constant evolution.

In a therapy session, any psychotherapist can enhance and self-train this skill of reflexivity. By practicing reflexivity the psychotherapist steps outside of the process. He takes a meta-view. The reflexive process of the psychotherapist grants the ability to decide to shift, or to maintain the direction he is taking with a client. In the effort to co-construct potentially helpful conversations with his client, the psychotherapist can, moment by moment, use this reflexive ability to control, assess and check the value of the process in which he is engaged.

My insatiable curiosity has been the fuel of this work. The questions that fueled this qualitative research are the following:

- What happens inside the psychotherapist's head?
- What is the therapist thinking, and feeling?
- How can I approach this secret place?
- How does a psychotherapist think in action?
- What are these processes like?
- How can I define the reflection-in-action of a psychotherapist, even if it seems automatic?
- What informs the next move of a therapist?

- What type of data does a clinician select?
- How does he process the information he receives? What is it that one calls clinical intuition?
- How does a therapist identify moments of movement (Rogers, 1942) in therapy?
- What criteria does the therapist use to identify them?
- Are these moments the same for the client, the psychotherapist and the researcher?
- How does a psychotherapist put this implicit, tacit knowledge into words?
- What can I do, or not do, as a researcher, to encourage RIA to happen?

Trainees and therapists in general may benefit greatly from the RIA of expert clinicians. RIA can be used to enhance the awareness of the psychotherapist. The exploration of RIA will broaden, I believe, our understanding of psychotherapy.

Before RIA is brought to language, it belongs to the domain of the tacit knowledge. I make the hypothesis that expert therapists[4] have a sense of what they are doing and how they are doing what they are doing at almost any moment of their practice. In other words, experts' RIA is elaborate and coherent. I also make the rather logical inference that the elaboration and coherence of RIA decreases along with the lack of training and experience.

---

[4] I define expert psychotherapists as clinicians who master their profession. They have demonstrated exceptional abilities. I define this concept in details in chapter 9.

There has been an almost occult quality to how the psychotherapists think in the midst of their work. My research is also an attempt to approach the "black box" (Watson, 1920), to unveil the mystery linked to psychotherapy. What do therapists do once the door of their offices is closed? Psychotherapy does not just happen. There is work behind what may appear as the magic of psychotherapy. There is a careful and methodic thinking behind each intervention. There is an immense body of knowledge, practical and theoretical. There are methods and an experienced articulation behind each good therapy session.

RIA is difficult to control and to predict. I am aware that my research may create wariness. There is something scary about this place of uncertainty. With this implicit form of knowing, how can we psychotherapists rely on our theories? We refer to theories, but not directly. Some psychotherapists may find it unappealing to participate in my research. It involves a kind of knowing that we are not clearly aware of. Theory can either be a helpful guide or an intrusion upon our ability to understand and formalize RIA.

This introduction will not be complete if I do not mention the major influence of Schön (1983) throughout my work. Schön is the first author to mention the concept of reflection-in-action. He examines the growing importance of RIA in today's professional field. He demonstrates through interviews how professionals think in the midst of their practice. Schön maintains that the best professionals know more than what they can articulate through language

(Polanyi, 1966). As Schön (1983) reminds us: "If applied science consists in cumulative, empirical knowledge about the means best suited to chosen ends, how can a profession ground itself in science when its ends are confused or unstable?" (p. 23).

My research belongs in the domain of a qualitative inquiry. Specifically, it is a *process research in psychotherapy.* Process research is a new field with a methodology in discovery. Until recently process research has created little research and its body of knowledge is rather small. Process research in psychotherapy can be traced back to the 1930s. Rogers (1942) has been credited as the first researcher to seek to identify "moments of movement". Years ago, Bannister (1981) explained the absence of publication in the field of process research in psychotherapy in a rather provocative way:

> "Its relative unpopularity may be due to the fact that it breaks the closed shop whereby only psychologists may psychologize" (p. 196). For the subject to talk freely during and after the experiment, for the experimenter to be aware of the subject's construing of the situation, for the subjects to offer their own hypotheses about what was happening and have the experimenter consider them: these are relatively rare phenomena in psychological research"(p. 197).

# An overview of my research

In chapter one, I review the interest and the purpose of this research. I present the applications and the possible developments of my research to the field of psychotherapy. Chapter two seeks an in depth definition of the notion of reflection-in-action (RIA). I review the literature on reflexivity and reflection-in-action. Chapter three, four, five and six address the different methodological aspects of my research. Chapter three discusses the founding theories of science behind the qualitative methods. I explain in chapter three the paradigmatic change that allows qualitative methodology to take place. I compare a positivist methodology to a postmodern one (or post-positivist) and what are the fundamental differences between these. In chapter four, I discuss how the field of Family Therapy and its latest development, the second-order cybernetic, informs the methodology of qualitative research. I discuss the implication of a shift from a linear paradigm of knowledge to a circular one. In chapter five, I give a history of the foundation of qualitative research. I review broadly the field of qualitative research from its birth to a well-respected (but still alternative) field of knowledge. In chapter six, I clarify and explain the methodological guidelines that I use to approach reflection-in-action. These guidelines are extracted from chapters three, four, and five. In chapter seven, I discuss the process of interview. I define an interview as a valid instrument to produce knowledge. I discuss my preparation for the interviews. I present the process of transcription and how I transform the verbatim interviews into legible ones. Chapter eight addresses the problem of interpretation of data.

Interpretation is not an isolated process at the last stage of the research process. It permeates the entire interview inquiry. I explain and define the process and the method I use for interpreting the data. I review the guidelines that assist me in interpreting the data, to overcome the obvious without adding unrelated information. Chapter nine presents the question of selection of data and the grounding criteria for this selection. I explain how I delineate the relevant units of information that will improve the description of RIA. Chapter ten discusses the definition of knowledge and the transition from a quantitative definition of knowledge to a qualitative one. The chapters eleven to thirteen contain the interviews commented and analyzed. The conclusion (chapter fourteen) summarizes the findings and presents some implications for the future. Based on these findings, I attempt to create in chapter fourteen a theory of reflection-in-action. The last chapter is an addendum. I provide the reader with an extract of my research journal. It is a more intimate approach to this research reflecting upon the inner conflicts and struggles throughout the process of this qualitative research. The last chapter may be read as a reflexive exercise during the process of writing a doctoral dissertation, or completing a research.

# Chapter I

# Why shall we study reflexivity in psychotherapy?

There are endless theories about psychotherapy, but none explains how they emerge from practice. None focuses on practical knowledge. In the field of psychotherapy, there is relatively little literature on the micro-theories of psychotherapy. As Greenberg and Pinsof (1986) state: "By and large the field of psychotherapy and the Family Therapy field in particular, lacks an explicit, specific, and behaviorally focused micro-theory" (p. 18). Hoshmand and Polkinghorne (1992) echo this statement: "There is a need for theories of action that inform practice and provide more adequate maps of the social realities of practice" (p. 62). They also support the use of reflexivity as a tool to generate knowledge: "Attention should be given to the reflective process used by skilled practitioners and field researchers as legitimate methods of generating knowledge" (p. 62). Gale (1991) encourages researchers to continue research in this domain:

> "Areas in which there continues to be a need for further investigation by Family Therapy

> researchers include: exploring the interactive talk of the clients and the psychotherapists, finding a common language of change, irrespective of the parent school of therapy, and working with the issue of the observer as helping to shape the research system" (p. 16).

The ability to reflect critically on our clinical practice when we encounter complexity and unfamiliarity is a vital element of a healthy professional practice. RIA is at the heart of what Gale (1991) calls the "interactive talk of the clients and the therapists". RIA may give psychotherapists precise information about the mysterious and sacred therapeutic alliance. RIA should inform the clinician in detail about procedures to obtain and maintain a therapeutic relationship. The development of RIA will help us clinicians to better understand, construct and maintain therapeutic relationships with our clients. The therapy office is a unique context in which the interaction between psychotherapist and client is constructed and maintained.

RIA may become a *bridging concept for the field of psychotherapy*. By enhancing and encouraging RIA, I cherish the hope for more conversation between clinicians from different theoretical backgrounds. RIA enables clinicians and researchers to discuss practice in a theoretical way, using a language relatively jargon-free.

In my daily practice and through my long training to become a psychotherapist, I have been daydreaming that a skilled psychotherapist would share with me what he is doing while constructing a therapeutic relationship. The absolute simultaneity of this exercise seems difficult to achieve. If the psychotherapist stops the session and shares his RIA, he will probably disrupt the therapy process. Such perpetual disruption of the session is an obvious obstacle to reaching a satisfying therapeutic relationship. The client runs the risk of becoming more of a guinea pig. The deconstruction of the therapy process, in the presence of the client, could disrupt and affect negatively the client. However, if the psychotherapist can share his RIA and if this process is delayed until after the session (using an audiotape or videotape), it seems manageable.

## Toward more conversations between practice and research

In essence, RIA questions and links theory to practice. RIA reminds the clinician to continually question what informs his next moves in the therapy process and from where the clinician's ideas and interventions are informed *(reflexive loop)*. RIA promotes a self-feeding dialectic between theory and practice.

Postmodernism, as a critique, requires the psychotherapist to be continually aware and to question what he knows and how he knows what he knows. Postmodernism also requires that psychotherapists question the influence of their knowledge on clients (see deconstruction in Derrida, 1967). How and what a psychotherapist knows is fluid, changeable and socially constructed. Many authors share similar concerns about the nature of knowledge and the necessity to be reflexive with knowledge (Anderson, 1997; Andersen, 1987, 1991; Brown, 1996; Danzinger, 1990; Grafanaki, 1996; Hoshmand & Polkinghorne, 1992; Kvale, 1996; Manicas & Second, 1983; Morse, 1994; Neimeyer, 1993; Polkinghorne, 1984, 1988; Reason & Rowan, 1981). These authors would like to see more links between the fields of research and practice Polkinghorne (1991a) worries about the increasing gap between theory and practice:

> "A series of survey studies has pointed out that present research in counseling and clinical psychology is little utilized by practitioners. Psychotherapists, in most instances, do not look at research to inform their practice; neither do they use the available data of research to challenge their current practice. The source of information about psychotherapy that practitioners found most useful, was their ongoing experience with clients. Only 10% reported psychotherapy research articles or presentations as their primary source of information" (p. 191).

The jargon used by researchers can be repulsive to practitioners. If one wants more permeable boundaries between the fields of research and practice, it is important that researchers "rack their brains" to make research more relevant and more readable for the clinicians. Polkinghorne (1991c) emphasizes the importance of using a common language for psychotherapists to access research: "To be useful, the results of both qualitative studies and quantitative studies will need to be reformatted and translated into the language of practitioners" (p. 111). Gale (1991) questions the very relevance of psychotherapy research if clinicians do not use it: "If psychotherapy research, whatever its multiple motivations, does not have a meaningful impact on practicing clinicians, its continued pursuit must be seriously questioned" (p. 612). Burley (1998) deplores that psychotherapists show little interest in research:

> "Until quite recently, psychology was a field made up of unrelated pockets of information that had a few clear implications for each other. While gossip travels with the speed of light, real news is very slow in circulating. Unfortunately, the same is true of science. In the last two decades, there has been an explosion of clinically relevant information coming from psychological research laboratories around the world, and unfortunately, little of it is getting to the clinicians best equipped to use that information" (p. 131).

Hoshmand & Polkinghorne (1992) explain the gap between research and practice not only by the concept of relevance or "readability" but also by the underlying philosophy of science. They encourage researchers and theorists to broaden their notion of knowledge. They invite us to realize how profoundly our notion of knowledge is colored by our a priori, our culture, and our epistemology. They highlight how the positivist mode of science has dominated the field, how it separated clinicians from researchers. They advocate, after Heron (1981), for the value of practical knowing and the necessity to study and theorize the knowledge of practice. Hoshmand & Polkinghorne (1992) emphasize the mutuality of practice and science. They propose another criterion for judging the quality of knowledge. Rather than being based upon the correspondence to reality, as the positivist science encourages, the quality of knowledge should follow a pragmatic test rather than a logical one (Margolis, 1984, 1987, 1989).

This new criterion for knowledge has immense implications for practical knowledge. In the field of psychotherapy, knowledge frequently serves to guide the psychotherapist in helping his clients. Hoshmand & Polkinghorne (1992) argue that the low interest of clinicians for research resides in the perceived incompatibility between the two fields. They defend the practical knowing as an important form of knowledge: "Practitioners depend on knowledge derived from experience and direct interaction with clients, a type of knowledge not formally admissible by the accepted scientific model" (p. 56).

Some twenty years ago already, Heron (1981) advocated for a form of science that essentially focuses *on procedural and practical knowledge.* He encouraged us to broaden the field of science and its definition:

> "Science as a process of inquiry, involves not only propositional knowledge, but also practical knowledge and experiential knowledge. Practical knowledge is evident in some skill proficiency or knack, whether physical or mental. It is knowing how to do something" (p. 27).

Schön (1983) is also in favor of a constant dialectic between research and everyday practice:

> "Clearly, then, when we reject the traditional view of professional knowledge, recognizing that practitioners may become reflective researchers in situations of uncertainty, instability, uniqueness and conflict, we have recast the relationship between research and practice. For from this perspective, research is an activity of practitioners. It is triggered by features of the practice situation, undertaken on the spot, and immediately linked to action" (p. 308).

Needless to say, extensive training is necessary to develop this highly complex, reflexive skill. Hoshmand & Polkinghorne (1992) with magisterial concision touch this crucial issue. "Reflective habits", they say, should have a central position in our professional training: "These approaches aimed at the development of reflective habits of mind should be central to our professional training. Professional wisdom should include the ability to evaluate and critique one's own understanding and actions" (p. 62). They show how RIA can enhance the clinicians' efficiency and assist them in controlling their own biases: "The purpose of developing a skillful reflection is to enhance the capacity of deliberative control over the biases that hamper full understanding and lessen practitioner's effectiveness in the context of practice" (p. 62). Further, the authors link RIA's benefits to the complex and necessary relationship between research and practice: "The implementation of these changes in professional training may narrow the gap between education for science and education for practice (...)" (p. 62).

Throughout my research, I will apply reflexivity and reflexive processes at a methodological level.

## More awareness, more reflexivity and better training

There are direct implications of my research on reflection-in-action on training. If the community of psychotherapists can approach the secret community of expert psychotherapists, if we could "read their minds" and listen to their RIA, we could better teach therapy. We could teach procedures, processes and not just content and leading theories. If we can access the narratives of the psychotherapists about the process of therapy if we can freeze the process of therapy, then we can understand, micro-analyze and teach therapy better. If we can approach therapy with a magnifying glass, we shall be more able to transmit this practical knowing to psychotherapists in training. RIA holds a fundamental role in the training of psychotherapists. They can learn form the RIA of expert psychotherapists. For further developments of our professional practices and a more proficient training, education needs to focus on the development of reflective judgment or expert RIA.

Psychotherapists in training (students, trainees or interns) should be taught to develop their RIA. By observing and understanding the experts' RIA, a therapist in training can start to build a *repertoire of practical knowledge*, a repertoire of how skilled psychotherapists think in action. Both the beginner and the advanced psychotherapist will benefit from the findings of this research by learning to broaden their awareness and understanding of the psychotherapist's process. My research can benefit the psychotherapist (new or skilled) for several reasons:

- RIA brings into awareness the implicit knowledge about therapy. This might take the form of "I know much more than what I thought I knew".

- It broadens the relationship between theory and practice.

- It helps avoid a dogmatic posture by escaping a rapid comprehension of the other without dialogical movement and enhance options for seeing the status of theories as they are: a simple approximation of reality to be integrated into a complex field. Theory is not the truth. It is just a lens.

- It encourages the very exercise of RIA and encourages the auto-corrective functions of RIA.

As a clinician, I defend the need to enhance the articulation of what I am doing in a therapy session. I believe that developing and understanding RIA is of tremendous importance. This enhancement of practical knowing is fundamental in my field. The ability to understand what I do in a session becomes crucial when I have a negative experience in a psychotherapy session. If a session goes wrong for the client I need to be able to articulate what happened and what was unhelpful (or hurtful) to the client.

This articulation and its re-mediation become an ethical duty: I *should* know what I said or did that contributed to making the session go wrong. My responsibility as psychotherapist is to provide and generate narratives that are potentially helpful for my clients. For that to happen, I have to heighten my awareness of what I do.

In this chapter I have shown how RIA can be one of the ways to enhance the efficiency of clinicians and quality of psychotherapy. RIA allows clinicians and researchers to bridge the gap that has existed between them for too long. It is a linkage between theories and practices and a way of elaborating *theories of practice.* With RIA as a focus, clinicians and researchers may together gather a better understanding of the dynamic elements of a therapeutic relationship. Finally, RIA plays an essential role in the protection of ethics, and the application of ethics-in-practice since it holds an auto-corrective function.

# Chapter II

# What is a reflection-in-action?

How does a therapist put his experience of the session, his RIA, into words? The underlying question of RIA is to understand how language brings thoughts and experience into awareness. Vygotsky (1986) discusses what he calls a shift between *inner* and *outer* talk. Vygotsky is one of the first to introduce the notion of meta-cognition (Vygotsky 1962, 1966, 1986). Vygotsky (1986) believes thoughts are formed in language. He sees language as a generative process:

> "The relation of thought to words is not a thing but a process, a continual movement back and forth from thought to word and from word to thought. (...) Thought is not merely expressed in words; it comes into existence through them. Every thought tends to connect something with something else, to establish a relation between things. Every thought moves, grows and develops, fulfills a function, solves a problem"(p. 218).

Vygotsky continues: "The connection between thought and word, however, is neither performed nor constant. It emerges in the course of development and itself evolves" (p. 255). Vygotsky's ideas are crucial to my research.

He highlights that language and thoughts are a process in constant development and a co-construction. RIA is a process, not a thing. RIA comes into existence with the language. Language is essential to RIA. Language makes the thought exist. Every thought, as Vygotsky states, is in relationship with another thought. Thought does not come out of a vacuum. Thought always evolves in a context. Therefore, thought both depends upon and influences its context. Shotter (1993) discusses Vygotsky's ideas:

> "As Vygotsky (1986) sees it, rather than issuing mechanically, from an already well-formed and orderly cognition at the center of our being, the expression of a thought or an intention, such as the saying of a sentence or the doing of a deed, first originates in a person's vague and unordered sense of the situation they are in (...). In other words, speakers are sensitive to the very act of speaking, to the kind of "links" - between themselves, their listeners and their circumstances - that they must construct as they speak" (p. 43).

Shotter (1993) highlights Vygotsky's idea about the importance of the utterance of words. Unspoken words do not have meaning. Meaning emerges from a context: "Unformulated in words, a thought-seed remains vague and provides only the possibility of having a meaning" (p. 44). Without the support of words, thoughts do not have the same strength. Thoughts become alive through language. Bruner (1986) echoes Vygotsky. He demonstrates the role of culture in shaping our thoughts and our language: "People have reasons for their actions and these reasons are contextualized and particularized" (p. 83). The works of Vygotsky (1962, 1966, 1986) Shotter (1993) and Bruner (1986) are important to comprehend the process of reflection-in-action. These authors clarify the connection between thoughts, language, and the cultural aspect of language.

The notion of tacit knowledge as created by Polanyi (1966) is important to my subject. With RIA, there is always an allusion to the tacit, the "not-yet-said" (Anderson & Goolishian, 1991b) or the untellable. Polanyi questions and redefines the complexity of human knowledge by addressing tacit knowledge: "I shall reconsider human knowledge by starting from the fact that we know more than we can tell" (p. 6). To illustrate his point, Polanyi uses the recognition of faces. For example, I cannot tell in many details why I recognize my friends' faces among thousands of other faces. Yet, in a microsecond, I can make sense of all these details and bring them to the meaning: "This is Sophie". The process is mostly tacit. The theory of Gestalt demonstrates well this global understanding that transcends the articulation of the constitutive details. The explanation of the details does not account for the whole. Only a part of the tacit knowledge cannot be put into words (the whole is greater than the sum of the parts).

For my purpose, I could classify knowing in two categories: a practical knowing (knowing how) and a cumulative (knowing what). Both knowing are important to refine the definition of RIA. Polanyi (1966) refers to the German distinction between "können" and "wissen" to further explain this difference. Neither in English, nor in

French does this subtle and crucial distinction in the use of the verb exist. "Wissen" refers to the cumulative knowing (knowing what), or intellectual knowing. "Können" refers to the practical knowing (knowing how). "Können" refers to a tacit form of knowledge. For example, swimming is a form of everyday knowing, in the sense of "können". If I am aware, when swimming, of all the moves I would probably drown. Yet, when I learned, I had to master separately balance, equilibrium, breathing and control of movement. I probably would not swim very successfully if I were fully aware of all of the sub-learning experiences involved in swimming. Once I know (kann) how to swim I can daydream or pay attention to the landscape around me. "Können" is used with actions that have become automatism, such as walking, speaking, running, swimming or driving. Much "können" become automatic and we have little interest in tearing apart its different components, unless we want to convey this knowing to somebody else. Teaching "können" knowledge requires that we take it apart into its different components.

RIA refers to a *procedural* and *practical knowing*: the knowing "how". To perform RIA a broad knowledge of the field of psychotherapy is necessary. This knowledge ("wissen") becomes integrated into the knowing "how", thus creating a skilled practitioner. Explaining the "können" or reflecting upon one's practice is essential in teaching therapists their work and how to develop competency. Therapists in training need to be aware of how expert therapists make sense of a practical situation and how they operate in the midst of a session (können). RIA also strengthens the skilled therapist and is essential to maintaining his own skills. These two forms of knowing (können and wissen) are usually interrelated. Polanyi (1966) refers to the diagnostic ability of the clinician to show how these two modes of knowing are interrelated "a knowledge which intimately combines skillful testing with expert observation" (p. 7).

## Reflexivity and awareness

Sometimes we reach a higher level of awareness when we know how we do what we do. The second level of awareness is hard to achieve. Reflexivity is comparable to the awareness of awareness. It belongs in the domain of meta-cognition: I know *how* I know and I know *what* I know. I also know what I do not know. For example, when I go to a long and boring meeting I know that I tend to become withdrawn and irritable.

With this second level of awareness the notion of choice and agency unfolds. Choice unfolds, because I know how I function. Since I am aware of how I function, I can change it. Knowing how I function gives me the freedom to act differently than if I was unaware. Having this acute level of awareness implies the possibility to make choices. To return to my example, I now have choices: Instead of feeling angry or resentful at my boss for sending me to this meeting, I recognize I have choices: I can bear with it or I could avoid it. I take responsibility for making choices. If I avoid this meeting, I may endure consequences, since it was clearly my boss's order. If I stay in the meeting, I still have choices: I could speak up, rather than withdrawing. Chances are that if I get involved, I will be less bored. When there is reflexivity the choices I face become almost endless.

With tacit knowledge we access a more constructivist ideology, which places us as creator of our world, rather than as actors in someone else's. Bannister (1981) stretches the importance of reflexivity and its impact on how we approach "reality".

> "Reflexivity is at the heart of personal construct theory. At the heart of most psychological theories is a fundamental distinction between scientist and organism. They provide different languages for the two. They imply that the scientist is psychologically a very different kettle of fish from the subject" (p. 194).

Bannister (1981) maintains that the reflexive process is profoundly compatible with a constructivist approach (Kelly, 1955). This reflexive function (or awareness of awareness) is essential in the psychotherapy process. I would be tempted to say it is almost within the job description of a psychotherapist. One of the common goals of a psychotherapist is to lead patients to become aware of their own processes. The practice of reflexivity is both fine and difficult. It requires an access to the procedural knowing and the processes of the patient.

The first challenge of tacit knowledge and practical knowing is our traditional logic. With tacit knowledge there is more information and, especially, more uncertainty than with Aristotelian logic. For Polanyi (1959), the participation of the knower in shaping his knowledge is "now recognized as the true guide and master of our cognitive powers" (p. 26).

We should not seek knowledge as an object to hold on to like an anchor, nor as a belonging. Rather, we should immerse ourselves in the personal, relational, circular, generative, sometimes even contradictory process of knowing.

> "I suggest that there is a tacit dimension of mutual gazing (and associated signs) that enables us at a basic level of awareness to agree about the use of words. That dimension involves a pre-linguistic experiential knowing that is primarily relational. What we know is the relation between the interconnectedness of our presence to each other, our world, our eyes, and other signs. Such knowing is tacit, inchoate, unfocused. It does not of itself give us explicit propositional knowledge of facts and truths about ourselves and our world, but it enables us to agree on how to use language to make such propositions. Nor, of course, does it do so alone: there is also touch, and, tangential to the gaze, facial expression, gesture of head, arms and hands, sounds and so on, which constitutes a ground for the figure of explicit knowledge" (Heron, 1981, pp. 25-26).

Heron highlights the relational nature of reflection-in-action (RIA). Heron (1981) notes that the tacit is only part of the interaction. The tacit creates a basis for explicit knowledge.

## Schön's categories of reflection-in action

Schön divides RIA into four categories: frame analysis, repertoire building, fundamental methods of inquiry and overarching theories and reflection-in-action. He also argues that professionals' practical knowing is trainable. Should a psychotherapist use Schön's four categories of reflection-in-action he will enhance his RIA; he will gain in competency. For each category presented, I give a practical example as applied to the therapeutic process.

*Frame analysis.* By frame analysis, Schön means how to identify and define a problem and place it in a sub-category of known phenomena, therefore creating a micro-theory to fit the new and unknown. When using frame analysis, the clinician strives to identify and describe ways in which he frames the problems, situations and roles. The practice of frame analysis enhances the psychotherapist's ability to be aware of and remodel his tacit frames. Frame analysis reveals possible ways of making sense of a unique situation. This form of reflection-in-action (RIA) shows the relativism of the choice of a particular frame. That is: If I take a psychoanalytic lens, I may frame a clinical question this way, but if I take a cognitive behavioral approach, I will understand this problem in another way. Frame analysis prevents dogmatism and rigid thinking. Schön explains the major advantage that professionals gain from practicing frame analysis: "When a practitioner becomes aware of his frames, he also becomes aware of the possibility of alternative ways of framing the reality of his practice"(p. 310).

*Example.* I have in my office a highly suicidal patient. I follow the logic: "Life is first, therapy second". First, I will, along with providing support, assess the acuteness of the crisis of my patient in his context. His context is essential because if my patient has a supportive and engaged family support he will be in less risk than a patient who perceives himself as having nothing to hold on to. First, I make a careful assessment of the suicide risk by asking my patient if he has a plan, a weapon, lethal medication or drugs at home, or a date for his death; I do so maintaining a strong therapeutic alliance that will allow me to serve my patient. Other factors enter into the assessment, the history of the patient, the history of loss, religious beliefs, impulsivity, command hallucinations, trauma, a history of substance use, a history of suicide attempts or suicide within the family, or a sudden feeling of happiness after a profound depression. I assess the necessary level of care to maintain my patient's safety. I discuss the need for hospitalization. If I judge it appropriate I treat my patient from the office, providing as much support as needed, but as little as necessary. I want to provide the least restrictive environment to protect maximum freedom. I construct with my patient and frequently his environment, a plan to maintain maximum safety for my patient. This plan may involve in some cases a 24 hours watch from the family members. I increase the frequency of sessions, and make myself availability to my patient. I may discuss, create and sign with a no-harm contract. I carefully monitor any threats to the therapeutic alliance, or possible ruptures of alliance. I can build with my patient a simple, step-by-step of daily activities schedule to assist him to reestablish a sense of a routine. This will help my patient access a sense of worth and "make it through the day". I may call my patient between appointments to check on him and to allow him to remember and maintain the work done in session. I provide emotional support and convey kindness and warmth, throughout each of my interventions. Throughout this crisis, since my patient is eminently distressed my position in the therapy will be different, more directive and structured than I would be otherwise. This will assist my patient in having a sense of containment that is probably momentarily not available. Once the basics are covered and the high risk of suicide is controlled (in reality it is rarely that linear), my frame analysis is that major depression involves on a very passive position. My frame analysis in this example can be that my patient uses all his energy to cover aggression and to turn inward the energy that should be directed outside. I ask myself: What may stop my patient from directing his aggression outside? What may be the constraining ideas (such as: It is mean to be angry with somebody, I should not feel that)? I suspect that a profound need is not attended to and the person is suffocating. Aware that I am doing a frame analysis, (i.e. aware that what I have is only hypotheses); I direct and create interventions to promote a more active stance for my patient. The methods I use vary. I may embrace a whole range of interventions. I custom-build interventions depending on my patients' needs, my hypotheses, their response, their need, the context, and the quality of our therapeutic relationship. Based on my frame of theoretical and clinical reference, I have several choices:

- I can help my patient be more aware of what he does to himself by telling him what my theories are about depression. In other words, I help the patient develop a meta-awareness of how he operates (or awareness of his procedural memories). I therefore give him the option of choosing to do something else. In Schön's words, I help the patient access an analysis of his frames.

- I can offer the patient a more active position by saying: "So you are really angry with your wife because she left you. If she were in the room right now, what would you tell her? What prevents you from being openly angry with her?" These interventions suggest a more active stance by having the patient work hard on unusual questions.

- If I have access to the family of my suicidal patient, I may work with the whole family and help the family to construct a "people sculpture". This concept invented by Satir (1983) aims to represent how the problem affects the whole family without using words. Sometimes, Satir said, "words are stuck". It is useful to use a different channel of expression, especially in the domain of trauma where the limbic system is involved and may not respond well to cognitive directives only. I may ask the family to construct with their own bodies a "living sculpture" of how the problems affect the family and my patient. This helps my patient visualize and experience differently how the problems affect him and his family. This helps the patient to perceive the problems as "outside" of him, as an isolated identity. Departing from the common mental health representation that asserts that the location of the symptoms is within our selves, this surprising intervention may help my patient to objectify his problems and fight *them* better. As defined by the Narrative Therapy movement (White, 1886, 1987, 1988a, 1988b, 1989, 1991, 1995; White & Epston, 1990; Winslade, 1997; Winslade & Monk, 1999), externalization is a helpful way to put metaphorically the problem "outside" of the person through the use of language. That may bring a more acute awareness of *how* the problem causes and maintains the suffocating feeling in my patient. The patient may do a physical action to pull away from the problem. This movement of physically pulling away from the problem forces the client to view the problem as a separate entity, as a negative entity, and as something that is *not he.* This is what White (1991) calls the "externalization of the problem". This process leads the patient into an active stance.

- I can also have my patient discuss with me the influence of his negative self-talk. I may assist him in understanding the catastrophic thinking he constructs. I may further investigate how this thought process affects his world and the narratives he creates about his life. I may reach the same goal by asking a set of questions that invites him in a more active position: "What do you do to yourself? What do you imagine this negativity does to your life? What is the history of this negative self-talk? What can you tell me about this negative self-talk? Who did you inherit it from? Where was it born? Who did it damage the most in your family? Who escaped it in your family, do you know? Has it always been part of your life? Have you ever been tired of it? Have you ever wanted it out of your life, even just for a moment? What do you think this negative self-talk stole from you? Are there any alternatives to suicide that this negative self-talk may hide from you?

Through these examples it is important to note that a therapist's interventions will take on meaning and pertinence in his contact with patients. The pacing of the interventions needs to follow the rhythm of the patient and the relationship with the patient, following the brilliant inspirational work of

Erickson (Erickson, 1962; Erickson, Rossi & Rossi 1976; Erickson & Rossi, 1979; Rosen, 1982). The patient's response to a particular intervention informs the therapist's next move. In other words, I know by the patient's response if an intervention works, or if I should offer another one. The problem of suicide in therapy involves multiple factors: ethics, responsibility, treatment, availability of the therapist, emotional response of the therapist, and legal issues. The success of treatment seems to benefit from having or developing a strong social support around the patient. The success of treatment depends on a strong therapeutic alliance.

Back to the frame analysis, the clinician who uses this sub-category of RIA needs to be able to articulate how he makes hypotheses and frames a clinical problem.

The various interventions I have suggested in this example are based on different approaches: Family Therapy, Gestalt Therapy, Cognitive Therapy, and Narrative Therapy. Frame analysis allows the clinician to realize that his interventions are not the only possible interventions. This nuance is crucial. When the clinician knows that he uses a lens (a theory) he is more flexible about shifting his lenses, than if he applies *the only possible and helpful intervention.* Frame analysis inserts awareness into our discourse and forces us to reflect on our practice. It inserts necessary and useful doubts about our daily practices.

*Repertoire building.* Building a repertoire is a way to store in the clinician's memory a great number of therapeutic experiences and interventions. The nature of this repertoire is therefore essentially practical, since it contains resolutions of clinical dilemma. When a practical situation does not fit the available theories of action, the therapists may feel stuck and confused. It is a method, which leads from initial framing to outcome. If a clinician associates this unfamiliar situation with a more familiar one he may regain a sense of control. This association is a helpful and a successful example of repertoire building, which is a sub-category of RIA. The greater number of familiar situations the clinician can refer to, the larger his repertoire is and the easier it will be for the therapist to maintain a sense of control in a confusing and new situation. Schön (1983) says about repertoire building, that rather than focusing on "the starting situation, the action taken, and the results achieved", cases of problem solving should also reveal the "path of inquiry" (p. 317). Repertoire building refers not only to its content, but also to practical and procedural information. Building a repertoire of RIA is building a set of "I know how" essential in the profession of a psychotherapist.

*Example.* Sarah, 16 years old, presents with a complex and apparently frustrating issue. She is struggling with a secondary form of encopresis. She also suffers from mild mental retardation. I reflect during the session: I have worked successfully with several cases of encopresis but only with young children. This may be challenging work. I have never had a situation just like that. I have worked extensively with teenagers and I rely on what I already know to build a strategy and a treatment plan with my client. I construct new interventions based on the ones I have applied successfully in the past. The situation seems *a priori* unfamiliar, but it reminds me of similar situations. I first focus on how to present the problem in a non-shaming way to Sarah, and Sarah's family, so that the family and my patient will all work *with me* on reducing the importance of the problem. I intend to avoid and/or dismantle the possible dynamic of exclusion and scapegoating linked to the most embarrassing problem (encopresis). I try to do the same with the larger system: school, friends, and the extended family. I join with Sarah and her family against the problem of encopresis. I encourage them to work with me against the problem rather than becoming resistant to my interventions. The use of externalization helps me in achieving this goal (White, 1990). I ask externalizing questions to reach this goal:

- ❑ How much of the time are you in control of your sphincter, Sarah?
- ❑ Is there any time Sarah uses the toilet successfully? How much of the time is encopresis in control?
- ❑ Who in your family hates encopresis the most?
- ❑ What is encopresis stealing from your daughter?
- ❑ Could you, Sarah, draw for me the ugly face of encopresis?
- ❑ If encopresis had a size, (a color, a shape, a smell, a texture) what would it look like?
- ❑ What would we see if encopresis were no longer part of the picture?
- ❑ Who would like to see encopresis disappear?
- ❑ How would Sarah be different if encopresis was no longer part of the picture?

With these interventions, Sarah and, ideally these around her will see the problem as outside of Sarah.

Second, I will explain the specifics of the training for encopresis (i.e. increasing the awareness of the sphincter functions and re-learning its control). I will underline with my client Sarah and her family that there will be rocks on the road and that, as in any kind of tough training, accidents are expected. I will also assist Sarah with remembering my interventions outside of the room; I will use her family support to do so, knowing her difficulty in building long-term memory. I will build charts, signs with the family to assist Sarah in remembering with signs, colors, even sounds in her home, that she may need to go. I have done several similar interventions in the past that have been quite successful. If this strategy does not work, I have other ideas of interventions to try. I also have a good network of supervisors and colleagues, with whom I can consult if I need more ideas or references.

This example demonstrates the general and simple idea of repertoire building. If I have a large enough toolbox of therapeutic interventions my level of confidence is as high as my sense of competence. When accessing repertoire building, the therapist starts with some pre-known schemes about how to react and what to do in a particular situation. This form of RIA is in construction, since the repertoire keeps building. The therapist uses the known to adjust it to the new situation.

*Fundamental methods of inquiry (or overarching theories).* They are the third category of reflexive practice. Fundamental methods of inquiry (or overarching theories) are connected to both repertoire building and frame analysis:

> "By methods and theories fundamental to a practice, I mean those that some practitioners have learned to use as springboards for making sense of new situations which seem, at first glance, not to fit them. In this sense, an overarching theory and a generic method of inquiry, which is inseparable from it, are used to restructure a situation so that, eventually, one can validly say that the theory fits the situation" (Schön, 1983, pp. 317-318).

Methods of inquiry describe the overall strategies developed by skilled clinicians to use in a variety of situations. Schön observes that frame analysis and a repertoire of strategies need a developing theoretical framework to support the clinical practice. For the clinician, the more explicit these fundamental methods of inquiry and overarching theories are, the better. A theoretical framework creates both a sense of coherence for the therapist and the ability of connecting seemingly different clinical episodes.

*Example.* I use the previous example of encopretic behavior to exemplify my overarching theories. Schematically, the overarching guidelines to which I refer include the notions of Family Systems, context-dependence, circularity, relationship, and responsibility, (and finally my three favorites: reflexivity, positioning and ethics in practice). These guidelines lead my interventions. Back to my previous example, I will make sure that she can first access the basics (i.e. toilet paper, privacy, sufficient supplies of underwear) to follow up on the basic requirements of hygiene and to apply my interventions. Thus, my interventions will be context-dependent. My approach is influenced by Family Therapy and Gestalt Therapy, I will therefore not invite my patients to discover the cause of the behavior, but rather I will be inclined to assist them in understanding the way they function (I will focus on the how instead of the why). I will highlight the procedural functions (encouraging the awareness of how you do the things you do), rather than why. I will focus on what needs to happen so that something different may happen.

*The process of reflection-in-action.* The fourth type of reflexive practice described by Schön is the exercise of RIA while the clinician works. This reflexive practice is more than mere observation of the process. The psychotherapist reflects on his theories of practice and modifies them when necessary. Reflexive practice includes the identification of the conditions that encourage or prevent RIA. Schön (1983) talks about the process of RIA as also a research method, which invites the researcher to be an active and involved participant. The therapist does not function as a mere user of the researcher's product: "In order to study RIA, the researcher must learn an art of experiment in which reflection-in-action plays a central part. Reflective research requires a partnership of practitioner-researcher and researcher-practitioner" (Schön, p. 323). Thus, RIA encourages flexible boundaries between research and practice.

*Example.* The more a psychotherapist stops during a session, or reflects after a session, the more RIA he practices.

The questions prone to generate RIA are:

- Wait a second... What did I do?
- What will I do?
- Why did I say that?
- How did I inform my intervention?
- What is my intention?
- What are my theoretical underpinnings?
- How do I make sense of that?
- If I were to do it again, what would I do differently?
- What would I do the same?
- Was this intervention helpful for the patient?
- How do I intervene ethically?
- How do I promote ethics?
- What could I have done that could have been more helpful?
- What was the client's reaction?
- Why did the client react this way?
- What is the effect of my questions?
- How do I influence the process?
- What is happening?
- What is the process? Does it remind me of something else?
- How do we connect?

The practice of RIA is demanding. This process requires ethics and discipline. It also requires a general desire to possibly change, improve and question one's daily practice. Schön (1983) warns us about the still fragile status of RIA as professional knowledge: "Nevertheless, because professionalism is still mainly identified with technical expertise, RIA is not generally accepted -even by those who do it - as a legitimate form of professional knowing" (p. 69). Schön (1983) describes RIA as the capacity to engage in a double vision that does not require us to stop and think. It is the capacity to keep alive, in the midst of an action, a multiplicity of views of the situation: "It does not interfere with action, but contributes to the inquirer's readiness for the mode of action I have called reflective conversation with the situation" (p. 281). This attitude of wondering about one's practice and expanding upon it is the essence of a good clinician. In other words, the psychotherapist is a researcher. He questions and aims to improve his practice. RIA is enhanced and deepened by its very exercise. The more I question my practice, the more articulate I become about how I inform my next intervention with clients and the better I am able to communicate with other clinicians or to look onto research for answers. This is a circle of knowledge. Schön (1983) comments:

> "Here, the exchange between research and practice is immediate, and reflection-in-action is its own implementation. Nevertheless, there are kinds of research, which can be undertaken outside the immediate context of practice in order to enhance the practitioner's capacity for reflection-in-action" (p. 309).

## Research as an everyday practice

Several authors hope to transform our professional attitude into a broader and more invested interest in research (Anderson, 1997; Brown, 1996; Hutchinson & Wilson, 1994; Lamb & Huttlinger, 1989; Rober, 1999; Schön, 1983; Speed, 1999; Tomm, 1983, 1987, 1988, and 1991; White, 1988b). These authors encourage clinicians to take on a more research-oriented attitude, not only by reading research, but also by doing research in their daily practice. They warn therapists of the risks of being on automatic pilot, instead of using RIA to guide their practices. Selekman (1997) says about RIA:

> " With RIA the therapist seeks new ways of approaching client's problem situation in a future therapy session, accepts the possibility that the client's problem situation may not fit any pattern of understanding in the therapist's present repertoire, or accepts that he or she has tried to make the client's problem situation conform to a particular theoretical orientation. (...) One famous reflective practitioner was the physicist Niels Bohr. Bohr was never found of axiomatic system and declared repeatedly: Everything I say must be understood not as an affirmation, but as a question ".

The use of RIA should be the cornerstone of our profession. Brown (1996) adds the meta-level and declares that not only should we reflect on our actions, but also on our RIA. Schön (1983) warns:

> "Many practitioners locked into a view of themselves as technical experts, find nothing in the world of practice to occasion reflection. They have become too skillful at techniques of selective inattention, junk categories, and situational control, techniques, which they use to preserve constancy of their knowledge-in-practice. For them uncertainty is a threat; its admission is a sign of weakness" (p. 69).

For Lamb & Huttlinger (1989), the reflexive process overlaps the research process as well as the therapeutic process. Both authors declare that reflexivity is "a self awareness and an awareness of the relationship between the investigator and the research environment" (p. 766). Tomm (1983, 1987, 1988, and 1991) presents an extensive and highly clinically relevant research on how therapists frame their questions. He maintains that therapeutic interventions come from different postures (overarching theories). Tomm (1988) notes that most therapists base their clinical decision on a moment-by-moment basis before asking a question. Tomm expands on the importance and the art of questioning by clinicians and the importance of using reflexivity as a constant scanner: How should I ask this question? What will the effect of this question be on my client? Is that a question, or a covert statement, or worse judgment? What effects am I searching for? White (1988b) talks about a similar process. He emphasizes the importance of the psychotherapist's reflexivity. White explores the effect of different styles of questioning on patients, as well as on the therapist. He advises clinicians to be aware of the power of questions and how words may shift the reality that the psychotherapist is trying to co-create with his patients.

Different words are used to describe RIA: meta-process, self-report, awareness of awareness or second-order change. Several authors (Anderson, 1997; Burley, 2000; Brown, 1996; Dreyfus & Dreyfus, 1988; Greenberg, 1984a, 1984b; Kuenzli-Monard, 2001; Piaget, 1950, 1956, 1970, 1974; Polkinghorne, 1991b, 1991c, 1994; Rennie & Toukmanian, 1992; Rober, 1999; Schön, 1983; Sluzky, 1985; Speed 1999; Tomm, 1987, 1988, 1991; Watzlawick, 1984) talk about the reflexive stance of the therapist. They have named the process of RIA differently, but they all refer to the same type of process. In this reflexive stage, a different figure-ground relationship becomes accessible. The therapist is stepping outside of the process. He is taking a meta-view. The reflexive ability implies eventually having the choice to change the behavior (i.e. pattern or action). Reflexivity brings into awareness the ability to choice involved in change. Family Systems theorists and Therapists call this reflexive ability "Second-Order change" (Sluzki, 1985). Gestalt therapists call it "awareness of awareness" (Resnick, 1995). For Piaget (1950, 1956, 1974), reflexivity is the culminating stage of cognitive development, what he calls "operations on operations".

Let me now examine in detail some definitions of RIA. Brown (1996) defines RIA as a process related to self-awareness: "Self-awareness and awareness of others lead the way to presence, responsiveness, direct communication and contact; provided one is able to put words to one's experience" (p. 66). Brown presents a powerful idea. She implies that presence is not a given; neither is it necessarily a natural ability of a psychotherapist. Moreover, she says that RIA could play a major role in developing and building presence for the psychotherapist. Brown (1996) provides a list of the purposes of what she calls meta-processes:

> "To unravel and puzzle out the events that have been taking place. To clarify the motivations and social dynamics behind the event. To reflect on and reveal the values, experiences, and observations. To allow conflicting views to surface and to highlight relationships, informal rules, and covert alliances. To share what has been learned and explicate the steps and operations that facilitated or interfered with the learning or task. To show when there has been no closure to the interaction, and to create the possibility to come to resolution and closure. To proceed with a new pursuit" (p. 73).

Rennie & Toukmanian (1992), in their qualitative research, use the word *self-report* to name RIA or similar processes:

> "The term *self-report* refers to therapy participants' representation of their experience of therapy. Self-report involves a variety of forms of representation such as choices among numerical alternatives on rating scales; selection among prepared items in inventories, endorsement of items on checklists and written responses to either structured or unstructured interviews. It is pertinent to both the paradigmatic mode and the narrative mode of explanation, depending on how self-report is used. Self-report then provides the researcher with an

> opportunity to get *inside* therapy, in contrast to opting to stay *outside* of it when using coding systems" (p. 243).

Rennie & Toukmanian refer to Rorty's earlier work when they discuss the importance of the reflexive process and what happens when the psychotherapist get stuck in his practice and does not know how to intervene with his client or just more generally how to interact:

> "At the level of a person, behavior is seen as an expression of agency in the form of intentionality and will. Within the phenomenology of agency, it is as if the person not only is *constituted of* beliefs, values, needs, and desires but *has* them as well. Thus, a person may not only act in terms of them, the person is determined by them; in acting upon them, the person is determining them. It can be maintained that neurosis may be seen as a state of being in which the individual is determined by beliefs and values and incapable of intervention on them" (Rorty, 1976, p. 238).

## The gift of neuroscience

The definition of RIA will be incomplete if I do not mention the contribution of the field of Neuroscience. The recent development of the research on memory and consciousness brings much to RIA (Baddeley, 1997; Cozolino, 2002; Damasio, 1994, 1999; Iacoboni, Woods and Brass, 1991; Schacter, 1994, 2001a, 2001b, 2001c; Sherry and Schacter, 1987;

Siegel, 1999; Squire, 1987, 1994; Squire & Zola-Morgan, 1991; Stern, 1995; Tulving, 2000). Tracing the development of research on memory, the early seeds were planted by Maine de Biran (1804/1929). Called at the time a philosopher, this French intellectual understood already the immense complexity of memory. He postulated that there are three different kind of memories: "They depend on different mechanisms and can be characterized by different properties: Mechanical, sensitive and representative memory" (p. 4). His three sub-categories of memory were:

- the mechanical memory, that is the non-conscious memory, (motor and verbal skills),
- the sensitive memory encompassing recollection of feelings, affects, or fleeting images (also non-conscious),
- and the representative memory.

The relevance of the information provided by neuroscience for RIA is the distinction made between the declarative or explicit memory and the "procedural" or implicit memory (Schacter, 1987). *RIA is a link between the two.* It is the ability to retrieve through conscious recollection and convey through verbal declaration procedural practices or knowing "how to". Practically if you as a therapist would like to encourage your client's recollection of procedural memories, you would ask questions like:

Do you remember what just happened a second ago?
Can you describe it for me in great details.
Could you put words on what you just did?
And right before that?
And right before that?
And right after that, what did you then do?
And right after that?
How did you do what you did?

The emphasis is therefore on the sequential aspect of an action. An action is deconstructed step by step and micro second per micro-second with one's patient to retrieve this form of memory called procedural.

In 1994, Schacter, a professor of psychology at Harvard University along with Tulving, a leading researcher in the field of memory research, from Toronto make a breakthrough. They postulate and formalize the presence of multiple memory systems. Schacter and Tulving (1994) clarify and redefine the notion of memory and knowledge. They discuss how these multiple memory systems refer to different neurocognitive structures. Tulving (1999) discusses the importance of what he calls "working memory" or so called "procedural memory" in the meta-cognition, the "knowing about knowing". His concern is at the heart of my discussion about reflection-in-action. Baddeley (1997) brings important contributions with his studies on memory and consciousness. He is the founder of the notion of "implicit learning". Squire (1987, 1994), professor of psychology at the University of San Diego divides the memory into "declarative" (where things can be told) and "non-Declarative" (things which cannot be told or most of the procedural memory). Baddeley and Squire of course bring us back to the saying of Polanyi (1966): "we know more than we can tell" (p. 6). Polanyi refers to what later Squire (1994) would call the non-declarative form of memory.

Several authors in the field of neuroscience refer to Schön's notion of repertoire building (Baddeley, 1997; Cozolino, 2002; Iacoboni, Woods, and Brass, 1991; Baron-Cohen, Tager-Flusberg, and Cohen, 2000; Schacter, 1994, 2001a, 2001b, 2001c; Siegel, 1999, Squire, 1987, 1994; Squire & Zola-Morgan, 1991; Tulving, 2000; Woods, Brass, et al. 1999). They agree that there is an important form of memory, which allows us to use previously encountered strategies of functioning, in unknown and new situations and to function in the present. Reflection-in-action is a form of knowing similar to what Squire (1994) calls this "implicit or non-declarative", similar to what Tulving (1999) calls "procedural" and finally similar to what Schacter (1994, 2001a) and Baddeley (1997) call "implicit". Damasio (1999) brings important clarification in discussing procedural memories. In Descartes' Error (1994), he explains that the feeling and the knowing that Descartes described as separate are interdependent. Humans do not learn well under high emotional distress. The need, the motivation and the emotional tone of a person deeply affect how and what he learns. Damasio 1999 defines procedural memory as something we know "how to do", but we are not conscious of the actual doing. After Piaget, Damasio (1999) asserts with his research in neuroscience and on brain-damaged patients, that the sense of self happens when there is a sense of knowing. After Vygotsky, he further states:

> "The idea that the self and consciousness would emerge *after* language is not likely to be correct. Language does not come out of nothing. Language gives us name for things. If self and consciousness were born de novo from language, they would constitute the sole instance of words without an underlying concept" (p. 108).

Damasio (1994, 1999) brings much clarification to the field through the construction of careful definitions of notions that are frequently confusing and confused (consciousness, emotions, feelings, and the unconscious). Damasio links his findings with philosophy and the history of science. Last and not least for this specific domain of neuroscience, Damasio is eminently readable. Damasio attempts to assist practitioners in using his findings and applying his research to treatment.

There could be an organic reason to the ability of humans to be reflexive: the amazing discovery of "mirror neurons" (Baron-Cohen, Tager-Flusberg & Cohen, 2000; Cozolino, 2002; Iacoboni, Woods, Brass, et al. 1999; Siegel, 1999, 2001, 2003a, 2003b). Siegel (1999) describes the discovery of the mirror neurons in a clear and concise manner:

> "As primates evolved, they were not only social and tuned into the state of others; they evolved a mirror neuron system that enabled them to respond to the intentional (rather than random) acts of other members of the species. *Mirror neurons* are a system that links perception to motor action (Iacoboni, Woods, Brass, et al. 1999). When an intentional act

> is witnessed (such as the raising of a cup to drink), the same mirror neuron will fire as when the individual observing the act enacts that same behavior. By responding only to the intentional acts, and not just to random motion, mirror neurons reveal the way in which our minds respond to the intentional state of another being.
> With our evolution as humans, we have taken the mirror neurons one step further into the world of representing in a more abstract way the internal state of others. This *capacity of having a sense of another's mind* has been called theory of mind, mentalizing, mind reading, and mindsight. This capacity for mindsight enables us to perceive the minds of others and to put ourselves in the "mental shoes" of another person, something other primates, though they have mirror neurons and can imitate, apparently cannot do" (pp. 4-5).

The scientific research literature on neuroscience is enormous. It seems to become a domain of much relevance for our practice. With the work of neuroscientists who are interested in psychotherapy (Cozolino, 2002; Damasio, 1994, 1999; Siegel, 1999, 2001, 2003a, 2003b) we have received extremely interesting, readable and clinically relevant research over the last five years in our field.

## Non-reflexive elements

Rennie, Shaké & Toukmanian, (1992) distinguish between reflexive and non-reflexive processes in psychotherapy:

> "The first form is reflexive: the client is aware of the event, deliberates on its significance, and decides what to do about it, if anything, and when and how. The second form of activity is non-reflexive: the event in the therapy may be thought of as being experienced as a *step*, a shift in the direction of experiencing things differently" (p. 245).

The authors go on to explain the benefits of non-reflexive processes in psychotherapy:

> "From that point onward, the client encounters the self and the world within the framework of the new step, assimilates new information into it, and furthers the evolution of the new construction. This evolution may occur in the context of the clients' relationship with the self, the therapist, and/or the world"(p. 245).

The trio defines the therapeutic episode as *non-monadic* that is an occasion with two forms of activity: reflexive and non-reflexive. Both are important in the therapeutic episode.

The qualities of RIA are multiple. Brown (1996) Polkinghorne (1991b), Rennie & Toukmanian, (1992) and

Schön (1983) mention the following qualities: self-corrective, self-evaluative, evolutive and encouraging creativity. Schön (1983) says about the auto-corrective function:

> "The process of reflection performs a crucial function for a science of practice by checking on the validity of practicing knowledge. Through reflection the practitioner can bring to the surface and criticize the tacit understandings that have grown up around the repetitive experiences of a specialized practice and can make new sense of the situations of uncertainty or uniqueness which he may allow himself to experience"(p. 61).

Polkinghorne (1991) shows how this reflexive process invites change:

> "When we reflect, we change from thinking with our patterns to meta-cognitive awareness. We focus on the possibility that the situation may not fit any pattern of understanding in our repertoire or that we have tried to make the situation conform to a pattern with which we are comfortable" (p. 61).

Polkinghorne (1991) encourages the use of these reflective practices:

> "They add to the therapist's body of background knowledge, patterns of understandings, and suggestions for possible actions. Furthermore, they help equip the practitioner with the evaluative and conceptual understandings needed for skilled reflection" (p. 111).

I would like to emphasize that RIA can be a methodology for learning. When using RIA the psychotherapist becomes more aware of how he functions, how he learns. There is a necessity for continual self-education in the practice of psychotherapy itself. So, what gets in the way of the practice of RIA since it holds so many advantages? Bannister (1981) shows how historically the very division of the field of psychology has prevented for a long time the type of research promoted by Schön (the process of RIA: fourth type of research).

> "The very division of psychology into a series of mini-frameworks (emotion, cognition, memory, sensory perception, social psychology, abnormal psychology, comparative psychology, physiological psychology, and so on and so forth) has segmented the discipline so that most commonly, we produce masses of micro-defining researchers which cannot be related, or more extensive researchers which ingest huge lumps of different and non-cross-translatable language systems" (p. 198).

Bannister's quote remains of contemporary. Science proceeds, but a tendency to segment and separate inherited from a positivist tradition remains in the field of psychology. In the last decade or so, there have been several encouraging attempts to reach a more holistic and integrative view of the field.

# Chapter III

## The founding theories of qualitative research

Historically, it is important to keep in mind that it is the same philosopher, Comte (1798-1857), who founded sociology as a science and introduced the term of positivism to the social sciences. His development of positivism was directly in reaction again "religious dogma and metaphysical speculation, and stressed a return to observable data" (Kvale, 1996, p. 61). Kvale reminds us that positivism was a gift to science, in that it contributed to "moving social research beyond myth and commonsense" (1996, p. 61). In organizing his ideas and offering methodological guidelines and theoretical background as a foundation for knowledge, Comte contributes to giving a scientific status to social sciences. Comte helped our field to attain the rigor of scientific argument. The very notion of science has oftentimes been juxtaposed with positivist assumptions, especially in the field of social sciences. The co-existence of these discoveries may have created the assumption that social science *is* positivist.

Let me schematize for you the major assumptions of positivism. Positivism affirms two ground rules: science is unified (Polkinghorne, 1991c, p. 106), and there is only one method to produce true knowledge statements. There is only one "right and true" way to understand one object. Unified means also that there is one science, one world, one system, and one language. If there is truth there is also falsehood, and subterfuge. Second, the method that yields this positive knowledge is the experimental method (Polkinghorne, 1991c, p. 106). This method uses both numeric data and quantitative analysis. So, science is unified and after Galileo quantifiable. Positivists' influence is important in the world of science. This positivist paradigm is currently the most influential in social sciences (Bakan, 1967; Danzinger, 1979, 1990; Polkinghorne, 1984, 1988, 1991a, 1991b, 1991c, 1994).

Positivism is so embedded in our culture, that it has become the only way. It is important to remember that the foundation of Positivism is based on a set of beliefs that creates a certain science. Positivism is no longer looked at for what it is: a paradigm, or a set of assumptions. Positivism has an effect on the way we view the world and on the way that we understand science. The exclusivity of the positivist paradigm will eventually restrain us from possibilities of knowing. It has frozen research in psychotherapy for decades. The catechism of positivism may keep us from challenging and broadening the definition of science and knowledge.

Like every other form of research, although we may prefer it to be bias-free, qualitative research is informed by a theory, explicitly preferably, sometimes implicitly. Schematically, quantitative research claims the positivist paradigm and qualitative research claims a more postmodern, post-positivist or socio-constructivist paradigm.

For years, positivism has rejected the qualitative research as a scientific method. Positivist researchers still sometimes do.

## Constructivism

The reaction to positivism, before contemporary authors, has a long history (Bakan, 1967; Brentano, 1874; Dewey, 1896, 1950; Giddens, 1976). The seeds of the postmodern critique are to be found in the constructivist position (Bannister, 1981; Danzinger, 1979, 1990; Heron, 1981; Kelly 1955; Kvale 1993, 1996; Polkinghorne, 1984, 1988, 1991a, 1991b, 1991c, 1994; Reason & Rowan, 1981; Vico, 1668/1744). The constructivists argue that any research is done *with* someone rather than *on* someone. Bannister states: "Viewed reflexively the psychological experiment is simply a formal instance of people trying to understand people and psychologists might do better to experiment conjointly with their subjects rather than on them" (p. 195). Heron (1981) echoes Bannister's idea that in social sciences, research involves an interaction *with* the other:

> "Research is a process of systematic (and not so systematic) inquiry that leads to knowledge stated in propositions. In social science research, this inquiry involves an element of observation of, of interaction with, persons in order to offer empirical evidence for the research conclusion" (p. 19).

Polkinghorne (1991a) offers an interesting definition of science that has been inspirational throughout my research. He stresses that research is a continual effort to correct and refine the description until it fits the experience:

> "Science is an extension of the ordinary cognitive process used to make experience meaningful and inform everyday human actions. (...) The result of scientific efforts is simply knowledge proposals until they have been judged by the community of scholars as worthy of inclusion in a discipline 's body of knowledge" (p. 175).

The constructivist position involves a constant negotiation of the kind of reality found with the object of investigation. The constructivist research is context-related and context-dependent:

> "The research process is not a mapping of some objective social reality. Research involves a co-constitution of the objects investigated with a negotiation and interaction with the very object studied. Conversation and social practice become the ultimate contexts in which the validity of knowledge is negotiated and ascertained" (Kvale, *in Corsini*, 1996, p. 101).

As Polkinghorne notes (1991a), knowledge gains the status of science, as a result of a consensus among the experts in the field. Heron (1981) warns us about the positivist reflexes that are almost engraved in our genes. We remain, Heron says, tempted to try to approach "reality":

> "Science, as a product, is in the domain of propositional knowledge. The outcome of research

> is stated in propositions, which claims to be assertions of facts or truths, a contribution to the corpus of knowledge statements. A claimed fact or truth is a propositional entity, a construct, an artifact. It is a statement about the world. It does not constitute the world. It is not part of, or found in, the world (...) Science as a process of inquiry involves not only propositional knowledge, but also practical knowledge and experiential knowledge" (p. 27).

## Hermeneutism

In the philosophical tradition, hermeneutics has significantly influenced much the field of qualitative research. Hermeneutics has been described as a methodological tool of research. The philosophical movement borrows its name from Hermes, the Greek messenger who translated information back and forth from the gods to the mortals. "Hermeneutics" means to translate and to interpret. This was one of the earliest questionings of the Enlightenment tradition ("Le siècle des Lumières"). It is a clear departure from the positivist claim of knowledge. Hermeneutics questions the causal paradigm of science. Hermeneutics may have been the first philosophical movement to bring forth debates over the dualistic aspect of knowledge (as first introduced by Descartes). Hermeneutics asserts that all understanding is interpretative (Gadamer, 1975). Since understanding is an interpretation, one cannot separate the knower from the known. Each interpretation is only one version of the truth. Seeking interpretation is a never-ending process. Finally, Hermeneutics bring us out of the causal paradigm; it asserts that understanding always involves a reference to the known. This is what Heidegger (1962) called a "hermeneutic circle". We can only understand somebody else, as Heidegger asserts, by immersing oneself into the other's "horizon". This "horizon", Heidegger continues, constrains and limits our interpretation, and our understanding. However the notion of "horizons" for Heidegger is not a fixed one, through dialogue and the active process of interpretation these horizons can expand and transform. In that meaning-making process hermeneuticians assert that we should never omit the other part of the equation, i.e. the "meaning maker".

## Phenomenology

Husserl's ideas on phenomenology (1913) have influenced my research. In my interviews, I try to focus on each individual phenomenology. For the phenomenologists, knowledge starts with experience and ends with it. My training in Gestalt Therapy, since 1993, has helped me to gain a broader understanding of Husserl's notion of phenomenology in practice. Notions such as presence, availability and commitment to dialogue have always been in my awareness throughout the interview process. I have made an ongoing effort to accept and allow differences to emerge and to co-exist, rather than to reduce them. I do not agree with Husserl's ideas that language is separated from experience. As a researcher from the phenomenological tradition, I am interested in reaching direct experience: naive, raw and sensory-experience. I am even more interested in reflexive experiences. In interviewing, I try to translate sensory data into meaningful experiences. In accordance with the phenomenological tradition, I try to stay as close as possible to the experience of the clinicians. When I make an interpretation, I name it as an interpretation. I make an effort to describe and watch. I offer my interpretation back to the clinicians, to see if it fits their own experience and intentions. I favor extensive descriptions of the observed processes over interpretations. My interpretations are always careful and tentative. After the phenomenologists, I maintain faith in human beings. Phenomenologists believe that experience organizes itself *organismically* (rather than requiring the therapist's interpretation for example). The way I interview encourages this "organismic self-regulation". It translates in practice in:

- Accepting and respecting the clinician, where he is, rather than having a preconceived agenda on what he does.

- Allowing and welcoming the clinician's own view of the therapy, as well as allowing mine to be. In order to have a contact between the clinician and the researcher, a dialogical encounter, one needs to state our differences.

- Limiting my assumptions, as a researcher, that some parts of the story are more important (or interesting) than others. If this is not possible, I choose to share my lack of interest politely: "I

> am more interested in that part of the story, because..."

## The postmodern critique

The body of theories emerging from the constructivism continued through the post-modern critique. Derrida, 1967; Foucault, 1980; Lyotard, 1979, 1988; Ricoeur, 1984; and Rorty, 1979 are among the main authors who create a grounding theory for qualitative research to emerge. Today, postmodern thinkers prefer to view reality as "multiverse" (Gergen, 1994b). Qualitative research almost consistently appeals to authors who are interested in the postmodern critique (also called post-positivism, post-structuralism, deconstructionism). The postmodern critique has links with authors interested in constructivism (or with an accent on social procedures: socio-constructionism, or social constructionism).

Where the positivist point of view sees "reality", the postmodern critique asserts that there is no theory that can account for everything. As we previously said (Kuenzli-Monard & Kuenzli, 1996a):

> "Reality explodes or implodes in a multiplicity of "realities", that are not objectifiable. Where positivism looks for rules and regularity, postmodernism encourages multiple perspectives and differences. Where modernism encourages dualities, polarization and simplifications of the

> world, postmodernism tries to question and displace dualities such as rational-irrational, subject-object, form-content, subjective-objective, normal-pathology, assessment-intervention, structure-function, and masculine-feminine. Postmodernism challenges dualistic views of the world. It critiques dogmatism and polarity. Postmodernism suggests that dualism is socially constructed and that it favors one side of the dichotomy over the other (for example normal vs. pathology)" (p. 38).

Anderson (1996) provides an interesting definition of postmodernism:

> "Postmodernism is an umbrella term that refers not to an era but to a philosophical perspective that includes an ideological critique of the foundation of literary, political, and social thinking a continual questioning and reexamination of the familiar (Derrida, 1978; Foucault, 1980; Lyotard, 1984; Ricoeur, 1984, 1985; Rorty, 1979). It questions the taken-for-granted and universal givens, including dominant discourses and cultural practices-beliefs, truths, laws, and social institutions. From a postmodern perspective, everything is open to critique, including postmodernism. Said differently, postmodernism is occupied with everyday discursive practice: how we construct and attribute meanings to our realities and how our cultural practices are created and set in social agreement. Postmodern favors the idea that a knower participates in creating the world he or she

> lives in, observes and knows; that what is created and known, or believed to be known, changes through creative interactions (Berger & Luckman, 1966; Gergen, 1982, 1985, 1995; Harré, 1979; Shotter, 1991b, 1993a, 1993b; Vygotsky, 1986). Some postmodernists are occupied with broad cultural discourses and practices and how they influence and express themselves in our everyday lives (Gergen, 1982, 1985, 1995; Rorty, 1979). Others are more occupied with local knowledge as it is generated through and within the interactions of persons (Polkinghorne, 1988; Shotter, 1993a, 1993b)" (p. 195).

Positivism does not take into account the context in which knowledge evolves. It tries to minimize the influence of people in the construction of knowledge. Kvale (1993) highlights the trend of postmodernism for multiplicity, diversity: "Postmodern does not designate a systematic theory or a comprehensive philosophy, but rather diverse diagnoses and interpretations of the current culture, a depiction of a multitude of interphenomena" (p. 33).

In art, the postmodern movement was led by artists such as: Becket, Ben, Ionesco, Lichtenstein, Duras, Warhol or Wenders. The metaphor of collage is offered as a parody of postmodernism. In postmodern art, the illustration of aestheticism becomes an explosion of different images. Aestheticism is no longer defined in a comprehensive or global manner. In postmodern art, polarities and dichotomies reunify.

To give an example of persistency of positivist ideas, I quote Rennie & Toukmanian (1992), two researchers in the field of qualitative inquiry. Their saying is especially disconcerting in that they clearly think of themselves as post-positivists researchers. In their statement, it is obvious that they still believe that the only way to do good science is to maintain an external position:

> "In psychotherapy process research, three vantage points can be used in the attempt to understand the phenomena in question: the perspective of the external observer, client or therapist. By the external observer, we mean a third party involvement at all levels of the research extending from conceptualizing to data generalization, analysis and interpretation" (p. 239).

Their comment about the "external observer" implies that they believe that one can hold an external, neutral, and uninvolved position, a typically positivist idea. Further Rennie & Toukmanian (1992) underline the credo that in order to know, one has to be distanced from the object. This is also a positivist assumption. This example is without intending criticism. I want to show how present the paradigm of positivism is, even with well-trained qualitative researchers.

# The postmodern era: An hazard to our mental health?

There is a danger in entering the postmodern world such as the one that Kearney (1988) describes as the "postmodern disease of endless circularity". Kearney offers an interesting analysis of these three eras: the premodern, the modern, and the postmodern. He describes the paradigms and metaphors that derive from them. The premodern times are characterized by a mimetic paradigm. Everything is replicated. The invention of the printing Press by Güttenberg has probably something to do with this tendency to reproduce. Imagination is imitative as well as turned toward reproduction (bibles, icons, and portraits). To the modern epoch, Kearney attaches the symbolic object of the lamp (in French: "Le siècle des Lumières"). The lamp is there to highlight and affirm the creative power to invent the world and discover truth. In attributing to the postmodern epoch the metaphor of the mirror, Kearney (1988) warns of the seductive danger of being one 's own object of reflection, of turning the mirror inward. Kearney declares dead the modern concept of imagination as generative, productive and original: "With it has died a philosophy of truth, with its corresponding notion of interpretation, meaning, reference, narrative, history and value" (p. 360).

In the postmodern era, Kearney cautions that imagination becomes a form of self-parody, where reflexivity becomes an "end in itself" (Lawson, 1985). Lowe (1990) states that reflexivity is a dangerous tool and the metaphor of the mirror could lead to: "a mirror, which mirrors nothing but the act of mirroring. The central metaphor that Kearney offers to qualify the postmodern era is a looking glass or rather the interminable interplay between multiple looking glasses" (p. 4). Kearney shows the risk of the postmodern condition: "Imagination takes the form of a labyrinth of mirrors extending indefinitely in all directions, where the image of the self and the reality dissolves into self-parody" (p. 253).

## Escaping the vicious circle: Ethics and play

The only way out of insanity in postmodernism, Kearney declares, is a move toward ethics. The author (1988) affirms that the only way to get outside of the vicious circle is by taking a stance, by positioning oneself, and by making an ethical decision: "Here I stand" (p. 361). In other words: "Ethics has primacy over epistemology and ontology, or in simpler terms, good comes before the question of truth and being"(Kearney, 1988, p. 362). For Kearney (1988) the ethical statement "I stand" surpasses the epistemological statement "I think", in that it includes the concern for the other as its basic precondition". Kearney's metaphor of the mirror and a new form of imagination encourages us to use a reflexive posture, to put ourselves in the shoes of others in order to "embrace the multidimensionality of meaning" (p. 312). Lowe (1990) further explains the relationship suggested by Kearney between ethic and play:

> "Such an imagination would value the importance of play, parody, and reflexivity but not as ends or activities in themselves. It would seek to balance

> the undecidability of play with the ethical readiness to imagine which forms of play are liberating, and which are incarcerating of the other. Play without ethics leads to an attitude of anything goes, and everything is the same because, ultimately it is nothing at all. But if play requires ethics, ethics also require play. Ethics without play shrinks into a posture of cheerless moralizing. The ethical imagination needs the poetry of play to ensure that it is ethical, in a liberating way, one that opens possibilities for the other and enlarges our own response to the other and to the world beyond" (p. 5).

If meanings are multiple, it means we will not ever be able to grasp them all. It implies that the more we are able to put ourselves in the shoes of others, (in other words to practice reflexivity), the more we become aware of our multiple worlds, of our multiple meanings, and of our multiple selves. If meanings are multiple, we may become more comfortable with holding multiple truths at the same time. The point that Kearney makes about reflexivity is key to my research. Reflexivity, he says is essential, but it cannot become an end in itself. Reflexivity involves an ethical posture and becomes necessary so that a person takes a stance and declares, "Here I stand".

Giddens (1991) attributes the "reflexivity of modernity" to the technological advancement and globalization rather than to a direct reaction to positivism. Content of information is now accessible from our home on a worldwide scale. We access nearly everything on this planet through the Internet and compare it with everything. We have a wide access to comparison, and multiple choices. Therefore, Giddens says (1991) we become reflexive because we have access to more information and are exposed to more contexts. Giddens's central thesis is that absolute and definite postures decrease as the complexity of reality and contexts increases. Defining oneself at each moment is, in a postmodern world, a difficult and demanding exercise and a very important one. Giddens' ideas about how the high-speed information system that surrounds us affects and changes our perceptions are similar to Gergen's developments (1982, 1985a, 1985b, 1991a, 1991b, 1994b).

Concluding this chapter, I have discussed how, in the field of psychotherapy process research, the restriction to the solely paradigm of positivism can limit our possibilities of knowing. Ultimately the positivist paradigm favors quantitative information. I expressed my preference for the co-existence of different paradigms of knowing. Postmodern paradigm should not replace the positivist one. I have also discussed the grounding theories of qualitative research: constructivism, hermeneutism, phenomenology and the postmodern critique. Postmodernism challenges dualistic points of view and opts for a deconstructive stance toward knowledge. I explore the danger and the seductive temptation of Postmodernism, and how we could sink into an "endless circularity" (Kearney, 1988). Through the constant invitation of ethics and play in our discourse one can escape this danger and create generative knowing.

# Chapter IV

## Beyond linearity
## *(Family Therapy and Qualitative Research)*

Family Therapists are the ones who plant the seeds of qualitative research. They offer a paradigm that moves the researcher beyond linearity. In this chapter, I explain how the field of Family Therapy and its latest development, the "second-order cybernetic", informs the methodology of qualitative research. Qualitative research attempts to follow a "circular" (non-linear) paradigm. This paradigm evolves out of Family Therapy theories. These founding theories are essential in understanding how and why qualitative research developed. Like the Family Systems Theory, qualitative research emphasizes context-dependence, social contexts and multiple approaches. For Wynne (1984) the theories of Family Therapy should be regarded as "an approach or a paradigm, and not just another treatment modality" (p. 298).

I have been trained in the field of Family Therapy (or Systems Theory) since 1993. My ideas have been influenced by the epistemology of the second-order cybernetic. These ideas influence the way I do research. I present the complex developments of Family Therapy, its multiple influences and its direct effect on qualitative research. The implications of the "new epistemology" (second-order cybernetic) are profound and radical for the field of qualitative research. In a prophetic manner, Bateson stated almost thirty years ago:

> "The new science will form around profoundly non-physical ideas: the nature of the relation between name and that which is named, the nature of recursive systems, and the nature of difference" (1972, p. 337).

The Family Systems Theory has always been more interested in the process than in the content. By definition, this field is interested in how relationships develop within families. The accent is placed on the process and on the way a relationship forms and is maintained. Family Therapy looks at the way people act and "re-act", rather than at "facts".

## The pioneers of qualitative research

The early work of Family Therapists has planted the seeds of today's qualitative research. When comparing the work of early Family Therapists and how they then made sense of the complexity they encountered, we may confuse it with today's qualitative methodology. In Palo Alto, Bateson, Jackson, Fisch, Haley, Siegel, Watzlawick, and Weakland, began their work using a qualitative methodology without naming it at the Mental Research Institute (MRI). They worked as a team, took turns, conduced and criticized their own work, their own assumptions, as well as their colleague's. They studied their practice and kept modifying it. They reviewed their interventions and transformed their practice along with their theory as they questioned it. At the

Mental Research Institute, the bridge between practice and theory was evident and ongoing. Fish, Segal, and Weakland (1982) described their work as a daily research process: "Live observations of therapy sessions through one-way mirror, and detailed study of audiotape (...) extensive discussion and efforts to generalize" (p. 10). Until the mid seventies, in the field of Family Therapy, nothing much exciting happened. Doherty (1991) shares:

> "From mid sixties through the seventies probably, the most influential theory in the Family field was Structural Family Therapy which assumed there were universal organizational patterns in families" (p. 40).

Three decades ago, Minuchin (1974) founded the Structural Family Therapy. Since then, the field of Family Therapy has grown "from a reductionist perspective to a more globalistic approach during the period from the mid-late 60's to the 80's" (Kuenzli-Monard & Kuenzli, 1996a, p. 15).

## Second-order Cybernetic: The circular paradigm

Using the word revolution to qualify the paradigmatic shift from a linear to a circular epistemology is not an exaggeration. Within approximately forty years (1960 to 2000), Family Systems Theory made giant steps. For centuries, our western culture has taught us to explain phenomena and behaviors linearly. The importance of Freud (1921, 1922, 1930,

1951) and his remarkable ideas is still vivid. The linear derived idea, that problems are located *inside* people, for example comes from the psychoanalytical tradition and probably earlier (Foucault, 1972). Another common example is conveyed through this common saying: "If you understand where your problem is coming from and why it occurs, then you will heal". Those two examples are typical of linear reasoning. In the field of Family Therapy, the reference to the cybernetic model goes through rapid changes (Kuenzli-Monard & Kuenzli, 2000). The first-order Cybernetic goes through two sub-phases:

- The first "wave" of the first-order Cybernetic puts the accent on the negative feedback. This means that Family Therapists (previously, the cyberneticians) are interested in how the system *maintains* its organization in order to keep its *homeostasis.*

- The second "wave" of the first Cybernetic focuses on the opposite movement: the positive feedback. The interest shifts on how the system *modifies* its movement and organization to be able to adapt. *(Homeorhesis).*

Different approaches ensue from these two waves. The therapists trained under the first "wave" focus on how people maintain their sense of self, regardless of what happens outside. What is cherished is the idea of stability throughout time (homeostasis). The therapists of the "second wave" are interested in how people constantly adapt and readjust: (homeorhesis). The notion of health, by means of consequences transforms and adjusts. From a preferred stability, health is now defined by adaptability. The Family Therapists of the first-order Cybernetic (first and second waves) missed an essential component of their understanding of the field of psychotherapy: the inclusion of the therapist in the very system they saw as the therapeutic system. Under the first-order Cybernetic, the therapist remains *always outside of the system he treats and un-influenced by it.* For obvious reasons, the first-order Cybernetic placed the psychotherapist outside of the therapeutic system. The therapist maintained therefore a strong posture of power and neutrality. The first-order Cybernetic left the therapist in the external and uninvolved position of "treating patients".

The change to the second-order Cybernetic is a cultural revolution in the way one thinks and perceives and makes sense of reality. In order to fully understand the intensity of this change I will provide a few metaphors: it is similar to showing impressionist art to people who were used to appreciating realist paintings. Their first reaction was one of a shock. They could not see a thing. They could not comprehend the image. Another metaphor is the transition from Neutonian physics to Quantic physics. It is an enormous paradigmatic shift. It challenges the mind. The transformation from the linear to the circular paradigm is so profound that it takes some education to start grasping what this change is about. It brings a new paradigm of knowledge (which has been called the "new epistemology"). The second-order cybernetic (confusingly called "the third wave") recognizes that the therapist cannot stay outside of the system and just observe without changing it. Each encounter with a system transforms and changes us. The paradigm shift brought by the second-order cybernetic has tremendous implications for research. This shift directly questions the position of the researcher and his involvement in research. I describe some possible effects of this epistemic revolution:

> "This new epistemology denies the legendary privilege of the psychotherapist to his neutrality. It is now admitted that the therapist transforms the system he approaches and is transformed by it. Dangerous and daring, is for the practitioner the adventure of being constantly changed by the encounters with patients. The second-order cybernetic encourages the psychotherapist to maintain interest in the concepts of reflexivity, responsibility, autonomy and "complexity" (Von Foerster, 1983)" (Kuenzli-Monard & Kuenzli, 2000, p. 4).[5]

Applied to research, the second-order cybernetic transforms:

- The way I consider the participant as a co-researcher (rather than as an object, a subject or an informant).
- The way I am willing to transform and change my ideas and methodology, depending on the occurring contexts. (Context-dependence)

[5] This is my translation.

- The way I consider my data, not as an approximation of reality, but rather as detailed narratives about the researched phenomenon.

The huge and violent rupture between a linear and a circular paradigm is often underestimated. Mc Kinnon & Miller (1987) make an excellent summary of the shift from linear causality to a circular paradigm:

> "The new epistemology refers to the incorporation into Family Therapy of the cybernetic approach of Bateson, 1972, 1979; Maturana, 1980; Von Foerster, 1973a, 1973b; Varela, 1976, 1979; Varela & Maturana, 1973. Theoretically, this has been accomplished by writers such as Dell, 1982, 1985; Keeney, 1983, and in practice, by among others, the Milan associates Boscolo, Cecchin, Selvini-Palazzoli, and Prata, 1978, and their proponents Hoffman, 1981; Tomm, 1984a, 1984b,). The new epistemology has seriously challenged the field of Family Therapy in that it has (...):
>
> - Provided a description of the therapist/family system from a cybernetic perspective. Second-order cybernetics, or the cybernetics of cybernetics, emphasizes the observer's inclusion and participation in the system (Keeney, 1983).
>
> - Proposed an ontology, i.e. a theory of how the world is (Dell, 1985). This ontology emphasized the circularity and autonomy of systems and challenged notions of linear causality. The new

> epistemology differs markedly from generation systems theory (von Bertalanffy, 1968). Second-order cybernetics is of a higher order than simple, or first-order cybernetics, which emphasizes the homeostatic and adaptive properties of systems and higher than second wave of the first-order cybernetic (Maruyama, 1963) which emphasizes positive feedback in system transformation (morphogenesis)". (Mc Kinnon & Miller, pp. 140-141).

Like qualitative research, the second-order Cybernetic is interested in social context and the importance of social components in the construction of truth. Family Therapists of the second-order Cybernetic maintain a tight relationship with feminists such as Hoffman, 1981, 1985, 1990, 1991, 1997; Hutchinson & Wilson, 1994; Mc Namee, 1992; Morse, 1994, Papp, 1980; Penn & Frankfurt, 1994; Taggart, 1985; Weingarten, 1991, 1995.

Pinsof (1981) cites three reasons for the dearth of process research: the difficulty of the task, the lack of good micro-theory of psychotherapy, and the fact that process researchers, in general have been "individually oriented" and have ignored Family Therapy as a new theoretical orientation. Gurman (1983) argues that the circular paradigm challenges the very definition of the "dogma of science" (p. 231).

It seems important to keep seeking for methodologies that suit the moving object of process research and reflect the circular paradigm of this new epistemology.

# Chapter V

## Qualitative research: From birth to individuation

Only recently has the scientific community accepted qualitative research as a viable way to explore and understand phenomena in social sciences. Qualitative researchers owe a lot to the brave pioneers who opened the trails that have enabled qualitative research to achieve its current status. We can find the early traces of qualitative practice in the work of Wilhelm Wundt, in his Volkerpsychologie (1832/1920). Wundt offers the use of qualitative data as the only appropriate approach to the study of higher mental processes. It is not until the late 1930s, with the advent of phonographic recordings that the actual content and process of therapy was examined. The first to investigate with rigor the actual content of psychotherapy was probably Rogers (1942). Rogers hopes that "psychotherapy could become a process based on known and tested principles, with tested techniques for implementing these principles" (p. 434). Unfortunately, Rogers's dream did not materialize until years later. The "known and tested principles" mentioned in 1942 by Rogers have been rather elusive, keeping what happens within the therapy room highly secret. Rogers's interest (1942) in what he calls "moments of movement" in psychotherapy was way ahead of his time. Fifty years ago,

Rogers predicted the current cutting edge research on change in psychotherapy (Duncan, Miller & Sparks, 2004, Hubble, Mark, Duncan, Barry & Miller, 1999; Horvath, 2001; O'Loughlin, 2003; Paula, 2003). After Rogers (1942), qualitative research probably owes its growth to authors such as Bakan (1967) Garfinkel (1967) and Danzinger (1979, 1990). These three senior scholars devoted their career to qualitative research. More recently, advocates of qualitative research include: Andersen, 1991; Anderson, 1993a, 1997; Bannister, 1981; Chenail, 1993, 1994, 1997; Elliot, 1986; Gale, 1991; Hoshmand, 1989; Hubble, Mark, Duncan, Miller et al., 1999; Kvale, 1989; Mc Leod, 1994, 1996a, 1996b; Mc. Namee 1992, 1999; Moon, Dillon & Sprenkle, 1990, 1991; Polkinghorne 1981, 1983, 1988, 1991a, 1991b, 1991c, 1994; Reason, 1994; Reason & Rowan, 1981; Rennie, 1994; and Smith & Heshusius 1986. Danzinger (1991) highlights the importance of reflective practices; he states that research should start to investigate the tacit and implicit part of therapeutic practices:

> "The realm of practice involves a great deal of that tacit knowledge that has long been recognized as applying a crucial role in scientific investigation. In fact, the tacit component tends to be much larger on the level of practice than on the level of theory" (p. 13).

Human sciences refer to research qualitative procedures using various names. Anthropology calls it ethnography. For sociology, qualitative procedures become a participant observation. Psychology refers to it as qualitative research. I refer to qualitative procedures, qualitative research, or qualitative inquiry to encompass all procedures borrowed from these disciplines. They contrast with quantitative methods "(...) which uses data that consist of statements presented in numeric language, and analytic processes based on mathematical operations" (Polkinghorne, 1991b, p. 163).

Unfortunately, for too long academic researchers and psychotherapists split their bodies of knowledge. This schism had direct consequences on the production of research: for decades, we have had almost *no research on clinical practices*. Until recently, psychotherapy has been confined to literature *about* therapy. The art of psychotherapy has mainly been conveyed through an oral tradition, transmitted through mentoring, supervision, and the sometimes still called didactic psychotherapy. The skills and practices of psychotherapy are transmitted through internships, field training, workshops, case study, and of course personal struggle with one's daily practice and questions. Discussing psychotherapy, Polkinghorne states "this body draws its inferences from case studies, rather than from academic research" (1991, p. 168). For decades, the body of research on clinical practices has been a land of nothingness. Only a few universities offer coursework in qualitative research design. Almost none have well-developed programs.

Recently, Hoshmand (1989) presented a proposal for integrating the teaching of qualitative research design into graduate research training programs. It is likely to take a minimum of two decades for her recommendations to become standard fare in Family Therapy doctoral programs.

Echoing this comment, Rennie (1996) adds the political difficulties encountered in choosing qualitative research:

> "Most departments of psychology at Universities do not offer courses in qualitative research methods and discourage their use by students. Beyond the universities, mainstream journals have been cautious about accepting qualitative research manuscript" (p. 317).

Qualitative research is time and labor intensive. It does not lend itself well to the "publish or perish" environment prevalent at many universities. During the last 20 years, boards of psychology and professional associations have striven to add rigor and professionalism in the training of psychotherapists. They elaborate codes of ethics, clarify legal responsibilities of our profession. They attempt to standardize training and curriculum. A trend toward a more unified and rigorous training is appearing. These transformations may account for the appearance of research in psychotherapy process research (Atkinson, Heath & Chenail 1991; Bordin, 1979, 1983; Breunlin, Schwarz, Krause & Selby 1983; Carey, 1994; Duncan, Miller & Sparks, 2004; Eliott, 1986; Gale, 1991; Galley and Droz 1999; Gelso, Betz, Friedlander, et al. 1988; Germain, 1979; Grafanaki, 1996; Greenberg & Pinsof, 1986; Gurman & Kniskern, 1978; Hill, 1984, 1990, 1991, 1996; Horvath & Simons, 1991; Horvath, 2001; Hoshmand, 1994; Hutchinson and Wilson, 1994; Lamb & Huttlinger, 1989; Locke, 1989; Morse, 1994; Odell & Quinn, 1998; Ogles, Lambert & Fields, 2002; Pinsof, 1981, 1989, 1995; Pinsof & Wynne, 2000, Pope and Tabachnick, 1994; Toukmananian & Rennie, 1992; Rober, 1999; Schwartz and

Breulin, 1983; Shoham & Salomon, 1990; Spradley, 1979; Stiles, Honos-Webb & Surko, 1998; Strupp, Horowitz & Lambert, 1997a; Tripp-Reimer, 1983; Warkins and Schneider, 1991; Worthen and McNeill, 1996; Yin, 1989, Zichi-Cohen & Omery, 1994; Zinberg, 1986).

The field of qualitative research has been in many ways a land of reconciliation between research and practice. One of the most seductive aspects of qualitative research in psychotherapy lies in creating a continuum between research and its direct application to clinic. Qualitative inquiry is well suited to the immense complexity of the process of psychotherapy. Authors encourage the integration of these two disciplines (Hoshmand & Polkinghorne, 1992; Hoshmand, 1993; Kvale, 1993, 1996; Morse, 1994; Polkinghorne, 1991a, 1991c). Polkinghorne (1991a) points out that the same skills are necessary to be a skilled qualitative researcher and a fine clinician:

> "One of the advantages of including instruction in qualitative procedures as a part of scientific training is that the conceptual skills required to carry out these procedures are closely related to those required to work successfully with clients" (p. 169).

# Getting ready for a revolution in the world of science

Already in 1983, Polkinghorne declares that there has been a radical change in the philosophy of science during the last decades. Science now validates different systems of knowledge that can produce knowledge:

> "The essential idea of the new philosophy is that there is no sure and certain foundation for knowledge claims (Rorty, 1979). The primary implication of this idea is that no single system of knowledge acquisition has cognitive privilege, and thus that various systems can produce worthwhile and useful knowledge" (p. 106).

Qualitative research is certainly not the main stream of research in psychology. However, its body of knowledge of qualitative research has grown tremendously and has grown a solid reputation. Among the most frequently quoted research are: Agar, 1980; Bakan, 1967; Bogdan & Biklen, 1982; Bordin, 1979, 1983; Danzinger, 1979, 1990; Denzin, 1978, 1994; Duncan, Miller & Sparks, 2004; Eliott, 1986; Hoshmand, 1989, 1993, 1994; Hubble, Mark, Duncan, Barry & Miller, 1999; Gale 1991; Goetz & LeCompte, 1984; Grafanaki, 1996; Greenberg & Pinsof, 1986; Greenberg, Rice & Elliott, 1993; Guba & Lincoln, 1981, 1988, 1994; Hill, 1984, 1990, 1991, 1996; Kvale, 1993, 1996; Marshall & Rossman, 1999; Miller, Barry, Duncan, Mark & Hubble, 1997; Mc Cracken, 1988; Mc Leod, 1994, 1996a, 1996b; Morse, 1994; Orlinsky & Howard, 1986; Orlinsky, 1999; Pinsof, 1981, 1989, 1995; Pinsof & Wynne, 2000;

Polkinghorne, 1988, 1991a, 1991b, 1991c, 1994; Raskin, 1999b; Reason, 1981; Rennie, 1992, 1994, 1996; Rennie & Toukmananian, 1992; Schön, 1983, 1987; Seidman, 1991; Sprenkle, 1994; Strupp, Horowitz & Lambert, 1997a; Wolcott, 1990, 1994; Yin, 1989). I have witnessed the increasing number of publications in the domain, with satisfaction. Kvale (1996) highlights the privileged status of quantification in our field and the lack of publicity that qualitative research had for years. He underlines the constant interaction of qualitative practices in quantitative researches:

> "In the modern social sciences, quantification has often been considered as the very criterion of science, and when not taken as self-evident, is legitimated by referring to the natural sciences. This argument overlooks the role of qualitative descriptions in fields such as botany, zoology, and geology, as well as the qualitative analysis in chemistry. In the practice of research, qualitative and quantitative approaches interact. In published social science reports, however, there has been a tendency to downplay the qualitative aspects of the research process: a dichotomized conception with hegemony on the quantitative side may still prevail" (p. 288).

## Qualitative versus quantitative: "Add, but do not mix!"

There is today in the field of qualitative research an important discussion around whether or not these approaches are cumulative and compatible. I see these approaches as cumulative but not compatible. They are informed from very different theoretical frameworks. Their assumptions about science, knowledge and reality make them profoundly incompatible (see chapter III). I can provide an analogy with a poorly–informed eclectic therapist who chooses to believe both the psychoanalytic assumption of the Unconscious and the humanistic principle of responsibility. Both essentials and core beliefs are profoundly *incompatible*. Consequently, the therapist will put his clients in a complete state of confusion due to his incompatible beliefs. This is ethically damaging to his patients. Picking "both/and" (Smith & Heshusius, 1986) instead of "either/or" in this particular example induces confusion and anxiety for the client, rather than a creative support for change and growth. These philosophical assumptions are different and irreconcilable. Both perspectives are neither right nor wrong. However, the application of "both/and" is ethically unacceptable. Separately, these assumptions taken by different therapists can be a useful and constructive approach. These perspectives produce singular positions in the world. They produce different understandings of human interactions.

Smith & Heshusius (1986) qualify the early relationship between the advocates of each perspective as "uneasy". Rist (1977) states that the early discussion was based on "simple and rigid polarities" and there was a continual "fixation on what is good about one approach or bad about another" (p. 42). To get outside of this sterile debate, Guba and Lincoln (1981, 1988, and 1994) were among the first to develop a list of criteria to distinguish good from poor qualitative research (transferability, dependability, confirmability, and credibility). The authors make a clear analogy between their criteria and the procedures of the positivist side. Guba and Lincoln (1981) present in their writing an explicit parallelism between credibility and internal validity, dependability and reliability. After such hostile debate, a few qualitative researchers felt under much pressure to conform to the previously established norm of science (the positivist one). They somewhat lost their identity and their founding theories. In order to sell their qualitative research they make it look like the quantitative one. The works of Goetz & LeCompte (1984) or Miles & Huberman (1984) are typical examples of researchers who went back to their early positivist training. As Smith and Heshusius frame it (1986):

> "The two approaches become variations in techniques within the same assumptive framework, to reach the same goals and solve the same problems. The attempt to develop criteria and procedures for naturalistic inquiry has had the effect of blurring philosophical distinctions and has left the impression that the differences between the two perspectives are primarily those of techniques. (...) These disregards of assumptions and preoccupation with techniques have had the effect of transforming qualitative inquiry into a procedural variation of quantitative inquiry (p. 6)".

The title chosen in 1986, by Smith and Heshusius seems to be somewhat premature: "Closing down the conversation: the End of the Quantitative-Qualitative Debate among Researchers". Fourteen years after Smith & Heshusius' publication, we seem to have reached a more serene climate favorable to collaboration between qualitative and quantitative inquiry. The increasing number of publications in the field of qualitative research adds credibility to qualitative researches and makes them worthy of interest for the quantitative researchers.

Similar debates happen simultaneously in different sister domains. In anthropology, Geertz, 1983 in the domain of linguistics with Lakoff & Johnson, 1988; and Vygotsky, in the domain of philosophy of Sciences with Bernstein, 1983; Giddens, 1984, 1991; Polkinghorne, 1984, 1988, 1991a, 1991b, 1991c, 1994 or Rorty, 1979, 1989, 1998 and finally in ethnology with Garfinkel, 1967; Heritage 1994. Each of these authors offers a vibrant and clever critique of the mainstream in their field. They permit our field to reflect upon its own practices, to progress and evolve.

The commonality among all qualitative researchers is that they all reflect a phenomenological perspective. Qualitative researchers attempt to understand the meaning of phenomena as they naturally occur (as opposed to an experimental, controlled plan). The actions and interactions are viewed in their context (naturalistic) and the point of view of each participant is respected and explored. Goetz and LeCompte (1984) present four continua, which underline all Social Sciences research.

| | |
|---|---|
| Constructive | Enumerative |
| Generative | Verificative |
| Inductive | Deductive |
| Subjective | Objective |

These continua represent different epistemologies. Qualitative research is of course located closer to the left pole. Qualitative research favors constructive, generative, inductive and subjective methods. At the other end of the continuum, one will find experimental research with its enumerative, verificative, deductive and objective aims and methods.

## The "plus" of qualitative research

The questions asked should lead to the method chosen and not the other way around. Polkinghorne (1991c) states:

> "These procedures, although lacking the precision of mathematical analysis, are able to discover patterns within the interlaced metonymic and metaphoric links of everyday speech and actions." (p. 112).

This type of research focuses on what happens in a therapy session. What can the numbers really say about the very process of therapy? What can numbers say about the most complex domain of reflexivity? What types of information can numbers bring compared to the richness and the complexity of narratives? Along with Polkinghorne (1991c), I agree that:

> "The primary reason we need to add qualitative research methods to the field of counseling psychology is that important questions in our field are not easily addressed by quantitative methods alone. (...) Qualitative methods are crafted to work with data that retain the multiple levels of meaning of ordinary language" (p. 112).

The narratives of qualified therapists and the exploration of these will enlighten our domain further than numeric data. Numbers will provide different information, but will not highlight the complexity of those narratives. Polkinghorne (1991c) discusses why qualitative research is so important to our field and will ultimately add rigor the clinicians' practices:

> "Perhaps the most important contribution qualitative research can make to clinical practice occurs at the level of conceptual utilization. Because the analytic tools of qualitative research are directed at uncovering themes and meaning structures in ordinary language date, they overlap the clinical task of understanding a client's interpretive patterns" (p. 111).

*A fortiori*, in the domain of reflective practices and RIA, the choice of qualitative research is most relevant:

> "Two areas in which qualitative methods are particularly useful are the generation of categories

> for understanding human phenomena and the investigation of the interpretation and meaning that people give to events they experience" (Polkinghorne, 1991c, p. 112).

## What are the criteria of good qualitative research?

Communicability and in-depth understanding are important criteria indicating the quality of qualitative research. Reason (1981) describes qualitative research as a process of inquiry that relies on the researcher's ability to make sense of the data creatively. The quality of the research depends on the creative ability to make sense.

> "Typically qualitative research yields a large amounts of complex data. It is hard enough to find order in this kind of material. It can be even harder to communicate the outcomes of this analysis to others. By the time a qualitative researcher has completed analysis of the data, he or she should possess an intimate and fine-grained understanding of the phenomenon being studied" (p. 313).

Guba and Lincoln (1994) offer four constructs to mirror the assumptions of the qualitative paradigm. Credibility is the ability to define and place clear boundaries around the study. Dependability defines the researcher's attempt to account for the context of a phenomenon. Transferability insures that the findings can be used in similar situations. Finally, the confirmability of a research allows another research to replicate the same kind of findings.

## Transcending the obvious

I conclude my discussion on the criteria of good qualitative research with Gale (1991). He highlights the possible double-bind where qualitative research stands: staying close to its subject, yet being able to reflexively look at it, question and analyze it.

> "A good qualitative study should in some way take us beyond that we already know. It should illuminate our understanding, and offer fresh insight. However at the same time, one of the touchstones of any piece of qualitative research lies in the degree to which the slice of the world it describes is recognizable, credible, or authentic. In other words, a qualitative study must depict a world we already know, a reality we can recognize, while at the same time leading us toward a new understanding of that phenomenon. This can represent a cruel paradox for the qualitative researcher. On the one hand, his or her work is judged on the basis that he or she has produced statements that no competent person would regard as obviously or self-evidently true. On the other hand, there is also a judgment to be made over the 'surprise-value' of a piece of qualitative writing: the extend to which it transcends the obvious" (Gale, 1991, p. 196).

In the field of qualitative research, I select the following criteria: a clear and in-depth definition of the subject as well as clear boundaries and delimitation of the field, communicability, clarity, and transcending the obvious.

The importance of developing instruments and research tools that are sensitive to context and pattern is also a crucial indicator of the quality of qualitative research.

# Chapter VI

## Guidelines for a qualitative methodology

"Creativity and orthodoxy are oftentimes incompatible"
*(Lowe, 1990, p. 2)*

Several typologies of qualitative research have been offered and accepted by the academic. In order to build my methodology I have looked into the literature and have selected the traditions that are the closest to my research method. I found ethnomethodology (Garfinkel, 1967; Heritage, 1994), phenomenology (Giorgi, 1985; Polkinghorne, 1989), and the grounded theory or symbolic interactionism (Chenitz & Swanson, 1986; Strauss & Corbin, 1990). The typologies for qualitative research are numerous. Unfortunately, the content of these methods remains frequently unclear, and how these methods differ from one another, apart from their jargon. Amongst the most frequently mentioned methods are: case studies, clinical research, ethnography, ethnomethodology, personal accounts, conversational analysis, historical inquiries, grounded theory, phenomenology, hermeneutics, biographical, interpretivism, social anthropology, collaborative social research. There seem to be as many evolving categories as there are researchers. These typologies leave me perplexed.

After reading several qualitative methods and researches, I have concluded that my method follows the main principle of the *grounded theory* and the *hemeneutical method*. It definitely falls under the category of clinical research. I use conversational analysis and the principles of collaborative social research. I define a method that suits the complex and moving object of reflection-in-action (RIA). I build a reflexive method that is sensitive to the evolving contexts. The kind of method generated is dependent on the object searched. I could call my method a "reflexive method" should the field need one more word of jargon.

> "These procedures *(the qualitative ones)* need to be understood as activities that cannot be separated from the context of a particular research project" (Polkinghorne, 1991a, p. 181).

As a qualitative researcher, I follow and inherit an important tradition. The authors who influenced me have all applied their ideas to the field of research. Most of them are also clinicians. They are involved in the exchange between theory and practice. Most of them have not created a new category of research methodology instead they adapt their new ideas to the existing methodology and modify them. These authors guide my judgment, and influence my ideas. There is no need to reinvent the wheel each time, especially not when the invention resides in a neologism. Anderson and Goolishian 1988a, 1988b, 1990, 1991a, 1991b; Anderson, 1997; Bakan 1967; Braten 1986; Brown 1996; Danzinger 1979, 1990; Garfinkel, 1967; Hoshmand, 1989, 1992, 1993, 1996; Hoffman 1990; Hubble, Mark, Duncan et al. 1999; Hutchinson & Wilson, 1994; Kvale, 1993, 1996; Manicas & Second, 1983; Mc

Cracken, 1988; Morse, 1994; Neimeyer, 1982, 1990, 1993; Polkinghorne, 1984, 1988, 1991a, 1991b, 1991c, 1994; Reason & Rowan, 1981; Sandelowsky, 1994; Schön, 1983; Sterlin, 1987; Tomm, 1987, 1988, 1991b; Wolcott, 1990, 1994; and Yin, 1989) apply their ideas to the field of research. These authors question the historic assumptions of neutrality and the external position of the researcher. After the hermeneuticians, they assert that research is always interpretative. Research is guided and influenced by the researcher's set of theories about the world. These authors are somewhat close to the feminist tradition. Following Dell (1989), they argue and discuss that research involves issues of power.

The Feminists (Hoffman, 1981, 1985, 1990, 1991, 1997; Hutchinson & Wilson, 1994; Mc Namee & Gergen 1992; Morse, 1994; Papp, 1996; Penn & Frankfurt, 1994; Taggart, 1985; Weingarten, 1991, 1995) address the influence of power in research and make explicit its influence. The feminists critique the fact that traditionally, research silenced and marginalized various group of people, treating them as passive objects of inquiry. The feminists develop paradigms that are openly ideological. They try to design their research to democratize and empower the research participants. I borrow some of their ideas although oftentimes, I am tired of their excessive positions.

From the previous chapters (chapter III, IV and V), I extract the methodological guidelines of my research. These concepts have a profound impact on the way I do, conceptualize and understand research. There are presented here by order of importance. These concepts will be interlined in my text as a guideline, methodological tool and a reminder. This has been for me the most profoundly unsettling element of qualitative procedures. There is no set methodology to apply. I construct and custom-design the methodology to fit my object. Here a my methodological guidelines:

## Reflexivity

Fearless, risky and challenging are the steps to reach the second-order Cybernetic. Reflexivity is a meta-process. It forces us to think outside of the nine dots' square. Watzlawick offered this interesting exercise at the Mental Research Institute in Palo Alto (Watzlawick, Beavin Bavelas & Jackson, 1967). In order to expand our knowledge we often need to stretch it outside of our constraining and created reality. Watzlawick asks us to connect these nine objects with lines using four lines only, without lifting the pen.

Problem:

Resolution:

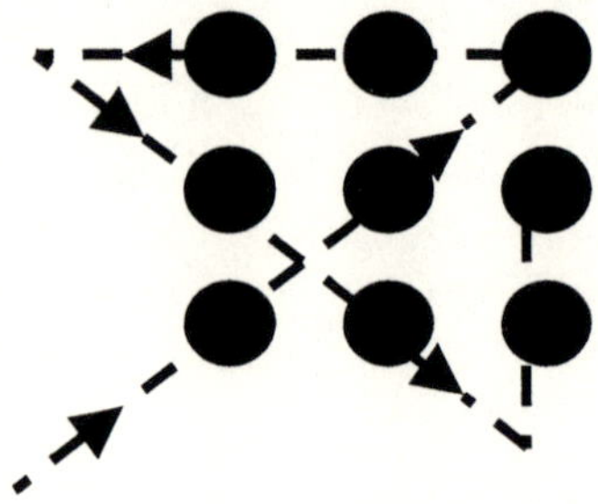

The only way to perform the task is to get outside of the imagined and constraining frame you *invented*: the square (Watzlawick, 1984). If you free yourself from this constraining rule, if you go beyond it, you have solved the task. In the same manner, reflexivity will be used at each level of my research, as an instrument. I will also use the ongoing support of external "reflectors" to reflect upon my work and improve it.

## Context-dependence

The second grounding methodological guideline is context-dependence. I try to be sensitive to how contexts shape and transform what and how I see. This is a truly systemic stance, where we start paying attention to everything around us, to the evolving contexts. The researcher recognizes that we are all part of an Eco-system. We cannot remove ourselves from a context. Everything that happens in a context has an impact on us, just as we have an effect on this very field. One of the sub-categories of the notion of context-dependence is the inclusion of the researcher in the system he wants to explore. The notion of context-dependence is a corner stone of qualitative procedures. In application, it means that qualitative research will be more fluid, more flexible, and finally more responsive to data than most of the quantitative designs. The design of the research will be frequently reviewed, questioned and modified.

## The constant positioning of the researcher

The third methodological guideline for doing qualitative research is linked to the one of context-dependence and reflexivity. It is the notion of positioning. In each context, as a researcher, I learn that it is fundamental to clearly position myself. It is especially complex and relevant because I have a dual status. Not only, am a researcher but I am also a psychotherapist, meeting with psychotherapists. I suspect that welcoming me as a whole (with my doubts, questions, challenges, differences, similarities and interests) of "who I am" in conversation with my interviewees may help them to be a fuller "them". We may therefore construct together richer narratives about RIA. Mc Leod (1996) agrees that the positioning of a researcher has a tremendous impact on the data obtained:

> "The frankness and honesty with which an informant discloses aspects of his or her story will depend, in part, to the extent to which the researcher is perceived as trustworthy and safe" (pp. 310-311).

The form of my discourse is important. I use the "I" throughout the text: this will affect my positioning toward the research process. My position in the text will also affect the nature of the constructed knowledge and the reader's response to it and the type of data obtained. I learn to use my own voice instead of hiding behind the impersonal "one" or the almost majestic "we"; I bravely say: "I", instead of: "The truth is". In personalizing my discourse, I gain visibility (Giddens, 1991). I take responsibility for my ideas, my positions, my opinions, my choices and my beliefs. Several authors highlight the importance of the "I" statements, in the writing process, among them Mc Leod (1996):

> "The word "I" is a stranger to most psychological journals. In some ways, the symposium, which this paper introduces, can be regarded as an attempt to encourage a group of qualitative counseling researchers to allow themselves to be more reflexive: to disclose the hidden stories that bring research to life" (p. 312).

Rennie (1996) shares the opinion that the use of the first person is important in this type of research to enable the reader to interpret the researcher as an "interpreter":

> "The plausibility of a qualitative research manuscript is increased when the author makes assertions reflexively, but with balance. (...) Extensive reflexivity takes space from other sections of the manuscript and the reader away from the phenomenon, while the absence of reflexivity creates a false objectivism that is easily noted, promoting skepticism. In striving for balance, I use the first person singular liberally when referring to my role. I also make it clear that I

> know what I am claiming is my interpretation. (...) In short, I try to enable the reader to interpret me as an interpreter of the phenomenon" (p. 322-323).

## Standing in the uncertain

Another important methodological guideline that I use throughout my research is to accept the unsettling, and to learn to accept the uncertainty. Any research path is somewhat unknown. As exciting as any new path is, it is also scary. I am constructing knowledge in a qualitative way, not in a quantitative one. This truism is important. What I do, what I find, and the narratives that I will gather will not be countable, addable. The nature of my data is therefore approachable in terms of their quality and not numerically in terms of a reference to a norm. For Reason (1981), "the myth of certainty" is one of the results of positivism:

> "Behind the perennial urge to retreat from the depth to surface, lies another obsession: the strong urge to certainty. (…) In philosophy the quest for the kind of certainty, which would serve as a defense of absolutist claims to knowledge inevitably leads to impasse" (p. 9).

Reason traces this explanation back to Hume's theory of regularity:

> "A particular theory of causality is one of the important consequences that flows from following the positivist retreat in the face of epistemological difficulties. Traditionally associated with positivistic epistemology is a view of causality, the

> regularity theory of Hume. According to this doctrine, the only empirical content of a causal law is the set of actual concomitance of events that have been and will be observed. An event is identified as a cause by its temporal priority on a later event and by a statistical fact that events of that type regularly precede events of the type identified as effects. Neither the activity of a productive power of an agent, nor implicit reference to the workings of a generative mechanism, are admitted as part of the meaning of a causal law. To say that something caused something else, is only to say that an event of a certain kind regularly precedes an event of the kind to be explained" (p. 13-14).

This law implies that even if we accept events as following the law of causality, most often it is simply the order of their occurrence that creates artificially their cause and effect relationship. We should therefore pay attention to the common and sometimes insidious assumption that we make where we understand causality literally, as an event provoking another one. I will attempt to discuss the assumptions of causality. I will offer them to deconstruction and continual critique. In qualitative research, the process is the challenge. Its exploration is the very challenge of qualitative inquiry. Polkinghorne (1991) shares how demanding it is for the researcher to "go" qualitative:

> "Conducting a qualitative research requires a significant degree of flexibility. Qualitative research designs are fluid and require researcher choices throughout the process" (p. 110c).

I hold like *mantras* sentences that lead me through the interview process. I owe my first mantra to a regretted and extraordinary clinician: Harry Goolishian used to say: "The familiar is to be explored from a new point of view". Goolishian challenges himself: "I find ways to talk to people in ways they have not talked to themselves or to others before". His comment is a direct reference to Bateson's (1972) concepts of news of information: "A difference that makes a difference". To be accepted by any new system, a difference must be neither too similar, nor too different.

## Questioning the stance of a researcher

During the collection of data, I watch out for the continual risk of slipping into the interviewer role, into the neutral role. This is another important methodological guideline to keep questioning the stance of a researcher. I wonder about that position of neutrality. How will I choose to welcome the information I gather? I challenge the construct of what a researcher "should" be: distant, cold, contained, uncontaminated, in control, knowledgeable, constant. There are at least two different ways of interacting with people in research. The traditional way to interact with one's interviewee is to guard against their making direct contribution to the formulation of my propositions that purport to be about them. In this interaction style, there is a split between the inquiry part (being all on the side of the researcher) and the action to be inquired (being all on the side of the informant).

| The inquiry process | Action to be inquired |
|---|---|
| The researcher | The informant |

I prefer a collaborative research, where the "subjects" can become co-researchers at times. They contribute to the hypothesis forming, suggest analysis and conclusions and help me with the process of research. Collaboration cannot be forced, only invited. By informing the clinicians of my research propositions and my ideas at several stages of the research, I invite them to agree, to disagree, to comment and to reflect upon my reflections. Heron (1981) is ahead of his time when he asserts:

> "We should inquire through dialogue, interaction and cooperative endeavor, *how* they symbolize their experience of the world through scientific constructs and actions, and in the light of this understanding to explain their behavior" (p. 24).

Another advantage to using a more collaborative research approach is for me to receive corrective feedback, and to keep the critique open. I am willing to have my ideas modified and transformed by their responses and questions. I watch out for the temptation of wanting to set the frame. I avoid directing the conversation and therefore to give up this precious curiosity. I approach my interviewee with an attitude of curiosity (Cechin, 1987, 1993) and of not knowing (Andersen, 1991, 1995; Anderson & Goolishian 1991b). Heron (1981) declares: "Each individual is not necessarily the best authority on the validity of his own constructs and intentions" (p. 24). As I previously said (Kuenzli-Monard, 2001):

> "I am inspired by the anthropological method. Approaching the other with eyes and ears that do not already know. I try to believe the other instead of second-guessing him. Through my work, I sincerely hope that humanity takes over the technical aspects" (p. 4).

In order to assure coherence in my approach to research, I choose along with others the notion of co-researcher (Anderson, 1997; Grafanaki, 1996; Hill, 1984, 1990, 1991; Hill, Rhodes, & Thompson, 1996; Rowan, 1981; Tripp-Reimer et al. 1994). Rowan (1981) is the first author to have used this term:

> "A true human inquiry needs to be based firmly in the experience of those it purports to understand, to involve a collaboration between "researcher" and "subjects" so that they may work together as co-researchers and to be intimately involved in the lives and praxis of these co-researchers" (p. 113).

The word co-researcher implies to work with. I see my interviewee as at least as knowledgeable as I am. Within the choice of these words, I intend to carry less of a sense of a separation between the knower and the to-be-known. This language shift implies a different status given to the co-researcher, more equal, and more participative. This language difference implies that I see my colleagues as an active and potentially transforming part of my research, rather than being simply "data providers". Hill (1984) shares her preference to view the participant as a co-researcher:

> "Treating the research participants as co-researchers and collaborators made it easier for me to relax and enjoy the research process and at the same time gain more cooperation from them. It also adds the benefit in terms of cooperation gained from this more egalitarian positioning" (p. 101).

## Red flags on methodological danger

A common problem occurs in qualitative research. In the face of newness and uncertainty we are frequently tempted to adore one's own method to the point of idolatry. As Gurman and Kniskern (1978b) point out, to worship the traditional methodology may act against reflective and innovative science. When advancing in the dark, it is extremely tempting to use an already existing methodology. This methodology could become a "methodolatry" (Moon, Dillon & Sprenkle, 1990). If nothing is certain, then an already constructed methodology could lead the researcher, like a candle light in the age of stone, holding a manual of practice in the darkness of unexplored lands. Years ago, the eminent and provocative methodologist Bakan (1967) warned:

> "When man tarries too long; when man seeks to be completely fulfilled on the way towards the objective, when in effect, he allows the impulse to be bribed, then he commits the sin of idolatry" (p. 152).

Bakan underlines the danger of worshiping a methodology. Method may dictate and constrain research. Bakan explores the danger of becoming seduced by the conventional methodological purity at the expense of the questions one seeks to answer. It will be a challenge throughout my research to maintain a commitment to the grounding ideas of qualitative research. I will attempt to stay connected to these ideas at each level of the research, from the interview preparation, to the interview process, to the design of the research and finally in the analysis process and in the writing exercise. I will attempt to provide clarity and define with care the concepts I am using.

I suggest that the reader keep in mind throughout reading the interviews the ideas informing my research. I also recommend that the reader judge my research in terms of coherence and consistency to these methodological guidelines, rather than the positivist's criteria for science.

I use reflexivity as a meta-process throughout the research to guide, correct and review each move. The notion of context-dependence is fundamental. Contexts shape and transform the way we see the world. My methodology will continuously be reflexive and context-sensitive. I have presented the central concepts of reflexivity and the notion of context-dependence and positioning. The other methodological guidelines I have described are the personalization of the narration, accepting the uncertainty, questioning the stance of a researcher, and his constant positioning. These methodological guidelines derive from the founding theories of qualitative research (the postmodern critique and the second-order cybernetic). These guidelines are used throughout my text either explicitly, or implicitly. Finally, I have shown the danger of idolizing one's method, at the expense of asking other questions and placing the method into question.

# Chapter VII

## The interview process

*"The primary human reality is persons in conversation".*
*(Harré, 1986, p. 58)*

I use my interviews to obtain greater knowledge of the psychotherapist's RIA. As a research tool, an interview has a purpose and a structure:

> "The purpose of data production in qualitative designs is to accumulate sufficient depictions of instances of the phenomenon under study to permit the construction of a pattern that fully describes the diverse qualities of the phenomenon" (Polkinghorne, 1991a, p. 185)

Kvale (1996) defines an interview as:

> "(...) neither an objective nor a subjective method, its essence is intersubjective interaction. The issue of the objectivity of knowledge gained through an interview is linked to the pervasive dichotomy of objectivism and subjectivism in Western thought" (p. 66).

Kvale argues for the importance and the quality of this interaction: the interview. He says that an interview could enrich the object researched with new and alternative meanings. The research interview does not seek a truth. Graphically, Kvale shows his interest in this definition, when he writes "interviews" as a hyphenated word: "Inter-Views". Kvale expands on the importance of this moving and changing interstice. He highlights the importance of the "between". This exchange of views, this dialogue demands a duality of perspective. More concerned about the process than the product, Kvale explores the demanding aspects of an interview. He continues:

> "There is an alternation between knowers and the known, between the constructors of knowledge and the knowledge constructed. This dual aspect of the interview, the personal interrelation and the interview knowledge that it leads to (...) which alternates between the focusing on the personal interaction and on the knowledge constructed through the interaction" (Kvale, 1996, p. 16).

Historically the interview process has been used. It has been dismissed for long in our field as a valid means to generate knowledge:

> "Conversation is an ancient form of obtaining knowledge. Thucydides interviewed participants from the Peloponnesian Wars to write the history of the wars, and Socrates used dialogue to obtain philosophical knowledge. Within the modern social sciences, which originated in the 19th Century, systematic interview research is, however, a new phenomenon of the past decades. Conversations have belonged to the realm of the humanities and

> philosophy, whereas social science methodology has long been modeled on the natural sciences. The present emphasis on the interview as conversation and on the interpretation of its meanings brings the interview research closer to the domain of humanities"(Kvale, 1996, p. 8).

The research interview is a construction site for knowledge. It focuses on a theme, without leading to opinions about this theme. Like the therapeutic interview, the research interview is determined by a set of theoretical references and procedures that suggest appropriate questions:

> "Qualitative interviews are not in themselves progressive or oppressive; the value of the knowledge produced depends on the context and the use of the knowledge" (Kvale, 1996, p. 72).

## Interview and psychotherapy: Establishing an alliance

Several authors (Anderson, 1997; Hutchinson & Wilson, 1994; Kvale, 1996; Morse, 1994; Ramhoj & Oliveira, 1991; Polkinghorne, 1988, 1991b, 1991c, 1994) stress the necessity of establishing a rapport for an interview to be successful. For a research interview to be productive, a contact needs to be established between the interviewer and his interviewee. There is no single recipe for that contact to happen, no step-by-step guidelines to follow that might guarantee the establishment of this alliance. However, several ingredients will enhance chances for contact to occur. Contact

(Resnick, 1999) is the ability to have a connection with somebody. This encounter is of a genuine nature. It is potentially meaningful. Contact means the ability to be present (as a whole) with the other. Being "contactful" does not mean to agree with the other's perception. One can create contact in disagreement. Contact assumes the pre-existence of boundary between two people. These are elements of a methodology of contact established by the Gestalt Associates of Los Angeles (Resnick, 1999). These steps are necessary, but not sufficient for contact to occur:

- *Movement*: must occur between two persons in order for a relationship to be contactful.
- *Difference*: There must be awareness that the two persons are different for contact to take place. There must be an awareness of the existence of boundaries between people.
- *Sharing of the primary experience*: the person who wants contact shares what is happening, his phenomenological experience. He does not cover, nor hide his experience in the present. The primary experience is the perception of what happens in the "now", with this person.

An alliance with moments of contact is an essential component in the quality of information that the researcher will be able to gather in an interview. We know that an alliance is central to any therapeutic relationship. The quality of the therapeutic relationship is central in the positive outcome for therapy. Regardless of the type of approach chosen, the therapeutic relationship appears as a common factor accounting for therapeutic success (Bordin, 1979; Greenberg and Pinsof, 1986; Horvath & Symonds, 1991; Hubble, Mark, Duncan & Miller, 1999; Lambert 1989; Lambert and Bergin, 1994; Rogers, 1942).

Developing a strong and positive therapeutic alliance has emerged as the single best predictor of positive outcome in therapy. As defined by Bordin (1979), the therapeutic relationship consists of two main components:

- the therapeutic bond, mutual feelings of positive affectivity between the client and the therapist, and

- an active collaboration, a shared vision of the goals of treatment and collaboration on the tasks of therapy necessary to accomplish these goals.

Like the therapist, the researcher must be present and committed to the interview process, rather than being confined to the role of a distant observer. He should convey by his words and his expression an attitude that invites the interviewee to be reflexive, to wonder about his thoughts and to feel confident in searching for new knowledge. Throughout the interview, a researcher should convey an attitude of genuine interest and curiosity. This attitude invites the interviewee to develop questions about his own comments, to expand his own descriptions. Lamb & Huttlinger (1989) make the following comparison:

> "Both research and therapeutic interviews are reflexive in that they encourage self-exploration and attention to what the researcher-therapist is asking, feeling, and thinking. Reflexivity is a self-awareness and an awareness of the relationship between the investigator and the research environment"(p. 766).

Kvale (1996) describes two possible scenarios, in which different climates can be created:

> "The interview situation may, for both parties be characterized by positive feelings of a common intellectual curiosity and a reciprocal respect. The interview may also be anxiety provoking and evoke defense mechanisms in the interviewee as well as in the interviewer" (p. 35).

Both climates can be present in the same interview. Both positive feelings, trust and common intellectual curiosity can be present along with high anxiety and a need to perform to provide the "right answer". Central to my argument is the idea that therapy and research may have different aims and similar procedures.

## Reciprocity and equity

The issue of reciprocity is important, since an interview is unequal. I get more out of the process than the clinicians I interview. In terms of reciprocity, I allowed my colleagues at GATLA to develop an understanding and an awareness of the importance of practical knowing and reflection-in-action (RIA). The other form of reciprocity can be as Seidman states

(1991): "that which flows from my interest in the participants' experience, and my honoring their words when I present to a larger public" (p. 83). Much as in therapy, the research interview is not based on equity. The interviewer and interviewee are not equal partners. As a researcher, I define, control, and delineate the boundaries and the focus of the conversation. Equity can be aimed toward, when the researcher clearly states the rights and the responsibilities of the interviewer and the participants at the onset of the process. It becomes a contract, therefore a choice. The interviewee knows what to expect and how much investment I ask from him. I set up times and places that would be convenient for the interviewee. I offer financial compensation for the loss of income.

## Money and research

Money is always an important and sometimes burning issue in a research process. I discuss with each expert clinician the issue of a fee and their income loss, should they decide to participate in my research. My initial requests are various:

- That each clinician obtains a written consent from his patient(s) to exchange and use part of the content and process of the session for the purpose of my research. I tell each clinician that I am willing to come and clarify with their clients the exact nature of my research and the specific use of the data obtained. None of the clinicians asked me to do so.

- That each clinician audiotapes the session.
- That each clinician suspends their professional activity for an hour after their session, while I am listening to the audiotape. The possible interference of memory could make the exercise of RIA tedious.
- That each clinician be available for an additional hour after their break for the interview on RIA, and that they agree to this interview being audiotaped.
- That each clinician be available for reviewing the transcripts and my interpretations of the transcripts. That they add relevant reflections on this analysis process, or erase any if desired.

These are many requests. It means, potentially, three hours of income loss for each clinician. I think it is only fair to offer to pay their regular hourly fee to compensate them for the loss of income. Although I offered assertively and with conviction, all the expert clinicians refused this offer. Their rational was the desire to help research advance. It is also obvious at this time that our financial status is quite unbalanced I am still an intern working with a low income and they have a flourishing private practice. There decision may have something to do with that as well. They say that they wanted to help me in my research.

## Format of the interview

I choose a semi-structured interview. I have a clear idea of the process that I am investigating. I have built a repertoire of questions accordingly. During the interview, I can use some of my comments to maintain our conversation within the boundaries of the chosen topics. My questioning, however, transforms and evolves, along with the comments, needs, requests and questions of the interviewee. In my opinion, choosing a structured and standardized interview mode might have led to an important loss of information. My interviews are co-constructed. Each comment, questions and wondering attitude will influence the other. A process thereby develops between the interviewer and the interviewee of unveiling personal feelings, beliefs, wishes, problems encountered, comments, and questions.

## Each interview is different from the next

There is no such a thing as a research interview. An interview is not a definite object, but a moving concept. It is constantly evolving in shape and form, defined by the contexts in which it occurs. There is only unequal, nonreplicable interview. An interview is idiosyncratic by nature: an encounter, a meeting, unique and different each time. Along with Hutchinson and Wilson (1994) and following the ideas from the second-order cybernetic (Bateson, 1972; Dell, 1982a, 1982b, 1985, 1986, 1989; Keeney, 1983; Maturana et Varela, 1987; Von Foerster, 1984; Von Glaserfield, 1984) I believe that each interview has a transforming function. An interview influences both the researcher and the participant:

> "I tried to let the participants teach me how to retell their stories in a way that was closer to their experiential world. The whole process of asking, listening carefully, understanding and retelling what happened was an exciting, interesting and exhausting experience" (Grafanaki, 1992, p. 333).

## Reflexive interviews

Polkinghorne (1991) holds that the quality of data produced in an interview depends on the skills of the interviewer: "The reflective and recollecting capacities of the interviewee, and the relationship that is developed" (p. 188). Hutchinson & Wilson (1994) underscore the important function of reflexivity in creating an interview that is qualitatively valuable:

> "In addition, interviewers must transcend the interview process and observe reflexively themselves and the interview dynamics"(p. 307).

To describe the reflexive process of a researcher doing an interview, they use words similar to those of a therapist performing therapy:

> "An internal self-dialogue occurs throughout the interview process. A researcher is not only listening but also thinking about what question to ask next and how to ask it" (p. 309).

Reflexivity and the ability to use the reflexive process are replicated at each scale of the process and meta-processes of my thesis. One does not get out of reflexivity. The process of interviewing often requests RIA. Knowledge is created in context and is constructed in relationship with the interviewee.

## Self-report

Direct access to the "black box" (Watson, 1920) is impossible. I can only access the clinicians' discourse about their own experience of therapy and rely on their report about their RIA. Self-reporting involves a reconstruction of the experience and a narrative about what the clinician is ready to share with the researcher. There might be a myriad of information that the clinician chooses not to convey. Despite the high level of self-awareness of the clinicians I chose, they cannot be aware of all their mental, emotional and bodily awareness at all times. So only part of their experience is conveyed through self-report.

Schutz (1967) offers some guidance regarding the nature of the obtained data. He says, in essence, that it is never possible to fully understand another person. In order to do so we should enter their mind, their stream of consciousness and experience what they have experienced. If we could do that, we would *be* the other. The way to meaning, Schutz (1967, chap. 2-3) continues, is to be able to put a behavior *in context.* The nature of my data is a narrative about the clinician's processes. I will access the reflexive process of a psychotherapist about this practical knowledge, as well as the struggle to put that into words. Despite the loss during the process of transmission, my interviews give valid and important information about the clinician's process in therapy. Guba and Lincoln (1981) advocate for the real value of these data:

> "Because the inquirer himself is the instrument, changes resulting from fatigue, shifts in knowledge, and co-optation, as well as variations resulting from differences in training, skill, and experience among different instruments easily occur. But this loss in rigor, is more than offset by the flexibility, insight and ability to build on tacit knowledge that is peculiar province of the human instrument" (p. 113).

## From interview to transcription

Taping transforms the therapeutic encounter and adds to it an unusual dimension. The further use of this therapeutic encounter to serve research transforms the nature of this conversation by placing it into a larger context and a different purpose. I ask the clinicians to use the audiotape before the final recording, to get used to the audiotape, and to help the patient become more comfortable with it. The sound of the audiotapes is generally good. Only minor and short segments are difficult to understand. Some segments are inaudible due to external noise covering up the voice of the interviewee. In the transcripts, I mention, when a segment is inaudible.

# Preparation of the interviews

There is no specific school, nor training on interviewing, that I know of. If I look back it took me several years of informal preparation to perform these interviews. I read Seidman (1991), he reassures and inspires me:

> "There is no solid, unmovable platform upon which to base our understanding of human affairs. They are in constant flux. Heisenberg's principle of indeterminacy speaks at least as directly to human affairs as it does to the world of physics" (p. 19). Preliminary ideas about research often stay locked in one's inner speech. They are fleeting, predicated, and unstable (Vygotsky, 1986) making communication of them difficult" (p. 23).

I start by describing my stammering with my close friends, with my husband. They help me clarify my thoughts and language. Then, I share my questions with my colleagues, at work, at a party, at a restaurant. Just anywhere. It becomes all that I do outside of my work. I observe and listen to their reactions. I remember discussing my passion with a gifted computer designer. I discuss with a philosopher. I discuss with a professor of Medieval Literature. I discuss with an expert in Linguistics. I discuss with a theologian. I discuss with a radiologist. I discuss with a researcher in oncology, my interest for practical knowledge. Everywhere I discuss my methodological concerns for qualitative methods. I discuss the postmodern critique and its impact on sciences. I assume our field could not communicate for failure of having the bounding language; to my surprise, they respond with enthusiasm. I am amazed that in such completely different fields we can speak a similar language. We share similar questions, interests and passions.

I gain assurance. I document in my journal their reactions, my reactions. I practice reflexivity. I document my questions and start building a repertoire. I know that I will never use this repertoire of course, because each question is context-dependant. There is no recipe for this process. It is rather an anti-phobic object for me. Moreover, constructing this repertoire is part of my training. I learn to generate sensitive and subtle questions. I find the courage to ask more questions. Now, I finally ask when I do not understand. This process of preparation for the interview is a struggle. It is emotionally draining. It is also a struggle to find a language that will account for what I want to convey. Reflection-in-action (RIA) is a revolutionary concept. There is no easy way of putting RIA into common language. I discuss with many clinicians. I adjust and modify my questions. I ask for help. I start to understand that I can recycle into interviewing many of my skills as a psychotherapist. I am skilled at asking questions, at framing ingenious questions and in the interview, I can use my talent. My language, my questions and the articulation of what I do and what I aim to do becomes clearer and clearer with time[6]. The more I talk about what I do, the more familiar I become with what I do, the easier and simpler the words come. Before the interview begins, I reflect on the following questions:

---

[6] I finally summarize the topic of my research to my five-year old niece! She explains it with her own words. She understands it! There is a clear assimilation of this complex set of information.

- What is the effect of this question?
- Does it open space for more possibilities?
- Does it close down conversation, inviting just a single answer?
- Does it invite clinicians to share?
- Does it carry an intention, a non-expressed assumption, inducing clinicians to answer as they are supposed to?
- What about the tone, the attitude I convey?
- Is it accepting of hesitancy?
- Does my attitude convey respect?
- Does my attitude carry blame, disregard or biases and shut clinicians off from other paths they would like to explore?
- Is the pacing of my questions fitting, leaving enough time for the clinician to process and think?
- Do I cut off silences that mean: I am done, or: I don't know ask me something else? Should I cut off such silences?
- Am I familiar enough with my biases, my strengths, my limitations, my interest (overt and covert) about this phenomenon?
- Am I clear enough about my own boundaries to invite the clinicians to define and shape, in front of me their boundaries?
- Will my questions offer the clinician support for a thought in process?

These questions are the fuel for my interviews. Building this repertoire of questions that I never used per se helped me to maintain curiosity and respect, and follow up on a question that was unanswered, hopefully without arrogance.

## Transcription

Transcribing means literally to transform *(trans-scribere)*. Kvale (1996) instructs the researcher in the qualitative field to pay attention to the necessary changes involved in shifting from the oral to the written and the transition to a new set of rules. The question is: "What is a useful transcription for my research purpose?" The choice of the audiotape disregards the visual and some nonverbal aspects of the interview. By making this choice to audiotape, I know I lose important information. I decide to do so, because my focus is on the discourse of RIA and the narratives of the clinicians. The audiotape captures certain expressions such as tone, rhythm, pacing that I transcribe in the interviews.

> "If the emotional aspects of the conversation are included, for instance: tense voice, giggling, nervous laughter and so on, the intersubjective reliability of the transcription could develop into a research project of its own." (Kvale, 1996, p. 164).

Transcription is a constructive and conventional activity. The transcriber is struggling to make clear decisions about what is said. As passive and unattractive as it may seem, transcription involves multiple judgments and decisions in order to go from oral to written. I make choices; when I think a segment does not add any relevant information, I skip it. I skip multiple repetitions. I fill in on rare occasions, on a specific word, difficult to hear. RIA is a type of knowing that is not normally expressed that is not often shared out loud. Therefore, the obtained data are probably more obscure and more difficult to understand than during any other interview. RIA by essence probably presents more hesitations, more repetitions and unclear statements.

In the tradition of qualitative research, transcripts are often tedious to read and hard to understand. They are verbatim transcripts, which are oftentimes unintelligible. The context of the interview is often poorly explained. I transcribe my interview to readable ones. The transcription phase is already an interpretation. Some see transcription as a long and boring clerical task. I however see transcription as a way of familiarizing myself with the material, and a way of controlling their accuracy. I first transcribe the material word for word. Verbatim transcription involves important judgments such as where a sentence ends. Is the sentence a question or a statement? I transcribe after listening to the audiotape segment of the session repeatedly (five to six times). I spend approximately seven to nine hours per fifty minutes session of repeated listening to the audiotape, in order to create a detailed transcription. I make qualitative choices. I remove the parts of the transcript that are not adding any information. I keep some hesitancy that I think is relevant.

# Interviews in context

Since the transcripts are de-contextualized, it is important to bring these conversations into the context of their emergence. The description of a context has much to do with judgments and decision-making. I selected the descriptive elements that I think are essential. I requested during my research a critical view from the clinicians, and from several readers on how my perception of the context fits and makes sense.

# Chapter VIII

## Interpreting qualitative data

In this chapter, I explain and define the process and the method I use for interpreting the obtained qualitative data. Rather than confirming a hypothesis, my intention is to generate a larger and richer description of the phenomenon of RIA. Schematically, I could divide the final stage of interpretation into two steps: the description and the analysis of data. The line between interpretation and description is blurry. It is not always clearly defined where analysis starts and where description becomes interpretative. A description always carries elements of interpretation. In the very act of observing, a qualitative researcher makes a myriad of choices in choosing to look at some things omitting others. Wolcott (1994) warns that a pervasive problem of interpretation lies in that we often try to reach too far beyond the case itself in speculating about its meanings, or implications. Hill (1984) suggests five assumptions to overcome what she defines as a crisis of faith. She offers the following guidelines:

> "There is no truth, rather there are multiple realities which are dependent on the vantage points, psychological filters, and predefined contours of the mind.
> Clinical phenomena are elusive and reactive.
> Clinical problems are often intractable.
> Human behavior should be studied holistically rather than in a piecemeal fashion.

> Cause and effect relationships or linear causality concepts may be of limited utility at this point of our understanding of human behavior"(p. 105).

The process of interpretation and analysis are not distinct and successive phases in the development of research. Frequently these phases are interlaced. Agar (1980) shows the importance of a dialectic process between analysis and interpretation (hermeneutic circle). To gather more information I may go back to the collection of data. This is a process of back and forth. The way I handled my pilot project is an example of these interlaced phases. Originally, I intended to create a pilot study. I then recognized the richness of these data. Agar (1980) describes this dialectic well:

> "In ethnography, you learn something (collect data); then you try to make sense out of it (analysis); then you go back and see if the interpretation makes sense in light of new experience (collect more data); then you refine your interpretation (more analysis); and so on. The process is dialectic, not linear" (p. 9).

The following guidelines inform my interpretation:

1) The goal of data analysis is to generate richer and more complete descriptions of the phenomenon of reflection-in-action (RIA). I favor the diversity of explanations of similar phenomena over a consensus of explanations.

2) The interpretation of the data must highlight a reflexive process at each step of the interpretation. Each step is informed by the previous one and will inform the next.

3) As in any reflexive process, I invite the clinicians to be involved in the process of interpreting the data. The interpretation of these data is also relational.

4) Interpretation of data is context-dependent. During the analysis, the context is explained as clearly as possible. These contexts influence the findings.

5) There is a continuum between description and interpretation. A description is always interpretative.

6) The interpretation of the data includes a critical analysis of the interviewer as well as the questions asked. Questions are never neutral and an interview is profoundly co-constructed.

7) The clinicians have the right to participate and offer feedback in the way their statements are interpreted.

The questions asked at the onset of the research, the leading questions and the questions asked throughout the interview will be the basis of a successful interview. However refined the process of the interpretation, it will remain sterile if the interview is not interesting.

Noting patterns of appearance, contrasting and comparing statements and understandings can also sharpen and add to the interpretation of the data. The interpretation of data will invite the clinician in a co-creation of meanings. I ask the clinicians to review and critique the interpretation that I offer. I encourage them to generate their own interpretation and reflect on my interpretation, if they so choose. This process of back and forth aims to refine the interpretation.

In concluding of this chapter, I have argued that analysis permeates the entire interview process. Kvale (1996) calls it "the pervasiveness of interpretation" (p. 205). The interpretative process is always in the background, since I am not neutral. Even in the transcription stage, as I will discuss in the next chapter, active interpretations are involved.

# Chapter IX

## Resistances, choices, and issues of selection

In this chapter, I discuss how I determine and delineate the relevant units of information that improve the description of RIA. I choose clinicians for the main interviews, based on the belief that they possess exceptional abilities. They are known for their precise and evolved articulation about their work, through multiple lectures, training and publications. They have outstanding training as psychotherapists. They hold an international reputation in the field of psychotherapy. They have achieved an international recognition through the teaching of their talent and proficiency in the United States and other continents (Europe and Australia). They have trained beginning and advanced therapists for over twenty years. The four selected clinicians have an impressive vita. They are well published. They possess a strong and persistent interest and dedication in learning about their evolving field. They prove it by their ongoing and updated readings, by attending workshops and training with other trainers. Their availability to my research is one example of their ongoing interest in research. That is why I consider them experts. Jennings and Skovholt (1999) identify common qualities of what he calls "master therapists". The clinicians I chose follow most of Jennings and Skovholt's criteria: they are voracious learners. They value cognitive complexity and the ambiguity of human condition. They have reached a balance between confidence and humility.

I initially wanted to interview clinicians from different theoretical backgrounds. I wanted to observe their discourses about their practical knowledge. How are there discourses similar to or different from one another and mine? Ideally, I would have liked to offer *more variety* in terms of the theoretical background of the clinicians. I regret that this has not been possible. I tried to interview a well-known and well-established colleague trained in a psychoanalytic orientation, who currently has patients under psychoanalysis. She showed clear interest in my research. She decided to ask several patients to participate to the study. However, she felt unable, or unwilling, to request taping from a patient on the couch. I respect this choice, but I wanted to know more about her choice. She did not provide an extensive response as to why this would not be possible, despite my questions. She stated that taping "just would not work with a patient in analysis". Despite my interest in working with this clinician, despite her interest in my research and after several months of going back and forth, I finally gave up on the idea of collaborating with her. To this date, I suspect the difficulty of taping has something to do with the clinician as well as with the patients. Maybe she was not ready to explore this process with me. I am still trying to figure out if, in some ways I might have made this process easier for her, more inviting, less threatening. I still wonder. There is in the psychoanalytical tradition of secrecy. In the field of Family Therapy and Gestalt therapy, showing one's work to colleagues is a tradition. I suspect this has something to do with it.

I asked three other colleagues, who would fall into the category of expert therapists to participate to my research.

They refer to three different theoretical orientations: Cognitive Behavioral therapy, and Ericksonian Hypnosis. I have not been able to engage them in my research.

These experiences show me the possible limits of my research. I work with clinicians who are closer to my own theoretical orientation. The expert therapists I chose are used to showing their work. They are used to being videotaped and audio-taped. They also are used to demonstrating their clinical work with clients in front of trainees.

After asking many therapists, I can almost predict who would be interested in participating in my research (expert or non-expert), or who may fearfully rejects the offer. I often face resistance to letting me into the secret and protected arena of therapy. Within the field of Family Therapy I also encountered resistance. Clinicians are often known to have a need for control. Clinicians do not like to be put in situations where they do not have control over the situation unveiling and exploring this tacit and emerging knowledge about practice must be *a fortiori* threatening. Along with Hill (1984), I agree that:

> "Though undoubtedly well-intentioned, counselors certainly have much less investment than the researcher in a study. They have other matters in their mind, and usually have more than a little ambivalence and reluctance to being taped and evaluated" (p. 101).

I include myself in the above definition. I have been interviewed, as a clinician, on my RIA. Before practicing reflection-in-action I have felt my heart pounding, my hands sweating, and the tension in my stomach. I can translate it as: What if I don' t come up with anything clever to say? My reaction is mixed with a profound excitement of discovering unexplored paths. So far, excitement has won over anxiety.

## Interviewing Trainers

Among the four expert therapists I chose, three of them were previously my trainers. This choice can be both an asset, and a limitation. I already have an alliance with these expert therapists. This alliance may facilitate the interview process. Before the interviews, my relationship with these expert therapist and trainers was a hierarchical one. I may limit myself out of concern for the relationship with these clinicians. I have reflected upon the particular relationship I have with each trainer, before each interview. I think I dared to question them, more than I would with an absolute stranger. Another less obvious limitation with an interviewee that I already know is to avoid exploring assumptions, and seeking clarity. With a pre-existing relationship, there may be assumptions "we understand one another". Mc Cracken (1988), Spradley (1979), Bogdan and Biklen (1982) warn about this important bias when there is a pre-existing relationship with an interviewee.

## Pilot project

At the Gestalt Associates Therapists of Los Angeles (GATLA), I first want to make a pilot project to practice interviews to answer the following questions:

- What are the questions and attitude that will generate interesting responses on RIA?
- How can I talk about RIA in a clear manner?
- What are the questions that open space, what are the questions that encourage clinicians to reflect upon their practice?
- How does conversing about RIA impact the therapist, the client and the supervisors?

I think that I may develop my interviewing skills with a pilot project. This pilot project would enable me to make a better final product. This idea of a pilot project does not take into account the fact that there is no replicable interview (as I discussed in chapter VII). The idea of a pilot project is informed by a positivist paradigm. Underlying the pilot project is the following assumption: If I try hard enough, if I prepare long enough; I may find the *right* instrument. I shall discover a reality that is more *accurate.* Behind the notion of pilot interview, lies the assumption that the type of information gathered will be of higher quality if I can learn to become "pre-programmed", to predict every subsequent step.

Having a clear focus on my goal and procedure is extremely important.

The use of multiple data collections and sources is an important concept of qualitative inquiry. In the qualitative research, it is called triangulation. Guba and Lincoln (1994) advocate for triangulation in that it increases the "trustworthiness of findings". I might have missed precious information, had I disregarded the content of the pilot interview. This interview is one of the lenses, one of the angles, one of the many ways to approach the definition of RIA. With multiple settings and contexts, I have co-constructed, interviews that are interesting in their own right. This multiplicity of interviews enriches the definition of the RIA. Using the pilot project as a valid source of information will allow me a valuable comparison between the expert RIA and the less expert clinicians' RIA. Selection is traditionally done *a priori*. A careful design of the qualitative study and its methodology is created ahead of time (Marshall and Rossman, 1999). I change these rules. I decide to use these interviews as part of the information. In this present research, I determine and delineate the relevant units of information that will improve the description of this phenomenon, *a posteriori*. It may be a dangerous choice, Seidman (1991) warns:

> "The danger of over-emphasizing the "emergent" nature of the design of the study is a looseness, lack of focus and misplaced nonchalance about purpose, method, and procedures on the part of those who do qualitative research" (p. 127).

Lincoln and Guba echo that the emergent nature of qualitative research cannot be used as a license to "undisciplined poking around" (1985, p. 251).

# Chapter X

## On knowledge

*"Man is an animal suspended in webs of significance he himself has spun."*
*Geertz, 1973, p. 5*

In this chapter, I discuss the status of knowledge in the field of qualitative research. Since the very first chapter of this research, I have redefined and challenged the canonical definition of knowledge. I present several authors who bring forth definitions of knowledge in qualitative research. The question of the status of scientific knowledge is a crucial one. In qualitative research, there is no reference to Galileo's adage (1564-1642): "Measure what is measurable and make measurable what is not". What makes knowledge scientific in the qualitative field? Several authors set as a criterion for knowledge a consensus (Anderson, 1997; Geertz, 1983; Gergen, 1985a, 1991a, 1991b; Kvale, 1993, 1996; Shotter 1991, 1993; Shotter and Gergen, 1989). A panel of scientific experts will ultimately pass judgment on the status of the knowledge produced. Just as you, the reader, will decide on the status of the knowledge, which I have generated. Ultimately you will be the judge of my contribution to the field: the rigor, the method, and the relevance of this knowledge. Is it sufficiently different from common sense to carry the label of science? Polkinghorne highlights (1991a) that doing research involves a stance and an ongoing methodical effort to correct and refine the original understanding of a phenomenon:

> "Doing science does not mean a different way of thinking or the use of special cognitive skill. Science is an extension of the ordinary cognitive processes used to make experience meaningful and inform everyday human actions. What differentiates scientific knowing from ordinary knowing is its deliberate and communal dimensions. Doing science is a purposeful and self-conscious activity: science involves a methodical effort to correct and refine the initial understanding until it clearly fits experience. The result of scientific efforts are simply knowledge proposals until they have been judged by the community of scholars as worthy of inclusion in a discipline's body of knowledge" (p. 175).

Polkinghorne (1991a) adds the importance of reaching a good-enough description of a phenomenon, a description that fits and clarifies the experience and provide enough details for somebody else to understand it:

> "The function of qualitative designs is to produce clarifying and integrating descriptions of patterns that make experience understandable and meaningful. Any description, whatever its source, that contributes to the clarification of the structures of experience can usefully be included as data" (p. 190).

Polkinghorne shows the thin border between a vernacular and a scientific knowledge:

> "For researchers trained in quantitative methods, perhaps the most difficult problem in comprehending qualitative research is its affinity with ordinary knowledge generation" (1991a, p. 178).

In the field of qualitative research, the notion of knowledge has expanded. Historically, it has come from several traditions. It is important to be aware of these fields of influence. To start with the constructivists, for example Piaget (1950, 1956), who portrayed the operations of ordinary understanding as involving two main processes: assimilation and accommodation. New events are understood by assimilation into previous acquired patterns or what he called "schemata". The constructivist approach to knowledge invites the subject into an active participation in the process of knowledge. The hermeneutic tradition (Gadamer, 1975) represents understanding by a circle. Understanding is a reciprocal interaction between the knower and the known. Understanding is context-dependent, and holistic. Speed, (1999) encourages clinicians to welcome common sense in the practice of psychotherapy:

> "Such life experiences contributes to what makes us good at our jobs, fuelling our curiosity about the dilemmas of others enabling us to empathize and understand our clients and similar difficulties more adequately and firing us with enthusiasm to try to help" (p. 134).

With the postmodern critique, knowledge comes into question, its canonical definition is offered to deconstruction.

Kvale (1996) underscores the increasing interest in practical forms of knowledge:

> "The recognition of the heterogeneous and noncommensurable contexts of the practical world involves a loss of hegemony for formalized experimental and statistical methods research. There is an acceptance of diverse ways of producing knowledge as abstract objective and universal to ecologically valid, socially useful, and local. More practical forms of knowledge are advocated elevating the embodied knowledge of everyday life over theoretical knowledge. And there is a move from the knower to the known, from the knowing subject to the subject known from the psychology of cognitive processes to epistemological investigation of the nature of knowledge sought. Narrative, hermeneutical, and deconstructive approaches are advocated. There is a multi-method approach with an emphasis on qualitative, interactive, and involved research" (Kvale in Corsini, 1996, p. 101).

In this manner, postmodern critique challenges the notion of knowledge related to research. The researcher is not distant, but a part of the interaction. Kvale (1996) continues to describe the move to knowledge as consistently colored by its evolving context:

> "This involves going beyond academic research to include the generation of knowledge by professionals and the epistemological, ethical, and political implications of this knowledge. In the current understanding of human beings, there is a

> move from the knower to the known from the inwardness of an individual psyche to being in the world with other human being" (p. 102).

Heron (1981) suggests including the notion of "relational knowing" in the general definition of knowledge. This form of knowing is essential in the profession of psychotherapy:

> "I suggest that there is a tacit dimension of mutual gazing (and associated signs) that enables us at a basic level of awareness to agree about the use of words. That dimension involves a pre-linguistic experiential knowing that is primarily relational. What we know is the relation between, the interconnectedness of: our presence to each other, our world, our eyes, and other signs. Such knowing is tacit, inchoate, unfocused. It does not of itself give us explicit propositional knowledge of facts and truths about ourselves and our world, but it enables us to agree how to use language to make such propositions. Nor of course does it do so alone: there is also touch and tangential gaze, facial expression, gesture of head, arms and hands, which constitutes a ground for the figure of explicit knowledge" (pp. 25-26).

It is a truism to assert that qualitative knowledge cannot be quantified. The criterion of scientificity chosen by several authors in the field of qualitative research is a social consensus of experts on what constitutes scientific knowledge. I have suggested that the boundaries between the common sense, the vernacular and scientific knowledge may be thin, sometimes blurred. It remains important, because the definition of knowledge in qualitative research is often challenged, to continue asking: What creates scientific knowledge?

# Part two:

# Interviews and Findings

# Overview of the interviews: How therapists think in action?

> *"P may very well be reflectively aware of his or her want of X and yet not actually describe it or talk about it. Only the ability to describe and talk about is involved here".*
> *(Smedslund, 1988, p. 22)*

I now present interviews that illustrate the concept of reflection-in-action. Reading these interviews, you will be witness to how a therapist makes sense and conceptualizes his work, constructing as he moves, a *theory of practice*. In the first part of this book, I have defined the postmodern (or socio-constructivist) epistemology that guides my practice of the interviews. These interviews are unique and non-replicable. The quality of the interviews depends on the quality of the relationship I establish with the interviewee, and the questions I ask. I use the principle of triangulation to create different settings and contexts for the interviews. Rather than repeating the same measure *ad nauseam*, I construct different interviews, reflecting upon different aspects of reflection-in-action. This triangulation method is commonly used in qualitative research to approach an object with different lenses.

*"One cannot not communicate"*
*(Watzlawick, Beavin Bavelas & Jackson, 1967, p.49)*

My presence in the interviews is not neutral. I influence the constructed knowledge, and define in part the context. I choose a semi-structured interview. I maintain the conversation within the boundaries of the chosen topics. My questions transform and evolve along with the interviewee's comments. To account for my part in the co-creation of these interviews, I carefully place each interview in context. I also position myself clearly as a researcher who is *also* a clinician. The interviews gain in quality, because of my training as a psychotherapist.

> *"Self-reflection and development should not be an optional activity for clinical psychologists, given the expectations we place onto others to develop"*
> *(Lavender, 2003, p.14)*

I apply reflexivity at different levels of the interview: I reflect on my questions and the effect they produce. I reflect on the therapist's reflections. I invite the therapist to reflect both on my reflections about their reflections and on their reflections about their reflections. I define with all participants clearly the contract of research before starting the interview. I define issues of confidentiality through an informed consent with the therapist's patients. I present three different types of interview to illustrate and understand reflection-in-action and how therapists think in their practice. Chapter eleven is a meta-process about reflection-in-action. I focus on the process of reflection-in-action and how the expert therapist uses reflexivity while practicing. Chapter twelve illustrates the reflection-in-action of less expert therapists. I present a set of nine interviews gathered at a training institute. This type of interview offers the rare opportunity to witness almost simultaneously the clinical work of the psychotherapist and his RIA. The unique setting of these interviews allows me also to explore the reaction of clients to the therapist's disclosure of RIA. Chapter thirteen illustrates the reflection-in-action of three expert therapists. Throughout the interviews, I insert my reflexive process and analyze the obtained reflection-in-action.

# Chapter XI

## First interview: An interview about reflection-in-action

### Context

This interview is at the heart of my work. It is an interview about RIA. In other words, this interview has a reflexive quality. I have three main purposes for this interview:

- My first purpose is exploratory. I am exploring what is the status of RIA in therapy. How therapists use RIA? How therapists consider RIA? How do they integrate RIA in the work with their patients?

- I also want to test the language that I use to bring clarity in the further interviews.

- My third intent is to test the reaction of a clinician to this subject.

I meet my first expert psychotherapist for the first time at a Gestalt symposium in November 1999, in Santa Barbara California. I previously heard about her work through her writings and her reputation. She trains interns and professionals throughout the United States as well as in Europe. She gives lectures internationally, has authored several books and articles. At the first contact, I am impressed by her personality, her intelligence, her clarity, her kindness, her presence. She connects easily with people. During the symposium, I approach her and ask her if she would be willing to spend an hour with me reflecting upon reflection-in-action. I explain to her the design and purpose of my research. She immediately agrees. She finds the idea "new and challenging".

This interview is not based on clinical work as opposed to the following interviews. It is a discussion about the process of RIA.

## Interview and analysis

**Therapist:** It is so interesting what therapists say they are doing and what they are actually doing. Does it go together? I think that, in the therapy process, the ends and the means must be the same. In my therapy sessions, I don't do one thing hoping that the people will do something else at the end. I want it to be happening right now. In terms of being equivalent to the meta-process or whatever words you want to use, to get in touch here (*points to her heart*) and there (*shows her head*). We, therapist and client, need to shuttle between the two and to have some sense of here *(shows her head)* of what we is going on here, *(points at the same time to her head, stomach and heart in a circular motion).* They *(the patients)* are not going to do it some day, by magic. We do it now. So in each therapy session I take some time at the end or even during the process to ask: "Let's talk about what we are doing right now!"

*Comment and analysis: The therapist highlights the importance of aiming toward coherence between the methods used in therapy and the ends of therapy. She encourages a continuum between interventions and goals, rather than a rupture. She highlights the need for the therapist to pay attention to how clients assimilate what is worked on, in the context of the session. This assimilation needs to start happening in the sessions, so that clients will utilize what they have learned outside of the therapist's office. Two types of learning need to occur for a transformation to happen: a cognitive learning and an affective learning. The clinician recommends including the therapist's reflection-in-action as a part of the treatment and teaching RIA to the clients. RIA should be used within the therapy session to encourage the client to reflect upon what happens in session (expressed by: "Let's talk about what we are doing right now"). It is the therapist's responsibility to bring awareness and clarity about how a client proceeds to have his needs met or unmet. It is a way of clarifying for the client the procedural method to achieve a goal. By procedural method, I mean a way to help the client understand the different steps he takes toward achieving a goal. This procedural method deconstructs the process with the client and assists him to bring forth his procedures to awareness.*

**Interviewer:** It seems like you stop the process, but you are still here. You are still inviting the client to step out too. Is this is an important part of the therapy for you?

**Therapist:** I interrupt the content and I disengage from the actual process, at appropriate times. I stop what are we doing now and if it involves me, personally, or me the therapist, or just me with the person in the here and now. Then, we talk about that.

*Comment and analysis: The therapist highlights that RIA involves a pause, a need to step outside and to direct and engage the client to do so. Reflected by the wording: "So let's talk about what we just did" is a frame inviting the client into a reflexive posture. This posture is useful in assisting the client to gather an understanding of how he does function in this relationship. The therapist discusses how to invite a reflexive attitude in therapy. She states that it demands a fuller involvement from the clinician, who has to explore her part in the creation of this relationship in process. I am not sure about what she means by her last comment and I should have asked some more about her comment and how she distinguishes her being personally and professionally.*

*The last three lines of her comments were added after her review of my transcripts, comments and analysis. The expert clinician clarifies what she means by this line between the personal and the professional. She says that she cannot separate her personal and her professional being.*

**Therapist's reflections after my analysis and comments:** When the client questions an intervention I have made, I reply as a therapist. When the client has an issue with me, then I reply not as a professional but as me the person.

**Interviewer:** I was wondering… Would you say that it is a way of assessing the process too, or would you define that as being something quite different? What words would you use to describe this process of reflection-in-action?

**Therapist:** Oh yes, to your question about assessing the process, the possibilities of this meta-process are endless. It means is to clarify, to position people.

**Therapist's reflections after my analysis and comments:** It is for clients to increase awareness of their behavior and whether their behavior is productive for them. Does their behavior support their neurotic habits? Or does it support growth and development? You can read something I wrote in my last book. I did a list. Although, usually I don't like to write in lists.

*Comment and analysis: The therapist defines RIA as a means to clarify and to position therapist and client in the process of therapy. RIA has a therapeutic effect and is a therapeutic element of therapy. The therapist highlights the richness and the endless possibilities of RIA.*

**Interviewer:** Do you think that reflection-in-action is teachable or trainable? Do you think there is a possibility of making people more aware of this process, more prone to using it? Are there some people who are more prone to watching what is happening with them and talking about it? Do you think there is a possibility of making people more aware of themselves?

**Therapist:** Yes, I certainly do. For me, it is part of the process of Gestalt Therapy. You left out one thing. When you said people watch what's going on and talk about it. I wanted to bring in something else then. It's not just watching and talking. It is involving yourself. It is talking about how you were then. Exactly, the process we are talking about is a moving back and forth, but it is not only cognitive. That is exactly it!

**Interviewer:** When you reflect about what you are experiencing, can you say something about the way you deliver the message to your client?

**Therapist:** Yes. What we are looking for in the delivery of the message is: "What needs to be there"? Very simply, the person needs to be there. There is also the listener, the responsibility of the listener in that.

*Comment and analysis: I was hoping for a more complete and refined answer regarding the way a therapist delivers a message and makes it more "audible" for the client. The clinician's response is that the therapist needs to be involved and present. I should have asked more about this statement.*

**Therapist's reflections after my analysis and comments:** This can be manifested by reflections, feedback, self-disclosure, and reporting one's experience in the interaction.

**Interviewer**: I am just thinking out loud. I hope I will make sense. As I hear you speak, I see this movement of the therapist trying to do some type of meta-process. You try to put yourself, as a therapist, first, in the shoes of the client and then wonder: How would it feel if I were to receive this message and how would I react? How do you, as a therapist, convey a message to the client in a way that is hearable for the client, rather than shutting down the person. What needs to happen for that to happen?

*Comment and analysis: This is a curious and inaccurate feedback that I just did. The importance that I put at this moment on language is not a reflection of the therapist's interest.*

**Therapist:** I cannot remember if Fritz Perls said it to me or wrote it. I was fortunate enough to hear him talking and to train with him. I don't know anymore what he said and what he wrote down but I remember his words: "Don't do for the client what the client can do for himself". There is one thing I often do, I'll say: "I'd like you to come out of your chair and stand up for a moment and I would like you to tell yourself what you see her/him doing now? So the client might say: Well, you know you are just kidding yourself all over again! Do you think you are kidding me too? Whatever it is, let her/him do it for her(him)self first. I really prefer to have people to discover by themselves what they are doing and not for me to tell them.

*Comment and analysis: This is a good example of what RIA is not. The therapist highlights her theoretical position. This is a theory a priori that does not explore what is happening now, nor the interaction between therapist and patient.*

**Therapist:** From the first moment, we build a relationship, not because the person walks in and I say: "I want to build a relationship". Of course, I am not always successful. People don't always come back. In building a relationship with a client, sometimes a client asks: "How do you work? I went to so and so, and I didn't like what he did". *(Turning to me)* You are nodding your head. You've probably heard these things or even said them before.

It is different with each person, but there is that first moment when they come in, where I do some kind of, I suppose, very quick assessment, conscious or unconscious, of what's going on with this person.

*Comment and analysis: The therapist clarifies the importance of building a relationship with a client from the very beginning of the encounter. The therapist recognizes the uniqueness of each relationship. Each time, as the therapist says, the relationship and the way to connect with the client is different. There is no ready to make cookbook about how to connect with a client. The therapist highlights the importance of the first sessions and the first few minutes of the first session and doing what she calls "quick assessment of what is going on" with this client.*

*Later on in this interview the therapist will come back and talk about the importance of the client's first sentence as well as the importance of being able to assess quickly what is going on right from a beginning with a client in order to build a solid relationship.*

**Interviewer:** Could you define what you mean by assessment?

**Therapist:** I look and see. What we call intuition is indeed a lot of experience. I think I have a lot of experience now. I see. I feel. I suppose, I do that, because this is what I teach. I teach the basics, you see. I see everything. I watch. I see. I listen. I ask them: "Why are you here?"

*(The therapist asks me not to tape this part, nor to put it in my research. She refers to a clinical example in her practice. I stop the audiotape until she allows me to put it on again).*

For example, when I see a couple I say to them: "I know you've probably discussed coming in here, but I would like you two to talk together in front of me, about what you want here". This is the way I work. I get my information from what you say and how you listen to one another and how you respond. "When a client comes in, sometimes he can't even talk. Sometimes he just starts crying, so I respond to whatever is going on, at the moment and my way of responding is my way. It's not right or wrong. It is just my way. It works for me. People who know me outside and in the group say: "But, you are the same in the group as you are outside". I love that. To me, that is the highest compliment. What else can we be but ourselves anyway?

*Comment and analysis: The therapist talks about what she refers to as "clinical intuition", which is a poorly defined concept. She asserts that there is a lot of experience behind "doing a quick assessment of where the client is". This assessment involves thinking, seeing, feeling and seems to be an integrative process using the therapist as a whole rather than being only cognitive. The therapist implies that observation is a trainable skill. The therapist talks about the importance of building a relationship, of being available and flexible to whatever comes, rather than having a fixed way of relating to clients. She clarifies that therapists should welcome their own style and their own subjectivity and personality in that contact. The therapist highlights the importance of being the same person in and out of the therapy room, rather than playing a role.*

**Interviewer:** *(Silence).*

**Therapist (continuing her previous comment):** My husband and I teach, as you know. We teach primarily in Europe. We usually use five days for training. In the morning, we work together in front of the group. When we finish a session with a client in front of the group, we say to the group: "Do you have anything you want to share about what was happening with you when this person was working". It is not giving advice. It is not a judgment. It is just: "How were you feeling?" Usually, in the group, people are very affected by the way somebody worked, whether they were stuck or flowing in their process. Then, we ask people in the group: "Do you have any questions or comments about anything we did, or didn't do". Of course, we are teachers, so they watch us carefully. They might say: "How did you think of saying what you said. It was just the perfect thing". How do I know? Experience, sensing something. We always know more that we can say. As Michael Polanyi says: "We know more than we can tell". That is the whole thing about tacit knowledge. We cannot always say what we saw. It is not magic that I know. When I say something I don't know that it will be the perfect thing, that it will facilitate the client's process, whether it is perfect or not depends on the response of the client.

*Comment and analysis: The therapist says that at times she is unable to clearly articulate why she intervenes a certain way with a client. At some point, there is no reflection-in-action behind what is done in therapy. Sometimes the articulation of RIA is lacking, but there is a sense that there is a tacit knowledge that leads to this intervention.*

**Interviewer:** And if somebody were to ask you at this very moment: How come you did what you just did? Do you think you could have put that into words?

**Therapist:** Sometimes yes. Sometimes it's a gesture of the client, or it's just a shrug of the shoulder or it's the way they looked at me before they said something. Sometimes and that's so crazy, in my most creative work it is off the wall as we say. It's not logical at all. We had a group of 20 people in Sweden and this woman came up to work and she walked in rather small steps. She had blond hair, she spoke rather softly, and she started talking about something. I don't even remember what it was. Usually what people say is not important to me, the first sentence: yes. Listen carefully for the first sentence. But after that, there is so much else of importance happening. I just looked at her and asked: "Was your mother a very sweet woman?" She really came to life when she answered: No. She certainly was not. And then it became this fantastic session. I asked her to do some exercises such as: Don't talk about your mother. Be her! Because talking about, as we already discussed, is not the best use of the time, as far as I am concerned. I remember after the session, the client herself asked: "How did you happen to ask me that question?"

*Comment and analysis: The therapist refers to a piece of work that she did in front of a group where she made an "off the wall" intervention. The therapist uses this example to explain that she may pay more attention to non-verbal cues, such as the way the client walks, the tone and the volume of the voice, the look, etc. The content of what the client says is not always relevant to her "there is so much else of importance happening". The therapist has no way of knowing that at this point whether the client had a sweet mother or not. What is interesting is that the therapist does not hold on to this comment, but rather uses as a "springboard". The flexibility of the therapist when using such statement is crucial.*

**Interviewer:** Hum.

**Therapist:** I don't know, I don't know. She never mentioned her mother. Sometimes there is a lucky chance.

**Interviewer:** What is most fascinating to me here, is that if this person had answered in a certain way such as: "Yes, my mother was indeed very sweet" or "don't go there" I think you may say: Let's change the topic.

**Therapist:** Oh! Yes. I drop it. There is no hypothesis that is true. Your response always depends on the response of the client, not only to the words but also the affect, the energy, the body movements, the facial expression. If there is no energy there, I drop it. I have no need in this interaction. There is no direction the client needs to go for me. There is always something else that emerges.

*Comment and analysis: The therapist emphasizes the need to take one's hypotheses lightly and not to hold on to them if they do not fit the client.*

**Interviewer:** So you let reality inform your work. Do you think that all the therapists are like that? What do you think?

**Therapist:** I talk about meta-process and meta-communication. I say, for example, that the therapist does a little self-disclosure first. You say something about yourself. Usually you include yourself in the communication, in the meta-process. Then, we come together at a different level. When a person self-discloses, it's contagious. It is like a disease. When I am reading to my husband, I can be reading something that I have read to myself. I say: "(...), I want to read you just a couple of lines...". It is so interesting. I read it to myself and then I read it to him out loud and I start crying. I didn't know that it was something that was so touching for me, until I read it to him. Or, I read something funny and I know he'll enjoy it. When I read it to him then I start laughing so hard that I can hardly read. What happens with that kind of things?

**Interviewer:** So, when you share an experience out loud with somebody else it transforms?

**Therapist:** Yes, it's so intensified, when it is shared; and that is what happens.

*Comment and analysis: The clinician explains how emotions can be intensified, by sharing them in the presence of another person.*

**Interviewer:** I believe, but this is my personal belief, that it does not even matter what language is used. You can be all over the world having people speak a different language and people have the same description.

**Therapist:** That is true, that is so true. It has happened to me.

*Comment and analysis: I state a personal belief in the universality of the process that she is describing. The therapist agrees with me.*

**Interviewer**: What is interesting and intriguing to me is: What happened just before? What allowed these things to emerge? You may just think it and keep it to yourself.

**Therapist:** What happened? How did it happen at this moment for you to just say it? Is that what you mean?

**Interviewer**: Yes.

**Therapist:** I am not sure we always know that.

*(The rest of the interview is not relevant to the present subject).*

## Conclusion

This interview has deepened the definition of the process of reflection-in-action. RIA is a meta-process involving the context and the content of the session. The therapist defines RIA as a means to clarify and position the therapist and the client in the process of therapy. When a therapist is committed to practice reflection-in-action in therapy what ensues is an internal demand of coherence between the methods and the ends of treatment. Practicing reflection-in-action involves an intention. It involves a pause in the process: taking a break and thinking outside of the box. The pre-requisite to practicing RIA is reflexive attitude toward knowledge and toward oneself. RIA is not a statement of one's theoretical position. This process involves an effort from the therapist who needs to explore his own responses and processes and, at times, share them. Practicing reflection-in-action demands a fuller involvement from the clinician who explores his part in the creation of this relationship in process. Therapist can engage their clients in a reflexive posture ("So let's talk about what we just did!"). The therapist highlights the relational and contextual nature of RIA. A therapist's response depends on the response of the client, not only the words but also the facial expression, the tone of voice, its volume, the body movements, and the posture. Sometimes the articulation of RIA is lacking, but there is a sense that there is a tacit knowledge that leads to this intervention. RIA has different properties. It is trainable, the therapist asserts. Sharing one's RIA will lead the client to become reflexive. Reflection-in-action should frequently be made explicit for the client, so that the client may learn and integrate this process. The practice of reflexivity, as the present expert describes, should be an integrated part of the therapy session. RIA is a highly useful instrument to generate a theory of a moving practice.

RIA can be used as a method. It is a way of clarifying for the client what happens implicitly and to make it explicit. It is a way to deconstruct for the client the steps toward a goal, steps that are outside of the client's awareness. RIA could be a method that enables the client to assimilate (Piaget, 1954; 1956). It is important to make what is happening inside the therapy room usable outside the therapy room. The therapist needs to find ways to test this assimilation process.

The effects of RIA may be multiple. First, practicing RIA invites the therapist to position himself in the system he is engaged in, and this almost moment by moment. The practice of RIA during the session can be utilized as an intervention for the client. The therapist may share his RIA with the client. Sharing the therapist's RIA may produce a therapeutic effect. It may strengthen the therapeutic alliance.

# Chapter XII

## Preparation of the interviews at the training institute

### Context

I have gathered the following data during a yearlong training program in Santa Monica, California (1999-2000). This program is designed to develop the skills of skilled therapists (licensed therapists who have a minimum of three years of practice after obtaining their license). This is an advanced training program within the institute. It means that all participants have at least two years of training with the Gestalt Institute. These clinicians therefore are used to showing their work with a client in front of a group. There are eight participants consisting of three men and five women (including me, the researcher). The therapists are from different cultural backgrounds (Caucasian, Asian American, European and Indian) and different training to become therapists (clinical psychologists, Marriage and Family therapists, social workers). The therapists perform individual therapeutic work (as patients or therapists) voluntarily within the group. Depending on the needs of individuals, the group participants can function in the group as client, therapist or as supervisor to other group members. There are two trainers therapists in the group at all times. All of the therapists are practicing psychotherapy on a regular basis, either in private practice or in a clinic.

This type of interview offers the rare opportunity to witness the clinical work and the RIA of the clinician almost simultaneously. We suspend the therapeutic process for a few minutes, discuss it, and then notice the influence of our sharing our reflection-in-action on the therapeutic process. This setting allows me to explore the reaction of clients to the therapist's disclosure of their reflection-in-action. When I present my interest in RIA in front of the group, I remember the reaction of the group participants. They were enthusiastic. The therapists manifest their interest in further exploring their ability to conceptualize their work in the midst of it. Rather than being passive subjects of my research, I invite the group members into a position of co-researchers with multiple questions on how to improve my research design, refine questions, and delineate the interviews. The therapists voice some anxiety, which is often projected onto the client in the form of: "I am afraid that if you interview me, the attention will be taken away from the client". As I hear them, I voice my own fears out loud: "What if I blank? What if I have nothing to say? What if my explanation of the therapy process is different from yours? I will look like a fool as the researcher, as a complete impostor". After voicing these anxieties out loud, several group members echo the fear of being exposed, seen, and scrutinized. They struggle with disclosing an unfinished or incoherent thought-process. Sharing my anxiety and my excitement for the process is, I imagine, reassuring for my colleagues. I am clear about not having any particular expectations, except trying to discover more about this process of RIA with my colleagues. I question them: "What does reflection-in-action look like? How can we describe it? How can we learn more about RIA? How can we put our thoughts in language?"

I share my ideas about the specific aspect of transforming this internal process of reflection-in-action into language. I talk about Vygotsky and how he thinks thought starts making sense in language (1986). The purpose of my intervention is to inform my colleagues that, hesitancies, confusions, or struggles with language are expected. I am aware that I am asking a difficult task, I ask the clinicians to talk about how they conceptualize their work, in the midst of it, and to struggle to put it unto language. The data obtained at GATLA are specific and context-related. They are only one example of how therapists think in action, with a particular training, background and theoretical framework.

## Therapy is first. Research is second

The clinical work comes before the research's interest. I request to be part an interviewee as well. I welcome opinions and feedback on the questions I plan to use and how to make them more interesting or more thought provoking. Before the interruption, I ask permission to do so, from both the client and the therapist. If a client or a clinician does not wish to be interrupted, I respect this choice. Twice during the interviews I do not interrupt. Once, I choose not to interrupt the session, because the client was in much turmoil. The other time the clinician requested not to be interrupted.

There are nine interviews based on nine separate sessions. Each therapy session is held in front of the group. The sessions are usually short to allow sufficient time for clinicians to work, as patient and as therapist during the day of training. The duration of the work ranges from twenty to thirty minutes. The duration is discussed with the group before starting a session. It does not exceed thirty minutes. At times, due to the intensity of the therapeutic work, the therapy session may last five extra minutes. The length of the interruption for the purpose of research never exceeds two to three minutes. I limit the length of the interruption, out of respect for both the client and the clinician. The questions relate to a therapy moment that just occurred. They are related to a specific context. Usually, after three or more questions, the clinicians have a chance to say what they want to say. The way I gathered this information is most often by some longer silence that I interpret as: I am done. If I am not sure whether the clinician is finished with his reflection, I may ask: "Would you like to add anything else?" Oftentimes, as you will see in the interviews the clinician signals the end of the interruption. On rare occasions, I decide that it is time to go back to clinical work, based on the time spent and the sense that enough information has been gathered based upon the redundancy of the response.

I audiotape the interruptions only (RIA). Each participant agrees to let me tape the interruptions. During each session, I take notes on the context of the therapy session and why I choose to interrupt.

## "Moments of movement"

The criteria used for the interruption are similar to the Rogers's description of "moment of movement" in therapy (1942). These are informed by both an intuition that can be verbalized by "there is something there" and by information emerging from the context of the session. I spend some time afterward reconstructing what raised my interest and how I chose to interrupt. Explaining why I interrupt is interesting since in doing so I practice reflection-in-action (RIA). Different indicators support this perception of information: a sudden change of voice, of affect, of rhythm, of pacing, a comment that stands out of the conversation, a raise of interest on my part, a comment that I do not expect, a different level of excitement, a movement, or a gesture. I sometimes interrupt the session because I am curious about a place where I, if I had been in the therapist's shoes, I may have done something totally different. On one occasion only, the interruption occurs for a reason only the interviewer knows. During the nine following interviews, I give the reader a context for these interruptions and the reason why I interrupt at a particular point in the conversation. I present these interviews in the chronological order of their appearance. The choices and the assumptions behind my interruptions may direct, transform and construct the data I obtain. If I choose a different criterion than the "moments of movement" I may obtain different information.

# Second interview

## Context

The session started ten minutes ago. The therapist seems to be looking to define the emphasis of the session. Several issues are discussed and dropped. The client presents an issue and then states: "I am not interested in exploring that". The session does not seem to have a clear focus at the moment. The client seems ambivalent about working with this therapist, as evidenced by statements such as: "I am not sure that you can help me with that". When the therapist asks what the "that" means, the client does not give a specific answer and moves on to another topic. Before the interruption, both the client and the therapist seem defensive and distant from one another. Finally, the client shares how difficult it has been for her to trust her parents and to get any positive attention from them. By saying that, the client seems to be aware that the previous interaction with her parents might have something to do with what is happening now in the session with this therapist. In response to this statement, the therapist discloses some of his issues with trust and his own parents. The client responds to this intervention in a harsh and cutting voice: "I am not interested in hearing about you!"

This is a moment of movement. I perceive an important turning point, an edgy and challenging situation that has to do with a potentially conflictual situation between the therapist and the client. In the client's comment: "I am not interested in hearing about you" I hear hurt and irritation. Much material for work is offered. I am curious about how the therapist will proceed.

*Comment and analysis: This last intervention from the therapist comes to me as a surprise. I imagine that if I were in the shoes of the therapist, I might have intervened quite differently. I probably would clarify the dilemma that the client experiences in front of the therapist. I may try to engage with the client, at this very level. I would discuss her reticence to share with me, and her request for help at the same time. I would present to the client her uncertainty about my ability to assist her, and her previous experience of difficulty with trust. I may focus on this impasse in a descriptive way. I intend by these comments to clarify the client's dilemma and to assist the client to choose more freely. My intervention (now that I have the luxury to reflect on it) may have been: "It seems as though you are not sure whether I can help you with "that". You mention how difficult and frustrating it has been in the past for you to trust your parents, and how often you missed their positive regard. There might be a connection in your mind between the way your parents treated you and how you are with me today. Right now, you may be just doing what is smart: checking me out, wondering what you want to tell me and wondering whether or not I can be trusted. It does not seem easy".*

**(Me as the) Interviewer:** Can I interrupt for a second? *(I ask permission from client and therapist*). Okay. Thank you. Would you be able to tell me in your own words what just happened for you during the last few minutes?

**Therapist:** I am aware of kind of a shift I guess. Actually… in her. The sense I got is that she was looking at me to sort out these pieces for her, or to give her some guidance or something like that. I was sort of feeling like: "I don't know what to do!" *(There is more energy in the tone of the therapist's voice)*. So, I wanted to start to try put together some pieces about what she knew about how this process works for her. I am not sure what else you wanted: What I was thinking, or the totality of my experience?

*Comment and analysis: My perception seems to match the therapist's perception that "something has shifted". It may be a way for the therapist to explain the interruption regardless of the content. The therapist seems to be bothered by what he perceives as an "expectation" from the client. In the comment "I don't know what to do" the therapist may be aware that there is something more than what he chooses to say. In the list of the omissions, the therapist does not mention a critical comment from the client ("I am not interested in hearing about you!").*

**Interviewer:** What you are saying is actually very informative. I am also interested in hearing if you have any awareness of what you chose to share or not share during the session.

**Therapist:** I thought my anxiety was rising at times and I think I chose not to share that. I was not sure what to do with that. Also now I am kind of wondering if maybe there might have been some parallel process with us, with my anxiety and her anxiety, maybe a kind of rising at the same kind of place.

*Comment and analysis: The therapist clearly identifies his feeling relative to the situation, in this case, anxiety. He seems to be stuck on how to bring that back into the dialogue with the client. Instead of struggling with this anxiety as a place of uncertainty, the therapist brings an overarching explanation. This overarching theory is not related to the client but seems to calm the therapist's anxiety. My questions lead the therapist out of the explanation about parallel process.*

**Interviewer**: Hum, So you are still questioning what you can share and not share? And now, when you reflect back on those things?

**Therapist:** Well... There might even be some ways to talk about it.

*Comment and analysis: The therapist questions his previous idea of avoiding sharing this important experience with the client.*

**Interviewer:** Hum... *(Silence)*

**Therapist:** Yeah ... There is.

*Comment and analysis: The therapist seems to have now a sense that his experience ("I don't know what to do") may be conveyed in a helpful way to the client.*

**Interviewer:** You were mentioning that you were not exactly sure about what I was asking. Is there anything broader that you want to share with us, that is beyond what we discussed, that you were aware of during the last few minutes of your session? Is there anything else that you want to share?

**Therapist:** Well, I think. I did. I mean, I felt like there was some kind of an emotional shift, where I was suddenly being called upon to do something and I think I got a little overwhelmed. I was not sure what to do or how to do it. I wasn't sure how to make it better. I didn't know how to make it clearer.

*Comment and analysis: What is interesting in this example is the important difference between the therapy "talk" and the RIA. Important information is not shared in therapy, creating a gap between what the therapist thinks within himself and what he conveys to clients. The therapist brings to awareness two conflicting thoughts that create a sense of anxiety "I need to do something" and "I don't know what to do". There seems to be confusion for the therapist between two different experiences: "What do I feel?" is confused with "What do I need to do?" Not voicing the "I don't know what to do" with the client confines the therapist to a passive position, where the therapist does not come forth toward contact. The therapist's insecurity expressed by the "what do I do?" creates a conflict with what the client has previously expressed "I am not sure you can help me with that".*

**Interviewer:** What did you choose to do at this moment?

**Therapist:** *(The therapist pauses five seconds).* To go back to her for more information?

*Comment and analysis: This long silence is a marked difference from the previous impulse to "do something". The therapist allows time to reflect and comes up with a different idea: I don't know enough. I will go back to the client for more information.*

**Interviewer:** Hum.

**Therapist:** I'm not sure if I made any comment about that.

**Interviewer:** In my recollection, but I may be wrong, I think you did share something to that effect. What do you recall?

**Therapist:** So, I said something about it? I wasn't sure if I did or not.

**Interviewer:** *(Silence)*

*Comment and analysis: I am not willing to take a corrective stance in re-collecting what the therapist said in the interview.*

**Therapist:** I am feeling kind of divided now. It's like... I'm almost feeling like it is more about me right now and I feel the need to go back to her.

*Comment and analysis: The therapist reiterates the same struggle: how much of himself enters into the relationship while maintaining a professional connection. It seems easier for the therapist to share this conflict with me (the researcher), than with his client*

**Interviewer:** Okay. Thank you very much.

## Reflections on the reflections

**Therapist's comment after the interruption:** I wanted to say that I am aware of so much parallel processes that were going on. You know. I mean, she was talking about issues that I certainly am dealing with all the time. They were going on for me too. Particularly, when you interrupted. I think after that, I didn't know what to do anymore. I was waiting for you *(looking at her client)* to tell me what to do. I deserted myself at that point. It is as if I didn't know how to do the work anymore. I just didn't know. I was very nervous and very aware of second-guessing myself in everything that I said and did. There were moments where I would just do something, then I was like: How could you have done that? *(His gestures show surprise and disgust)* What a terrible thing I just said. So, I found it really tough, really tough to try to stay with ..." *(client's name)* and at the same time to do this dual thing *(The therapist is referring to the exercise of RIA)*. The other part of me was trying to monitor whether I was being stupid or not, or missing an opportunity. The critical part of me was very active. *(Long Sigh. The therapist seems discouraged)*

*Comment and analysis: The fact that this interview is chronologically the first one in the group may have something to do with the experienced pressure of "doing right". I also say clearly that I am interested in how this reflection can be developed and translated into words. I am aware that in my question, I carry an expectation (Say something, preferably something clever"). This expectation may impede the therapist's creativity and ability to be present and reflexive. This interview demonstrates the fine line that reflexivity imposes. It requires from the clinician to be present in the interaction <u>and</u> to think and reflect upon his interaction. This dual track is demanding. If one becomes too reflexive, one loses sight of what one does.*

**Supervisor**: Keep that in mind, because you have a very nice way of staying with her *(referring to the therapist's relationship with the client)*, of supporting her and helping her move. But if you could replace the "Am I doing it right?" with the "What is going on?" and "What should I do?"

**Therapist:** Well, I feel like I could bracket[7] a lot of it.

**Supervisor:** No.

**Therapist:** But what are you saying? You are saying something else.

**Supervisor**: That is not what I am saying. I am saying something different. I am not saying: "Just bracket that off!". You *are* running a dual track. You are relating to a person and you are also thinking: What is going on? What is happening? How do I conceptualize it? Once you have conceptualized it, you ask yourself: How do I move with it? For example, when you say: "She is doing the same thing I often do! What do I want to do with that as you are listening? So, you are doing two things at the same time! I am just suggesting that you are replacing critiques of you with the conceptualizing of the work.

*Comment and analysis: The supervisor points out for the therapist that he uses reflexivity in his work. The supervisor suggests that what gets in the way of RIA is the self-inflicting critiques.*

**Therapist:** Yes. Yeah.

**Supervisor**: I am not suggesting that you stop doing these two things.

---

7 *Bracketing is a terminology of Gestalt Therapy. It refers to the effort to suspend strong ideas and to avoid quick judgments.*

**Therapist:** Yeah. I think it is harder to conceptualize when I am nervous.

**Supervisor**: That is a hard step for lots of people. It is a real prejudice, but many therapists pretend to be Gestalt Therapists because they know how to hang in there. They are not seeing the process. They do not understand the process. They are just posing as Gestalt therapists. They do not have any clear understanding of their work.

*Comment and analysis: The supervisor states that the reflexive ability is what differentiates good therapists from mediocre clinicians.*

**Another group member joins the conversation:** Are you talking about using this kind of meta-process? Using these meta-processes with the client at the same time that you are in dialogue with him?

**Supervisor** *(Nodding)*: Doing the kind of things that Fabienne is looking for: "What are you thinking? How are you conceptualizing your work? How are you making a decision, while still in the dialogue?"

**Interviewer:** It may be perceived as almost like a schizophrenic process, but this is what we do. We do the work and think about it at the same time.

**Therapist:** What we *try* to do.

**Supervisor:** It *is* what we do. You are right, but not always with so much awareness.

**Supervisor**: This is what excites me about the group. We are really struggling with that.

**Therapist:** So, this is what it is about ... conceptualizing the work, while staying in contact with the client. Is that right?

**Supervisor**: Yes.

*(The rest of the discussion is irrelevant to my present subject)*

**Interviewer**: I am grateful that you let me learn more about this process. It is very interesting for me. I am also interested in how to ask questions to provoke RIA. ? *(To the therapist)* How did you experience my questions during the interruption? Are you willing to share? Do you think I could have asked you other questions that might have been more helpful? I am happy to hear your comments about how you experienced the interruption. How did it then influence your work?

*Comment and analysis: I prompt reflexivity on my interviewing style.*

**Therapist:** I think there might even have been some relief on my part from the interruption. At times I was feeling… feeling, hum.... Inadequate... I think is the word. So, I think ...by talking to you about what was going on, I was able to step back a little and conceptualize a little more what was going on.

*Comment and analysis: This is an interesting comment that seems to contradict the previous ones. Maybe the previous conversation is responsible for this change. The clinician is now saying that the interviewer's interruptions and questions are actually a supportive process as opposed to being anxiety producing. This questioning seems to ground the therapist and informs him about the situation, and the possible next steps. In his comment: "I think there might even have been some relief on my part from the interruption. At times I was feeling, feeling hem.... Inadequate..." there is a clear allusion to Polanyi's comment: "We can know more than we can tell" (1966, p. 4).*

**Interviewer:** So, by talking out loud, are you saying that you felt you knew more than you felt you knew before you said so? Am I making sense?

**Therapist:** I think it was more felt sense stuff, before we talked together. Then when I talked with you about it. I ... you know… I started to see more patterns. But then … my fear became that I was going to be talking all about my experience and…and…I abandoned the client. I was getting into all my stuff, rather than doing the therapy. I did not want to lose sight of what it is about, and this is therapy.

*Comment and analysis: The therapist expresses how talking about tacit ways of knowing helped him organize his practical knowing. There is a clear enactment of Vygotsky's thesis (1986). Vygotsky claims that language powerfully refines raw processes (what he refers to as "felt stuff"). Language allows the sophistication of "felt stuff" onto "I started to see more patterns". The therapist says that using and struggling to put these unformed thoughts into language helps him to see a broader picture, to gather a richer definition of the phenomenon. The therapist seems to be afraid of stealing something from the client if he focuses on his own experience. In my opinion, this is the only thing he has: his experience. Maybe if he imposes his experience on the client he might take away something from her. It would have been interesting for me to ask: "How would you drawn the line between your stuff and her stuff?" This question might have helped me to clarify what the therapist means. I believe that it is helpful to ask questions to therapists about their "personal theory", a theory constructed by therapists. The therapist's personal theory, in this case, may be summarized as "I should not be too present with myself while doing therapy, it may steal something away from my client". This personal theory seems to limit the field of possibilities. Beyond the personal theories, I suspect that the clinician's response may have something to do with the client's comment that the therapist never addressed: "I am not interested in hearing about you!". This client's comment was powerful and aggressive. I believe that this comment, especially the fact that it was not addressed, has an impact on the therapist's continual concern for sharing anything. The therapist stays quite impersonal, for fear of displeasing the client. The therapist may just follow the client's verbal demand, without referring to it (I will not talk about anything that is of concern to me, for fear of upsetting you). If the therapist follows this implicit rule of communication, which excludes the therapist from the interaction, this will quickly get in the way of doing therapy.*

**Supervisor**: Interestingly enough what it may be, and I just realized this right now, is that it's really good training for the therapist: to take a time out and to do that conceptualization. There is no supervision of the conceptualization, except in retrospect.

*Comment and analysis: The supervisor seems to have an awareness of how practicing RIA benefits the clinicians.*

**Supervisor** (Second supervisor): I thought there was another interesting thing about that because at some point in the work you did start to share something about you and your process. The client's response was: "I'm really not interested in hearing about you!". I thought this was a fascinating piece. I was sort of reluctant to come in because I thought that ... *(the other supervisor)* was going to do this. So, I was sitting here doing this *(holds her arms, as if to use her energy to stop herself from interrupting).* One of the things she said earlier in the work is that she doesn't get support and that her family doesn't really respond to her. Then, when you move in to support her by sharing something about yourself, her response is *(the supervisor makes a movement as if to push somebody away).* So that is really interesting. Her word was: "I want to go somewhere else" and "I don't want to hear what you have to say about that". I would have liked to slow that down and see what was going on there. I think it was fascinating.

## Conclusion

The first observation is that RIA from less trained therapist carries hesitancies. RIA resembles much a thought creating and adding sense through its elocution. The therapist in training has often a poor positioning. For fear of displeasing or hurting the client, he puts himself on hold. He holds on to what he knows: the theories that he has learned to make sense of the complex reality he encounters. This first interview with a non-expert therapist demonstrates the fine line that reflexivity imposes, requiring the clinician to be present in the interaction and to think and reflect upon his interaction. Running this dual track of doing the work and thinking about the work at the same time is demanding. This interview also highlights the difficulty of practicing reflection-in-action, when one is not trained to do so. It shows the damaging effect of stress, anxiety or self-inflicting critiques on the process of reflection-in-action. I see the difficulty that the non-expert therapist has to find a clear focus to the work, he seems to wander around, unsure where to go and which direction to take. During this interview, there is a clear positioning on the importance to practice RIA, and being able to explain aloud: how we, therapists, think in our practice. The reflexive ability, as the supervisor indicates in this example is what differentiates good from mediocre clinicians.

Another interesting finding of this interview is the pure enactment of Vygotsky's thesis that ideas form and emerge through language (1986): "I think it was more felt sense stuff, before we talked together. Then when I talked with you about it. I ... you know… I started to see more patterns". Finally there is acknowledgment, and awareness that practicing RIA may clarify for the therapist what he is doing and how he does it. It grounds the therapist and informs him about the present moment, and the next possible interventions.

# Third interview

## Context

The client, a male in his mid-thirties, selects a male therapist for his session. As an introduction the client states: *"I want to work with a man"*. Before my interruption, the client states: *"I stop myself from crying in front of her. I don't know how come. I suffer from that. She is so sweet to me. I cannot cry in front of her."* It is, interesting to note that the client does not cry during the segment. His affect is depressed. His voice is low, at times with a tone of frustration. In the present relationship, the same process seems to be happening with the therapist. The client chooses to work with a therapist, he would like to cry with him, yet he stops himself from crying. The entire session lasts twenty-five minutes. I stopped the interview after seventeen minutes. I am interested in the therapist's theory about what is going on. I am curious about what the therapist intends to do, what will be his next move.

**Interviewer:** Could you say something about what just happened for you in the last few minutes? What informed what you did?

**Therapist:** I was very intrigued by what was going on ...by what I believe, and I am using a technical term, the "figure" is. *(This simply means that the therapist is not sure he can identify the focus of the work.)* I am curious about how... *(the client)* is willing to cry, but he is not able to cry. Crying is bigger than just crying. What are his meanings about crying with another person? In regard to... whatever he is experiencing...What does he think about when he is crying? So, I am really curious. I am really going with him in that. I am trying to let him, and be with him in the present. Hum... I am trying to explore that process with him: that which he is expressing so nicely and that which he is not aware of. That process intrigues me. If we can participate in looking at the process of withdrawing and letting go or retaining.

*Comment and analysis: The therapist's comment seems to gain clarity and information as it is put into language (Vygotsky, 1986). The RIA becomes increasingly sophisticated. I see the different stages in his RIA process:*

1) *The therapist first states his affective and cognitive involvement in the process: "I am interested".*

2) *He then focuses on the client's dilemma and sharpens the focus of the work to: my client wants to cry with another person he feels close to, and yet he feels unable to do so and experiences pain from it.*

3) *A third level of RIA is reached when the therapist understands that "crying is bigger than crying". The client's inability to cry is experience-related, and context-related. The therapist is interested in exploring these contexts with the client.*

4) *The therapist is curious to see whether or not there is a thought associated with the crying that may explain the trauma.*

5) *The therapist expresses an interest in exploring, in the present of this therapeutic relationship, the conflict between holding the tears or letting go.*

*The curiosity, openness, and willingness to explore in a non-judgmental way seem to be the strengths of this therapist. As opposed to the previous interview, the therapist's attitude toward "not-knowing where to go" is not anxious.*

**Interviewer:** Anything else that you were aware of? Anything else that was informing you?

**Therapist:** I am very aware that I am curious about ...*(the client)* experience.

**Interviewer:** How do you make that happen? How do you maintain this sense of curiosity? Do you know how do you do that? How does it happen?

**Therapist:** I think (that) it is because of his story. What he is says is very intriguing to me. It certainly reminds me of some of my old stories, but it is not at all in my foreground.

*Comment and analysis: The therapist may refer to a more general quality: he is able to maintain a genuine interest and curiosity in others' stories most of the time and in most situations. The therapist is not foreign to the feeling that the client describes, but this parallelism with his experience is not what he is interested in at this moment.*

**Interviewer:** Are you done or would you like to say something else?

**Therapist:** *(signals that he is done).*

*After the interruption, the client asks the therapist if the therapist was really "that interested" in him. The client reports being moved by the therapist's interest. Shortly after that, the client becomes teary.*

*Comment and analysis: In this example, the sharing of the therapist's RIA is therapeutic. The therapist's disclosure of his interest in the client, allows the client to open up. The client shows vulnerability when the therapist expresses genuine interest and curiosity with no expectations, no demands. I want to explore my hypothesis and asked the client right after the session:*

**Interviewer:** *(To the therapist).* I was wondering. I had a sense that the client was feeling some relief or satisfaction about what happened after the interruption. I thought that the interruption provided more space for continuing the session. I was pleased that you shared your experience. Do you think that it helped the session?

**Supervisor:** *(The supervisor intervenes).* Yes.

**Interviewer:** *(I first address my question to the therapist and then I turn toward the client).* Do you have anything to say about that? I guess, I am asking that especially from you *(to the client).* Do you have anything to say about that?

**The client:** *(the client is touched)* Well... Really, what you are doing here with the interruptions, I think helps the process. I did not know my therapist was thinking that about me. It's fascinating... Hum... It is like everything is going to help *(The* *next sentence is inaudible on the tape).* It just moved me. It moved the work along. Yes. Yes.

**Interviewer:** *(I look at both the therapist and the client).* I really liked what happened between the two of you. We may think this exercise is just an interruption for the sake of research. I really liked what you have created. It is like a springboard. *(To the client)* I am still wondering what in your therapist's comments triggered you to feel welcome in continuing. What helped you? Do you know?

**The client:** Well, I felt that even though, he described his process, he was still talking to me, in some way. In hearing about his process, it was just more of him to experience and that was helpful. And hum.... In some way, it underscores a little bit what ... just said *(the client refers to the previous therapist in the previous interview).* It seems to me that it is good that the therapist talks about the process in front of the client.

*Comment and analysis: Essentially, the client says that the more he feels the therapist is being "a person" with him, the more he feels he can open up in his presence. This is one of the keys to building a therapeutic alliance: the more the therapist shows himself as a whole the stronger the relationship. It is more than simple "modeling". The intention lies in the genuine and whole presence of the therapist and his willingness to be open in front of the client and show his humanness. Talking about the positive effects of disclosing the therapist's RIA, the client mentions the importance of "being talked to" as opposed to "being talked about". The language used in front of the client is inviting and inclusive, as opposed to an objectifying language, which may cut off the client.*

**Interviewer:** *(To the client).* Yes! Yes! I understand. I am so happy that you said that, because a few minutes ago, I had to bite my tongue. I wanted to intervene again in your session, just before your therapist concluded. There were three minutes left. I thought what happened was fascinating. I saw the therapist doing and saying exactly what I imagined he would have said, if I interrupted him. I believe that, well for me at least, it is a very good type of therapy: sharing your RIA with your client. When therapists choose to share some of how they think and how they inform their thoughts, it can be helpful. Your therapist did that when he said: "I'm now hesitating. I am hearing that there are three minutes left. I am also interested in what you want to talk about. I am not sure what to do". I thought this was a brilliant intervention.

*Comment and analysis: I share my preference: expressing the therapist's RIA, when facing a dilemma is especially helpful, so that the therapist does not have to choose for the client but can choose with the client.*

**The client:** Yes! Yes! Yes! This was helpful for me too. Definitely.

## Conclusion

This interruption brings clarification to the work. I gave the therapist an opportunity to clarify his dilemma in front of the client, with sharing his RIA. This is another example that shows how implicit knowing may gain clarity through language (Vygotsky, 1986).

At some point, we can even *follow stages of the RIA's sophistication*. As opposed to the previous interview, the therapist's attitude toward "not-knowing" is grounded and calm. In this example, the sharing of the therapist's RIA is therapeutic since appropriate and context-related. It is evidently a disclosure of the self that is for the client's needs. The therapist finds it clarifying and helpful to move the work along and to clarify his work. The therapist's disclosure of his RIA strengthens the therapeutic alliance. The client mentions the importance of "being talked to" as opposed to "being talked about" or "being talked at". The language used in front of the client is inviting and inclusive, as opposed to an objectifying language, which would have probably cut off the client.

# Fourth interview

## Context

During this session, a male client explains to a female therapist how he suffers from not being able to earn a living. The client refers to the gender issue: being a man and not being able to provide for his partner. He used the expression "I *should* provide" on several occasions. The client is teary. His body is tense. I stop the session after twelve minutes. At this point, the presence of the therapist is less and less obvious, almost erased. The client is alone in his monologue. It seems that the therapist could be exchanged and it would not make any difference. As the therapist disappears, the client speeds up his comments, disregarding the previous therapist's interventions. I find it an interesting "moment of movement".

**Interviewer** *(to the therapist)*: Can you please explain what just happened in the last few minutes? What were you doing?

**Therapist:** Well ... *(the client)* was talking about a real impossible situation for himself. He is qualified. Yet, they do not allow him to work and make a decent living.

Comment and analysis: The therapist tries to summarize the client's dilemma. The therapist seems to be impacted by the client's story, but does not say how the client's words affect her. I suspect that the therapist experiences frustration and powerlessness. The therapist does not answer my question: "What were you doing?"

**Interviewer:** Hum...

**Therapist:** One of the things I was noticing was that as he was feeling the frustration is that he was going faster, faster, and becoming more and more tense and ... Hum... It felt to me that he wasn't allowing himself to slow down enough, to say or to feel a little bit more what that was. So, that is what I was trying to do, to slow him down, to bring that more to a place of awareness, about that particular piece ... So, that is what I was trying to do. That is what I am interested in at the moment. I noticed, when I had him slow down, he softened and actually looked a little bit more relaxed, although that was not what he reports.

*Comment and analysis: The therapist analyzes and describes the client's process: the client hastens his speech and increases his physical tension. The therapist assumes that the client's pressured speech gets in the way of the client's getting in touch with what he feels.*

**Interviewer:** Do you have a guess about what may happen, if you slow him down?

*Comment and analysis: I ask the therapist what is her intent behind her intervention.*

**Therapist:** I thought it might affect him. It might affect him more. I thought it might slow him down enough so that he would be able to figure out his dilemma. That is sort of the goal here. I mean, just at the moment, just to feel what that is like, just to feel that a little bit more intensively.

*Comment and analysis: The therapist does not answer my question. I was hoping for a more specific answer maybe such as that slowing down the client may increase the awareness of sadness and fear.*

**Interviewer:** In regard to what *you* were experiencing *(I am addressing the therapist's emotional response to the client).* Is there anything that you would like to share with us?

**Therapist:** Before I told him or suggested that he might slow down: I was getting lost. I was feeling really scattered. Hum... I think... I partly said that to help me organize what was happening.

*Comment and analysis: It is interesting to note that the therapist refers to her cognitive process rather than her emotional response. When she says "lost", she refers to losing her own train of thoughts or her focus. In the Gestalt community, in which this training and session takes place, "slowing down" is a very classic intervention. Applying this intervention may be a way for the therapist to gain control over the situation, when she felt "really scattered". She indeed indicates that asking the client to slow down helps her to be better able to pay attention to the process. This intervention may serve the client, the therapist and ultimately the therapeutic alliance. It is interesting to note the shift from the previous comment, where the therapist explained the intervention of slowing as being only focused on the client's need.*

**Interviewer:** Anything else that you would like to share?

**Therapist:** No. That's fine

**Interviewer:** Thank you.

## Conclusion

In this interview and the previous ones, it appears challenging for a non-expert therapist to discuss his emotional response as a part of his RIA process, even when solicited. Yet, these same therapists often encourage an expression of emotions. There seems to be little awareness of the intent behind an intervention with this non-expert RIA. One of the most interesting findings of this interview is to highlight through *RIA that some interventions may hold a relational purpose.* The sharing of RIA may directly influence the "therapeutic alliance". The example provided here is: "I need you to slow down so that I can pay more attention to you" as opposed to "Slow down, so that you will feel more connected to your feelings.

# Fifth interview

## Context

At the beginning of session, the client complains about fatigue. She says that she is uncertain whether she even has the strength to address anything during this short therapy session. After saying that, the client presents to the therapist a current conflict with her older sister. She requests comments from the therapist: "I would like to know what to do, I am stuck". The client refers to a "known" situation for her. Her sister has always been critical of her. The client reports her sister took a parental role as she grew up. She would always tell her what to do and with whom to get involved. The client resents the sister for that. The client dates a former boyfriend. She admits that this relationship was previously "consuming and unhealthy". She thinks that her boyfriend has changed. The client mentions her own fears and doubts in getting involved with the same partner. She fears her sister's reaction if she keeps this news from her and fears telling with whom she is involved. The interruption occurs after eight minutes. The total length of the session is twenty minutes. Contrary to the previous interviews, the interruption is chosen randomly, before the session starts.

**Interviewer (second interviewer):** So, what led to your last question to her?

**Therapist:** Let's see. I am trying to explore with her the dilemma that she experiences with her sister. She seems to have an acute awareness of how she is in relationship to her sister. She seems to struggle with the news that she wants to discuss with her. She is hesitant and fearful to approach her sister. The dilemma she faces can be summarized as: Damned if I do, damned if I don't! So I am interested in exploring that ... My intention is to see how she can support herself in that process. How can I be helpful to her as well?

Then, I also have some inner thoughts and response. I wonder how can she protect herself from the sister or the sister's reaction, from harsh criticisms and things like that. I accompany… *(the client)* in this exploration. I try to go side by side with her rather than to lead or to follow. That is what I am hoping for. I hope to provide the environment for her to explore that dilemma safely. I hope, that is what I do, I hope I manage to convey that. At the beginning, I was not sure about what she wanted to talk about. What was really important for her? So, I said that I was a bit confused. I heard that she felt tired and I did not know if she just wanted to be tired or just… whatever.... And then she started talking.

*Comment and analysis: The focus of the therapist is on self-support. The therapist implies that the quality of her presence is important. The therapist highlights the clarity that the client has toward the situation. She uses some of the client's words to reframe the client's dilemma. The therapist presents her own dilemma, which is to allow client to have her own experience, and at the same time the therapist's desire to protect her client from further hurt. The therapist clarifies her position in the therapeutic system: she will not overprotect the client (as she experienced overprotection from her elder sister). The therapist wants to explore what the client wants, what is needed in the therapeutic relationship or in the relationship with the sister. At the beginning, the therapist felt confused. The therapist refers to the paradoxical theory of change (Beisser, 1970). Encouraging the client to stay where she is invites her to move to another place.*

**Interviewer 2:** What is your sense of what you want or need to do next?

**Therapist:** Well, I think it is going to be informed by... Well, I think at this point of the dilemma what is important for me to know is how she experiences this dilemma, and how she positions herself in front of this dilemma. One of my beliefs is that once she names it, she will know what to do about this dilemma.

*Comment and analysis: The therapist says that she will try to elicit from her client what her feelings are toward the dilemma not toward the boyfriend, not toward the sister but toward the dilemma (the stuckness, which she is experiencing). The therapist invites her client to put it into words first, clarify and then to take a position in this dilemma. To do that is to be in control of the situation again, rather than being a passive agent.*

**Interviewer 2**: Hum. Hum.

**Therapist:** So, I will put it on the table and then...

*Comment and analysis: The therapist refers again to an overarching theory Schön (1983) as a reflexive practice. This overarching theory leads her practice. She explains her underlying theory of how change occurs. Her specific reference is the paradoxical theory of change (Beisser, 1970). Applied to practice, this means that the client can only move when she is invited to identify and stay where she is.*

**Interviewer 2:** Okay. Thank you

## Conclusion

In this interview, the RIA of the therapist includes the experience of the relationship, while referring also to the therapist's theories of references. The therapist has a reflexive attitude on how her presence and intervention may affect the client. The therapist presents her own dilemma, which is to allow client to have her own experience, and at the same time the therapist's desire to protect her client from further hurt. The therapist positions herself clearly in the therapeutic system.

# Sixth interview

## Context

The client appears sad and anxious. She expresses concerns and fears about a written project that she wants to submit for publication. The client oscillates between polarized statements "I have spent so much time studying" to "I don't know shit". She says she does not know what she wants or what she needs. The client is withdrawn. She does not seem connected to the therapist. I interrupt after six minutes with a sense that not much is happening.

**Interviewer:** Can you please share with us, what happened during the last few minutes? How did you inform your comments?

**Therapist:** *(Laughter)* Daaah... a big daah...*(Laughter). (Long sigh).*

*Comment and analysis: The therapist says he does not know what he is doing, which matches my first impression.*

**Interviewer:** Okay. Maybe I could ask a different question then? What were you aware of? What were you sensing? What do you know about what is happening?

**Therapist:** I am not sure. Part of it is… I guess... There is something about that, that seems a little familiar to the last time we worked together, she and I. About wanting to have something and not having it, and feeling some sadness about that. I just feel like it is an exploratory stage. I don't feel like I can say that I am anywhere or go anywhere, or I make any definitive statement about anything.

*Comment and analysis: The therapist establishes a connection with the previous session with the same client. He notes that she experiences the same feeling. The therapist identifies the client's dilemma: to want something and not to have it. The therapist says that at this point he is gathering more information on the client. This is a different statement than the initial "daaah". This is a clear and lovely illustration of Polanyi's (1966) ideas about tacit knowledge.*

**Interviewer:** Do you have any sense of where to go right now?

**Therapist:** No. I think that ... *(the client)* may have more, more of an idea of what she wants to say.

*Comment and analysis: The therapist at this point invites the client into a more active position. Since the therapist cannot figure out what the client wants she will go back and ask the client to clarify.*

**Interviewer:** Thank you.

**Supervisor:** *(Interrupting).* Life could be easier. He said. He said that smoothly. I can assimilate when life is easier. Then he says that he is quiet and at that moment. He says that he becomes anxious. Anxious means melancholy, as he defines it, at this moment. After saying that he is anxious, he puts all these statement right into one small square and says: "I Know a bit. I did some good stuff". He starts to make some self-statements. Then, he comes in with a statement that is not an "I". It is a "You" statement, to himself: "You don't know shit!" *(The supervisor puts the emphasis on each word as he repeats them: You don't know shit).* He then follows that up with "I don't know why I can't feel the good stuff". The "you" is right there juxtaposed: "I know a bit. I don't know everything. I did some good stuff. You don't know shit!" Remind him of this sequence.

*Comment and analysis: What is interesting at this point is to note the difference of perceived information emerging from the session, between the supervisor and therapist. The RIA of the supervisor is evidently more elaborate. The supervisor focuses his RIA on a fine analysis of the client's process in relation to the therapist. The therapist seems largely confused by what is going on. He has a "sensed feeling" but has a really difficult time clearly expressing his RIA. The supervisor points out the client's process step-by-step for the therapist to use in his next interventions. The supervisor offers several possible interventions at this point. He invites the therapist to pay closer attention to the sequence of events: what the client says and how he tends to juxtapose "units of meaning" and make a collage of them.*

## Conclusion

The therapist's RIA refers to previous sessions and establishes patterns within the session. His RIA clarifies the client's dilemna. From an initial confusion, along with my questions, the therapist's RIA becomes more articulate illustrating Polanyi's idea: "We can know more than we can tell" (1966, p.4). The highlight of this interview is to compare the supervisor's RIA with the therapist's. The expert RIA is clearly more articulate and elaborate than the less trained therapist. The supervisor's RIA focuses the client's process in relationship to the therapist, when the therapist seems largely confused by what is going on. The supervisor points out the client's process step-by-step. The supervisor offers several possible interventions at this point. He invites the therapist to pay closer attention to the sequence of events: what the client says and how he tends to juxtapose "units of meaning" and make a collage of them. The expert RIA is able to deconstruct the process and describe for the therapist-in-training what occurred in a sequential manner. He seems to be teaching his therapist how to recognize and talk about a process.

# Seventh interview

## Context

The client, a male in his fifties, shares the turmoil of not having his birthday celebrated. He relates this painful experience to earlier ones, where his parents never acknowledged his birthday. The client chooses a female therapist to work with. I stop the interview after approximately six minutes. I find the session unfocused and do not understand what the therapist is doing or where he intends to go. I stop and ask for clarification.

**Interviewer:** Can you please tell me what just happened for you during the last few minutes?

**Therapist:** I am feeling like... I really need to figure out what the figural piece is, in his head. I feel… Instinctively, I feel some kind of emotion or feeling like... I just want to support him and not think about anything and, I want him to feel supported. I am feeling a conflict I guess with my intuition and I am trying to be also very analytical. So it's conflicting right now. I feel like I am struggling with that.

*Comment and analysis: First, the therapist manifests a desire to find what really matters for the client. Then the therapist shares her "gut feeling", what she calls instinct, to support and accompany the client, just where he is, in the heart of his pain. The therapist explains her conflict between following her "gut feeling" and being "very analytical". Then underlying dilemma could be: I follow my gut feeling but if I were a good therapist, I should be more analytical.*

**Interviewer:** In this conflict what do you follow?

**Therapist:** Well, I am following the… I am thinking a lot, and I want to know more about the piece of disclosure. What are his thoughts and feelings? How are they connected to her reactions to him?

*Comment and analysis: The therapist's statements are confusing. The therapist wants to explore the client's thoughts and feelings related to her mother not acknowledging his birthday.*

**Supervisor:** One of the things that you did, was that lovely expression of one part of you that you trusted. I had the fantasy that just expressing that helped you clarify what you were willing to do.

**Therapist:** Yes. It was important for me to put that out. I mean…It felt good to just put out my confusion.

*Comment and analysis: The therapist asserts that to verbalize her inner conflict clarifies and relieves the therapist's anxiety.*

## Conclusion

I notice an important effect of RIA on the therapist. The therapist simply shares her confusion with the patient; doing that apparently clarifies her RIA and reduces the therapist's anxiety. In this interview, I also note again the poor positioning of the therapist. The therapist has a hard time formalizing her thoughts and generating a theory of practice, while immobilizing herself with sterile conflict such as "should I follow my gut feeling or should I be analytical". RIA encompasses both.

# Eighth interview

## Context

The client, a male in his early sixties chooses a male therapist to discuss a difficult professional encounter he had with a female teenager and her mother. The client points out that, for unknown reasons that he ignores, he felt at that time a strong need to show off. He feels both saddened and disappointed about his reaction. He tells the therapist that he hates to have this urge for validation. After this first session, the clients never called back. During this segment of therapy, he explains with many details what happened during his session with this teenage girl and her mother. I intervene after fourteen minutes when the therapist stops the client from continuing his long and detailed description. I am intrigued by what happens. I perceive a change in the interaction: the pacing of the session is slower.

**Interviewer:** I was curious. Could tell me a bit about what led to your last intervention?

**Therapist:** Well, I was very interested in the fact that ... *(the client)* was stopping himself in that session with his young client. He wasn't obviously stopping himself, but he was certainly asking himself lots of torturing questions. He had a good self-observation as to what the dynamic… the underlining dynamics were between the two of them at that time. I was wondering if he was willing to explore that a little bit more, rather than to go on ... is a great storyteller and I am interested in the stories he tells most of the time. So I just wanted to see if he wanted to stop there and linger with that a little bit.

*Comment and analysis: Rather than letting the client continue with his narrative of what happened, the therapist refocuses the conversation on the client's emotional response. The therapist thinks that slowing down the pacing will bring out something interesting.*

**Interviewer:** Okay. Thank you.

**Supervisor:** I like that you to go back there and stop the story. I would have tried to go back there with a little tighter focus. When he starts his work, he is almost breathless. What I heard in the breathing was starting and holding, starting and holding, starting and holding. There is something there... whatever that might be. I don't know. I was really interested in what that was, because when he is done with his whole little piece of the story, that is what is left, this is a quote from him: "I feel disliked by everybody".

*Comment and analysis: I have one more opportunity to compare an expert RIA with a less expert one. The supervisor intervenes to highlight and encourage the therapist's choice. The supervisor adds a focus to the intervention. He invites the therapist to carefully explore the breathing of the client. At the beginning of the session, the client is short of breath as he speaks. The supervisor shows how the client is racing. He links the pacing with a short cut that the client makes toward the end of his story: "I feel disliked by everybody".*

**Therapist:** *(Surprised)* He said that?

**Supervisor:** Yes. This is, to me, a quite shocking statement. What is also interesting is the structure of what he does. He gets anxious here *(shows a place)* and this is where things deviate *(shows another place)*. Then, everything takes off from there and, sort of legitimate the trajectory. Where he goes and spends his time is: "What will happen" "Are they going to call?" There is no way to solve this, here *(shows the first place)*. And you brought him back to that. What are you doing there? You bring him back to that moment where he gets up to get his books. I might slow him down even further and ask him: What are you feeling just sitting there? What happened when you jumped for your books? What is it you wanted to do? I imagine he has a whole speech to give them at that moment: the pre-book speech? Such as: I want you to know… What is there? What is it that he spent so much time away from?

*Comment and analysis: The supervisor invites the therapist to pay more attention to the structure of what the client does. The supervisor refers to a specific moment, just before the client reaches for his books to show what a bright and literate therapist he is. The supervisor invites to explore what thoughts and words are related to this very moment: "The pre-book speech". The supervisor generates a list of questions to assist the clinician in exploring the "pre-book speech". The supervisor invites the therapist to explore how the client shortens the information to make cognitive distortions: "I feel disliked by everybody".*

## Conclusion

This interview offers another illustration of comparison between expert and less trained RIA. The supervisor deepens the therapist's intervention by moving past the content to identify the pattern and encourage the clinician to look at patterns of patterns. The supervisor focuses also on para-verbal elements (breathing, tone of the voice, level of excitement, rhythm…) to inform his RIA.

# Ninth interview

## Context

The client expresses a strong desire to work and to share the sadness resulting from feeling "alien in a lot of places". The client is close to tears. She relates that feeling of alienation to her family history. In this interview, the therapist is a supervisor. This interview should demonstrate a more expert RIA. The interruption occurs after nine minutes. I am not the interviewer on this piece of work.

**Interviewer (Second interviewer):** Can I stop you here?

**Therapist:** What I am thinking as I am hearing this schema is that: "In every place, I am an alien." When I begin to bring her to one place, she modifies it a little. She never really looks at it. We can never really look at it *(the therapist puts the emphasis on the "we")*. So, we cannot really check it out. She goes off on a tangent and it gets a little bigger: "I need to do this to satisfy them or this to satisfy them"... things that I don't know to be true. I want to bring her back to a place where we both have some sense of... something connected to reality.

*Comment and analysis: The therapist talks about the need to build a connection when talking about the client's concern. The therapist talks about how to initiate a shift from the "talking about" to the "talking with". The therapist refers to a similar process as in the previous interview, where the patient is not connected to the therapist.*

**Interviewer:** How did you choose to have the client talk about the belonging and loneliness out of everything she said? How did you decide that that was something that interested you?

**Therapist:** Those were the things that hit me the most sharply. It seems to run through everything that she says. She mentions some events. It seemed to describe the events again, being alone.

*Comment and analysis: Out of all the themes that the client presents, the therapist explains how he decides what to focus on in the session. The therapist first uses his intuition, as expressed by: "Those were the things that hit me most". He justifies his felt sense with the number of times that the client refers to same concept. The therapist picks the criterion of redundancy.*

**Interviewer (Second interviewer):** Okay. Thank you.

**Therapist:** *(To the client)* Go back and look at how: "You are an alien in any place". I am interested in how you would describe it.

*Comment and analysis: I kept this comment that came right after the interview on RIA. This illustrates the efficiency of the reflection-in-action. RIA allows the therapist to sharpen his previous ideas, in one single intervention for the client. RIA clarifies and encourages a precise intervention.*

**Therapist:** *(After the session, sharing more RIA).* For me the central piece was this sense of alienation. It was what kept coming in the fore of her experience and interrupting everything she was trying to do. It is where I wanted to focus to bring that to a level where we can work on it, whether it was here *(showing the interaction between the therapist and the client)* or here *(showing what belongs to the client).*

*Comment and analysis: The therapist makes an interesting analysis on the process. He thinks that the client recreates in many other settings the experience of "alienation" through something that she does or does not do in the therapeutic interaction. For this client, alienation is a way of interrupting contact with somebody else, in this particular case, with the therapist. The therapist sees two ways of working with this client: the first in the present and the second with the recollection of her past.*

## Conclusion

In this interview, the therapist highlights the importance of building first a therapeutic alliance before anything else. The therapist then explains how he decides what to focus on in the session. His RIA refers first to a felt sense and then he justifies his felt sense with the criteria of redundancy. After the interview, the therapist uses his RIA to produce a clear and effective intervention. RIA allows the therapist to sharpen his previous ideas in one single intervention for the client.

# Tenth interview

## Context

A female client in her thirties chooses a female therapist. I have a difficult time to describe what occurred before my interruption. I felt confused. The client and the therapist seem to be dancing: getting closer and then distancing. The client expresses on many occasions a wish to work on something in particular. As soon as the therapist shows interest, the client drops the subject quickly. The therapist seems uncomfortable. She mumbles; she hesitates; she has shorter eye contact with the client. I choose to intervene after twelve minutes into the session. I may have intervened before.

**Interviewer**: Could you please share with me what you know about what just happened, during the last few minutes?

**Therapist:** I feel just like my client said. I feel lost, frustrated. In terms of what is figural for me, I mean.... I don't know. There is obviously a dynamic. I think. I imagine that is more obvious to the observers than to me... or my stuff and what I think her stuff is and it works together. I perceive her holding back and I am doing the exact same thing. I think that before I ask her for more, I need to give more.

*Comment and analysis: This comment contrasts with what I see. The therapist demonstrates an elaborate RIA. She has a clear sense of what she feels: frustrated and confused. The therapist describes with ease the therapeutic impasse and her role in it. Unfortunately the RIA is not shared; it is not used in the therapeutic interaction. The reflexive ability of this therapist is fine; she knows that she does not know some things, but that other may very well see the dynamic more clearly. She knows how she parallels the client holding back. The therapist also discusses the therapeutic alliance and the need for the therapist to engage herself in this relationship.*

**Interviewer:** So... Do you have any sense of the direction you want to take?

**Therapist:** I am going to continue to be inappropriate again and say something non-therapeutic, but honest! Since it is totally f...up anyway! *(Collective laughter)*

*Comment and analysis: The therapist displays humor. She can distance herself and look at what she is co-creating. The therapist wants to stop what she is doing with the client. The expression of RIA creates a change.*

**Interviewer:** Thank you very much.

## Conclusion

The clinician's RIA contrasts massively with what I see happening in the session. RIA holds a relational value. The therapist's RIA is rather sophisticated, but if not shared with the client, the therapist's intervention remains sterile. There is information that the therapist was not sharing: about her client, about her relationship to the client, about herself as a therapist, and about the therapeutic impasse.

# Chapter XIII

## Interviews with the expert therapists

### Eleventh interview

### Context

This is the first interview of a series of three series of interviews with three expert therapists. There will be two interviews with this clinician. Rather than trying to change and unify the environment to fit my research, I always ask the clinician to work as closely as possible to the way he usually works. The first expert clinician teaches therapy to students and decides to have me participate in one of his sessions with the use of a reflecting team. A reflecting team is a way to expose clients to a meta-conversation. It involves creating a conversation about the conversation that just occurred in the therapy session. In practice, the use of a reflecting team translates into three moves in the therapy session. First, the session takes place with the therapist and the clients, while the reflecting team (usually three to six therapists) observes behind a one-way mirror. The clients are informed in advance about the reflecting team and may choose this extra therapeutic help. Second, after about fifty minutes into the session, the reflecting team switches rooms and starts offering reflections about what was said during the session, in front of the clients. The reflecting team shares their comments, reactions, and questions, in front of the clients. During this stage, the clients are in a listening position. They are discouraged from interacting with the reflectors. In the third part of the session, the therapists takes advantage of what has been discussed and generated by the reflecting team. He invites the clients to process and reflect upon what the reflecting team talked about. We owe the reflecting team to the original idea of a Norwegian psychiatrist, Tom Anderson (1987, 1991, and 1995). I have a rather long experience as a part of a reflecting team. From 1994 to 1996, I participated in approximately ten reflecting teams per week. I have also been trained and supervised by Tom Anderson in learning this practice.

I choose not to transcribe the reflecting team. I do not think it adds any relevant information to the topic of my research. However, it is important for the reader to know that a reflecting team was part of this session, since the context of this therapy session became much more "public".

In my opinion, the addition of the reflecting team was disruptive to the clarity and the success of this therapy session. The interview was done in the presence of four members of the reflecting team and a classroom of twelve students, who witnessed the session behind the one-way mirror. The reflecting team was of a mediocre quality with poorly trained student therapists. They offered lengthy and sometimes irrelevant comments as reflections. Even if protected by the legal and ethical boundaries of confidentiality, this therapy session did not provide a safe and private surrounding for the patients to feel safe and welcome to talk. This setting was however interesting in that it is typical for a learning context of Family Therapy training.

I gave each expert clinician the opportunity to choose the patient he wanted for this interview. The expert clinician invites me into one of his training sessions. He does not make any specific selection. This expert therapist has worked in the field of Family Therapy for at least the last three decades. He was trained by the founders of Family Therapy: Luigi Boscolo, Gianfranco Cecchin, Jay Haley, Chloe Madanes, Salvador Minuchin, Virginia Satir, and Carl Whitaker. I have been a student of him for three years. As a Family Therapist trainer, This expert therapist is used to using videotape and audiotape. He is comfortable with discussing his work in front of his students, even in a larger public arena. In the Family Therapy Institute where he works, any client who comes in also accepts to being videotaped or audiotaped for training. In exchange of that, the fee is based on a sliding scale.

## Context

The client, John, is seventeen years old. He comes in for a consultation at the request of his mother. During the interview, his mother is not present in the therapy room. She witnesses the session behind the one-way mirror. To complicate the situation the teen's mother is also a student of the expert therapist.

*Comment and analysis: From the beginning of this interview, I remember my reaction of surprise and reticence. There are uncertainties about the positioning of the participants during this therapy session, their intent, their need and what they want from this therapy session. I remember questioning who should participate in the therapy process, how and why? The initial request comes from the mother. She is not present during the session. Like most teenagers, John is not interested in coming to this consultation, and does not have any idea why he is here and what he should talk about. John comes in because his mother wants him here. I do not know exactly why mother wants him in treatment, since she is not part of the conversation. These uncertainties persist throughout the interview. I think that these uncertainties impede the therapist's ability to intervene. The therapist also has a dual relationship with the mother who is both the mother of the client and a student of the therapist.*

*The clarification ahead of time of some important aspects of this setting would have improved the quality of the session. Some of these situational elements (the role of each participant, their involvement, and expectation) could have been explained to solidify ground upon which a therapeutic conversation could have taken place.*

*Before the interview starts, I remember being preoccupied with these questions and comments. These concerns, I think, hindered my ability to interview.*

**Interviewer:** I would like to start by asking you, generally, what were the highlights of the session? If you were to talk about what you did in this session, what was your sense of this session as a whole?

**Therapist:** I guess I would use the phrase of being a witness. A witness who was not an inactive witness, but a listening witness. Also, I was a curious witness. There is some part of the session, where I felt *(hesitant)*... not invisible... I felt I was there, but I felt talked at, almost preached to. I do not mean that in a negative way, for it was such a place of passion. So that is the listening part, I think. I did not have or did not take much opportunity to interrupt him, to acknowledge what I was hearing, or question my own understanding or misunderstanding of what he was saying.

*Comment and analysis: The therapist highlights the quality of the relationship that is being initiated. The therapist defines his position as being "a witness". The therapist qualifies the quality of the conversation that he has with the client as being more of a monologue, as opposed to the dialogue he wishes to have with this client.*

**Interviewer:** Yes, I had a similar experience. I also have another question about some specific moments that I am curious about. Let me try to find them on the tape, so I can refer to them. Let's see...*(I am searching the part of the tape and playing it for the therapist).* When you asked him: "How did it affect your friends, your family, when you turned to God?" What were you looking for? What was your intention?

**Therapist:** I was exploring the field, the context in which he lives.

*Comment and analysis: The therapist formulates questions to explore the client's context.*

**Interviewer:** I noticed somewhat of a shift in the conversation and that raises my curiosity. I don't know if you would agree with that. I was paying careful attention to the opportunities you had to speak. I was noticing also how much he was speaking. *(I have the therapist listen to a part of the tape where the teenager talks about going to England for a month to study the Bible. In this section, the teenager speaks in a long monologue).* You responded to this declaration of faith by stating: "I hear your passion and I don't hear any concerns. Is that right?" What was your idea at that moment? Do you remember? Do you have a sense of what led you to say that?

**Therapist:** My experience of what he was saying was that there weren't any strong concerns, at least that he was presenting, in terms of following the path that he is on.

**Interviewer:** Why did you make this comment? Where did you come from?

**Therapist:** Well *(Pause).* He was not presenting a problem, a current problem. I was hearing his passion and excitement in the midst of transformation. He is in the midst of it at this point. And I did not hear him having any sense that there were any restraints to this or any obstructions to it at this point. So I used this word, whatever this word was.

*Comment and analysis: Therapist seems to be looking for something to work on. Therapist challenges some of the client's certainty to see if there is anything that, the client is struggling with.*

**Interviewer:** I just want to review and replay with you a part of the tape. *(We listen to a section of the therapy session where John* *talks about his heavy use of illegal substances including almost "everything you can think of, I've tried". John, the client, refers to his promiscuous behaviors with girls. John said during this time, he thought he was going to die. He then talks about his experience of a boot camp, where his parents sent him. He shares how hard it was for him to be in this hyper-structured environment. He quit all drugs without weaning. He adds: "I was clean for four months, I just came back and then… I slipped away, in that same destructiveness, all over again. I had an urge. Almost, not to get better.... It just kills me... I am just sick of it.... That was it. (He mimes with his hand going down a slope)... You can change somebody's behavior, but I do not believe you can ever... I don't believe anyone can ever change, until their heart is touched. Until they really experience the love of the Creator. I believe that is the only point where you really change". After this long comment from John, the therapist replies: "So are you saying that is something that happened to you or?")* Can you tell me what just happened the few minutes before you made this comment? How did you come to that decision? Do you remember anything about the context?

**Therapist:** I was curious about his reflections in terms of his purpose. That is why I asked that question.

**Interviewer:** Were you trying to highlight anything with your question? *(I should have asked more clearly: what was your intention? What were you hoping for when you asked this question?)*

**Therapist:** Hem.... *(Silence)*

*Comment and analysis: My question is obscure and the therapist may not understand my comment. Fortunately, I persevere in asking this question more clearly.*

**Interviewer:** Yes. I mean: "What was the intent behind the question that you asked?"

**Therapist:** I was interested in, given all the noted difficulties, how his heart was touched? What was this like for him?

**Interviewer:** It seems to me, as I was listening to the session, that there was an important shift between what he called "his previous life" and the life he is living right now?

**Therapist:** I don't know if it was at this moment, but frequently in my comments or sometimes in my non-comments, that was a question or questions I had about how he experienced himself.

*Comment and analysis: The therapist confronts his vision of change and responsibility to the client's. He tries to engage the client in realizing how much he experiences himself as an agent of change. It is unfortunate that I did not ask the therapist to be more explicit about his statement on "non-comment".*

**Interviewer:** Yes.

**Therapist:** Meaning his own involvement, participation, or cooperation.

**Interviewer:** You came back to this notion several times. What specifically were you looking for? Any stronger idea that you were trying to challenge him with?

**Therapist:** Hem. *(Silence)*

**Interviewer:** I noticed that several times you came back to this idea. Did you tried to elicit from him responsibility or personal agency, in making his decision?

*Comment and analysis: This is typically an example of a question not to ask in an interview. I do not ask a question but make an assumption and try to verify it.*

**Therapist:** Yes. It was just a curiosity. I don't present myself or see myself as a believer. I have my own spiritual personal journey of where he was at *(Short laughter).* I was his age as well. I am not trying to put him in a position. I don't think that people don't experience, that they don't have anything whatsoever to do with what happens to them. I was just very curious. Many times I wondered if that was a position he was really taking, or if he is seeing himself as having something to do with it. I think later on, when he began talking about his own struggle, he began talking about paying attention to the small voice in the back of his head, as opposed to the raging hormones or other feelings that were going on. That would suggest a shift in his self-perception.

*Comment and analysis: The therapist is searching for what he calls self-agency or a personal responsibility in that change. The therapist might be trying to challenge John's belief about how change can occur. Indeed several of his comments to the client try to bring him back to his part in the transformation process. I am doubtful about the therapist's statement: "It was just a curiosity". This would imply that there is no intent, nor direction behind this comment. I suspect that there was. (After reading the transcript, the therapist will add this comment in my margin "an invitation to other possibilities"). Again, I should have asked him more questions about his comment. I think that the therapist holds a preference for the notion of self-agency as opposed to the notion of change being operated by outside forces "when one's heart is touched". The notion of a magical transformation through spirituality challenges the long culture of change in psychotherapy. This notion of change as an external phenomenon, and as a grace puts the therapist in an extremely powerless situation about his role as "a witness" in a session.*

**Interviewer:** I have another question. That has nothing to do with my previous comment. You also said something about missing the presence of the mother during the session. She was behind the one-way-mirror. What stopped you from asking her to join you, explicitly? On many occasions during the session, I wondered: What was she feeling at this moment? What might her life have been like during her teenager's crisis?

**Therapist:** Personally, I was disappointed that the mother did not come. I thought she was. It was her idea to bring her son here. For her to sit on the other side of the mirror... There were some times, where I gave some thoughts about her sitting on the other side of the mirror and... I did not bring it up, because I did not find the appropriate moment to bring it up.

**Reflections after my analysis and comments:** *After reading the transcript, the clinician adds that the mother informed him just before the interview started that she would not participate in the reflecting team. This was related to an earlier comment about her being a mother, a student, a therapist in training, and a colleague of the other students present in the observing room. He also adds: "I* *usually choose to talk only with the person who wants to join in the conversation. However, during the pre-session conversation I could have included the therapist's pros and cons, as well as I could have shared some possible ambivalence toward a possibly more informed choice".*

**Interviewer:** I see.

**Therapist:** That was not again until our break and seeing her on the other side of the mirror. She chose not to come in on the reflecting team. This was her choice not to come in, her choice to stay outside.

*Comment and analysis: I disagree with this comment. I believe that the therapist hosts the conversations, and set and choose the context and the boundaries of the conversations he invites the client to join in.*

**Interviewer:** I see. I have the same kind of question on this section of the tape. Well, what I was going to say would be fairly interpretive, so I prefer to let you answer first, then I can tell you what I think I saw you doing. I may be off on that.

*Comment and analysis: I realize as I am interviewing this expert therapist how strong my ideas of leading the session differently come up in the interview and how these ideas influence my questions. This is not necessarily a negative comment but it shows how interviews are co-constructed. This interview also highlights my own training as a clinician responding to a clinician.*

**Therapist:** I wanted to have some specific sense of his struggles. What it was like for him? As opposed to this big generality, so I could better connect with him. So, I could understand what he is talking about and what kind of struggle he was possibly dealing with.

**Interviewer:** I had a sense, with the two interruptions you've made, that you tried to initiate some kind of connection, and shifting from "talking about" to "talking to"?

**Therapist:** I think that there were many times where my comments were an invitation for him to talk to me. I often felt that he was as I said preaching or talking at… You know.

*Comment and analysis: The therapist acknowledges that there is little therapeutic relationship with this visitor (not quite a client or a patient). There is little ground to establish a working alliance. The therapist confirms that he is struggling with establishing a more personal connection with the teenager. It seems to be the theme of his work.*

**Interviewer:** One of the reasons why I think this comment caught my attention is because I think I know your work. I have a sense of your style and my guess is that in your sessions oftentimes, most of the time, you highlight what works in people's experience. With John, you were often noticing his down sides. I noticed something very different. It is why I stopped you at these particular points. I had the impression that you were almost trying to have him see the balance, the other side of what he was saying and to challenge him, or at least to consider the other side of it.

**Therapist:** At this point, I don't know if I was trying to challenge anything.

*Comment and analysis: the therapist expresses maybe frustration in this comment. At this point of the session, it is possible that the therapist gave up trying to challenge anything. I may have upset the therapist by my comments, making guesses and interpretation rather than letting him speak.*

**Interviewer:** When the client says: "You know, change is a miracle!" You said: "It's a miracle and this means that in some ways you cooperate with it or is it outside of your realm?" I was curious about this comment. Can you say something about that?

**Therapist:** I think that it is similar to what I said in another comment. Again, I was wondering if in his own experience he has any awareness, or any sense of his own agency or of his own involvement or of his own cooperation or, that was outside his spiritual sense of God.

*Comment and analysis: The therapist states the same and consistent RIA. He tries to establish a more personal contact with the client. He attempts to generate a sense of self-agency from the client.*

**Interviewer:** I was also curious when you chose to have the reflecting team interrupt. Was it a specific choice, a specific time?

**Therapist:** Two things: one was that I had a sense of the time. The other was that I wanted to see if people might join in the group, including maybe his mother *(short laughter)*, people who might bring up some other questions or other comments that he might, or that we might bring into our own conversation. It seemed to me that they were going over similar patterns up to this point. If I had been alone at this point, I probably would have summarized what I had heard him saying up to this point. And maybe also I might possibly have brought up some of my own experiences, including that I was feeling at times that he was preaching, that I was like an audience to his preaching. Not that he was trying to convert me or anything like that, but the passion and the enthusiasm, he was almost swept up in it.

*Comment and analysis: The therapist looks for an intervention that would create a slight move, a difference from what he calls: "going over a similar pattern". He chooses to interrupt the session at this point to bring in the reflecting team. The therapist introduces a possible intervention that he may have used, he says, had he been alone with John: sharing his experience of being "preached to". The therapist stops himself, because of the context.*

**Interviewer:** Can you share your reaction to being "preached to"?

**Therapist:** There was a familiarity that I have experienced with different people who have experienced "finding the truth". It happens often and is very common in spiritual and religious contexts, but also in other contexts as well. So, it was a familiar experience. Also it was familiar in terms of my own experience, when I was his age. Actually, I was a little bit older but not much, when I found the truth. I was on my own spiritual quest. I saw myself in him. Perhaps not as colorful as he was with his green hair and everything else. My hair was bleached. *(Laughter)*

**Interviewer:** So how did it affect you?

**Therapist:** Kind of like a warm smile. It was memories. I have seen lots of people, whose lives turned around because they found Jesus or they found peace with meditation, or other practices. I certainly do not mock it. It is important. I just want to say something else though. After we came back, I don't even know if it was on the tape because the tape went off. This struck me: he was talking about, at least that was my understanding of it, his theory about therapy.

*Comment and analysis: I asked twice the same question, but the therapist does not immediately answer how he is impacted by the client. I am not sure what a "a warm smile" means. The therapist connects his reaction to his previous experience of being an adolescent and "finding the truth". We will not know more about his personal reaction to John. The therapist switches to the way that John understands change and therapy.*

**Interviewer:** Yes, what about John's comment on "people helping"?

**Therapist**: Yes, I imagine his sense of God might have a sense of the pain of people. We really have to come from a heart felt place to connect with people on a very deep level, and experience their pain and have a sense of their pain in order to be able to assist them in any way.

*Comment and analysis: The therapist relates this comment to how the teenager perceives change in therapy. The therapist did not notice that comment during the session. This is an interesting illustration of the importance of maintaining reflexive practice. When two clinicians review an audiotape, or videotape of their work, there is much material for RIA and learning.*

**Interviewer:** That is very interesting.

**Interviewer:** Another question I have is, maybe not in regard to what you did but more about what you did not do. I was very aware, as I was listening to your session, that maybe some other therapists might have jumped in places, where you chose to stay quiet. The first moment that raised my curiosity was when John mentioned his diagnosis of Attention Deficit and Hyperactivity Disorder (ADHD) and his medication, at the beginning of the session. You did not respond. The second was right after the reflecting team, when he mentioned his long history of being suicidal. There again, you chose not to intervene. So, I was really curious about your choices.

**Therapist**: Well I would not see that as… I would have seen that as being very disrespectful at this point, a person meeting with you there in a more public place *(i.e. in the presence of the students)*. Even if I were alone with him in the first session, I certainly would not have highlighted that or punctuated that, or inquired about suicide attempts or thoughts. I don't see that it would have brought any benefit at this point.

*Comment and analysis: The therapist explains that he chooses not to ask John any further questions about his diagnosis of ADHD and taking medication or having a history of multiple suicide attempts. It seemed to me that at these moments John talks about himself rather than preaching. Maybe it is difficult for the client to figure out what is expected of him. The therapist often times remains silent, despite his desire to initiate a dialogue and a connection.*

**Interviewer:** Would you have brought that up in other instances?

**Therapist:** What do you mean? With other people?

**Interviewer:** Yes

**Therapist:** Oh! With other people, of course.

*Comment and analysis: I should have asked for further explanation of this answer. What would need to be different for the therapist to be more direct?*

**Interviewer:** You did not have any concerns regarding the suicide for example. Is that what you are saying?

**Therapist:** I mean, there were invitations on his part. When he started going back in his whole story about trying to convince me of how awful things were for him. He talked about all the drugs he took and how he tried them all, and so on, and so on. There was a part of me saying: "I got it! I got the picture already! I got the picture! You know…But I think there were no reason to go there. I bring that up because to me it was similar to suicide.

*Comment and analysis: There is slight annoyance from the therapist in response John's comment regarding his previous history of self-destruction. I still do not understand why the therapist judges that it was not important to ask more questions about that period of the client's life. The therapist says that the client would have liked to discuss in detail this chapter of his life. I did not ask more, but I am still confused by the therapist's response.*

**Interviewer:** This was one of these moments where I really missed the presence of the mother. I think she would have added a dimension to the session.

**Therapist:** Yes. You are right. I agree.

**Interviewer:** Is there anything else that you would like to add?

**Therapist:** No. That is fine. Thank you. It was interesting for me.

**Interviewer:** OK, thank you so much for your precious time. This conversation was really interesting. I almost lost sight of the time. I really appreciate you giving me the opportunity to do this interview.

*(This is the end of this interview.)*

# Twelfth interview

## Context

In the second interview, the expert therapist chooses the same client a month later. He calls me back to inform me that he wants do a second therapy session this times requesting the presence of the mother in the session. John, 17 comes back with his mother Tina, 47. Initially, John's father is scheduled to be part of the session. He calls a few minutes before the session starts to inform us that he is stuck in the traffic of Los Angeles. The mother assists the father, a pastor in his ministry. They run a private church. Mother also completes her studies in the field of Marriage and Family Therapy. As in the previous interview, he decides to use the reflecting team. I choose not to be part of the reflecting team.

**Interviewer:** I want to start by asking you what your general sense of what you did today was. What happened during this session?

**Therapist:** Let's see. I know that, since John and his mother did not come forward to say anything that they wanted from this session, I expressed some of my interest from the last time we met, and some of the things that I have thought about. They were related to the past. I asked about some history that I was curious about. After a short period, he seemed clearly not interested in talking more about that. I think that the expression he used was "That was then, and now is now".

Mom said something similar. It was my sense that, especially with mom, there was still a lot of pain. That was still very close. *(Silence).* It could be accessed very quickly, since it was such a public place and that was not their intention to go there, I respected that. My sense of the overall session was that I experienced him being himself more, in contrast to the first time we met. More, in terms of with me... The last time it was just he and I in the room. This time, it was he the mother, and I. Yet, I felt there were times where I was talking with him. There were more connections with him being there. He was less in his head, in his own monologue. That stood out for me.

*Comment and analysis: The context of the session is interesting to note. The therapist chooses the same client, aware that the session had not worked out as he wanted he invites the same client in. The therapist focuses on the area he previously struggled with. This is an example of using reflexivity about one's practice. The therapist demonstrates a commitment toward his clients. The therapist first establishes a comparison between the last session where he could not establish a connection with this teenager, as opposed to this session where he experiences that John is talking at times "with him". The therapist does not say how he may have encouraged that to happen. The therapist pays attention to the client's emotional response, a pain easily accessible. He respects the teenager's request not to explore the past.*

**Interviewer:** I agree.

**Therapist:** I felt very touched, as he talked. Especially as he talked about his relationship with his father, his newfound relationship with his father and what that was like for him and reflecting on, or guessing what that was like for his father and how special that is. Even more so, when he talked about how he, his dad and his brother are able to be together in a different kind of way today. This was an example of that important change in this relationship, and his experience of this relationship. *(Long silence of seven seconds).* Let me ask myself right now: Is this a meeting that has opened possibilities for him? For mom? For them? Or, for him, and other people who weren't here? I don't know.

*Comment and analysis: The therapist talks about the new alliance between the teenager and his father, after his transformation through his faith. The therapist shares his emotional response. This comment marks a contrast with the previous session, where therapist felt being "preached to" and almost irritated. The therapist tries to assess the helpfulness and the quality of his session. He does not come to any conclusion.*

**Interviewer:** Would you like to add anything else, or are you done?

**Therapist:** Yes. I am done.

**Interviewer:** When you mentioned that you had a sense of John having more of a relationship with you, more of a contact with you today, which by the way I agree with. I sensed something similar. Do you have a sense of what you did that could have encouraged that to happen? Or something that you said that made that happen more?

**Therapist:** The first thought that comes to mind is that the last time when we met, if his mom or somebody else from the family had been there, that would be more of a grounding experience. I thought that last time too, at the end of the meeting. When I heard that his mother was more willing to be here and also, initially the father who, however, got stuck in the traffic and could not make it, I had a prediction. My prediction was that John may be more grounded. It was larger than just his relationship with me.

*Comment and analysis: The therapist seems to establish a connection between the presence of a family member in the session and the quality of the connection that he establishes with the client. I am curious about his theory.*

**Interviewer:** Do you have a sense of something that you did in the room that encourages that to happen, or to happen more? Is there anything that you purposefully did so that this relationship would be more alive and shared with John?

**Therapist:** Hem. *(Silence).* What comes to mind at this point and this wasn't purposeful was my letting him know, him and his mom, what I was interested in. Indeed, I invited him into a relationship with me about what I was interested in *(Short laughter).* He connected there and I thought mom connected there too. I was before asking: "what are you interested in" and he was interested in preaching.

*Comment and analysis: The therapist suspects that his clear statement of "what he is interested in" has something to do with getting something different from the client. Instead of letting the client follow a path that the therapist is not interested in, a monologue that does not seem to include the therapist, the therapist decides to take a more directive stance "let me tell you what I am interested in". This comment initiates a closer connection between*

*John and the therapist. That is a good illustration of how the positioning of the therapist may influence and transform the therapeutic alliance.*

**Interviewer:** There is something else. I guess there was an easy invitation for you, the therapist, to discuss their past between the mother and John. You chose not to take this path. At this point, several therapists might have chosen others directions. When John mentioned the past, the pain, you did not intervene. I had a sense of the very acute pain, the closeness and the availability of the pain especially with Tina, the mother. I felt at times she was close to sobbing.

**Therapist:** Yes, a couple of times.

**Interviewer:** At one point especially, I was curious about your choice "not to ask". She mentioned a report from a psychologist on her son. However, she did not go into further details. She said twice: "It was awful. It was simply awful". My question is: Was she, or was she not eager to talk about it? Why did she bring that into the conversation? I was curious about your choice not to address it. What informed that choice?

**Therapist:** Well, as you are saying, at this point it certainly would not have gone against any kind of theoretical belief nor do I think that it would not have possibly been helpful. At the time, what I experienced more was an indignant anger, more than sadness on her part. I thought that she was very clear about that. I had a sense that he was clear about what she was clear about. I think it was shortly thereafter that I went back to what he had already said in the previous session and about not being really interested in discussing the past, but being more attuned to what is going on now. So it was not one of the instances where I asked myself: "Would that be helpful or not?" I did not. I just didn't.

*Comment and analysis: It is interesting that we seem to have different interpretations of the client's feeling. The therapist reads the emotion of the mother as being one of indignant anger. I, the interviewer read it as sadness. I am not sure how to explain this difference of interpretations, I have noticed several times that with the presence a one-way mirror; there might be dramatically different interpretations of reality. It shows us something important about therapy: we should never assume that we know how to read emotions/mind. We should maintain the position of a researcher in the presence of a client, rather than assuming one knows. The therapist also recognizes that if he were to have asked more questions about this period of time, that might have brought interesting information into the session, but he chose not to.*

**Interviewer:** So, let's see.

**Therapist:** As I am saying here, though, I think it could have been useful or helpful to have asked the mother if this was something she would like to talk some more about. Since she still has very strong feelings when she thinks about it at this point, I might have asked: "What was it they said about your son that was so upsetting to you?

**Interviewer:** Are you saying that if you were able to just rewind the tape and do the session all over again this might be a question you might have considered asking? As an option? A path?

*Comment and analysis: My comment is a useless repetition.*

**Therapist:** Absolutely, there was so much energy there. There was so much energy.

**Interviewer:** That is what I felt.

**Therapist:** And they said it twice.

*Comment and analysis: The therapist reflects back on what he could have asked and said at certain points of the session.*

**Interviewer:** This is also something I love about this ability that we have to think about our work. There are many times, I reflect upon my work and wish I could have said this, or done that. I guess your saying that gives me the license to say: "That it is all right" to look at my work and wish that I had done things differently.

**Therapist:** Yes. You are saying that in other ways. I like saying that during the session I receive invitations from the clients to go somewhere, but I don't always take up the invitation. I am not sure, where I go instead. I acknowledge it.

*Comment and analysis: The therapist reflects on how he could have gone in a whole different direction, just with asking one question, "following one invitation" from the client, as he says.*

**Interviewer:** You mentioned something that was also important to you: the context of the session. Maybe in an individual session you might have taken this offer more promptly, but given the fact that they were trainees on the other side of the mirror…

**Therapist:** And more than that… I think the fact that the mother is also one of the trainees and one of the students makes it an even more public place.

*Comment and analysis: That is an interesting explanation where the therapist talks about privacy. It is, after all, the therapist who is responsible for this setting. He created this original setting and then uses it as a justification not to intervene.*

**Interviewer:** During the session I was wondering about the father. How is this new relationship that John describes linked to Christianity? What if John was not Christian but a Muslim or a Buddhist? Would John have this same ideal relationship with the father who is a pastor? I don't know exactly why I was asking myself these questions; they were really loud in my head as I was listening to the session: What about you? Did anything similar cross your mind or not?

**Therapist:** It is interesting. It is something that I haven't given any thought to. No. It didn't come to mind. What stood out for me more was that people who come in may want to talk about their relation to religion or spirituality and how it affects their lives. Therapists find that religion is not the arena for therapy. It should take place outside of therapy. A lot of times, therapists and maybe I will change the subject or try to get to the "real issues" instead of staying at the level of talking about religion, spirituality and their relationship to prayers or whatever people are talking about. I thought that John was at a place where his relationship with his father had something to do with a shared religion: Christianity. Yet that he was also saying something much more than that. In terms of what he missed and how he was able to look at his father in a different way and to take his father in and to reciprocate. In response to what you are saying, I might have asked: "If your own father was Buddhist, instead of Christian, what difference do you think that might make?"

*Comment and analysis: The therapist acknowledges that we are restricted by our very ideas of what is therapy and what should be talked about in therapy. This restriction is probably higher if we are not aware of these restrictions.*

**Interviewer:** I had a question not only about what was said in the room, but rather about what was not said. Is there anything really important that you chose not to share with the clients?

**Therapist:** This may not be relevant. One of the things that struck me was when he was looking at this picture from New Mexico on the wall. A couple of times, I was going to make a comment about that, but then things moved on and I did not. The last time he was looking with such intensity, his mom was speaking at this moment, so I did not say. I think that this is the first thing that comes to mind.

**Interviewer:** Anything around the last few minutes where he took the bible and read it to you. Anything that you thought, but did not say?

**Therapist**: Oh! Yes! Yes! The preaching place that he is in.

**Interviewer:** *(Wide smile).*

**Therapist:** *(Laughter)* The preaching place that I was in one time in my life: the study of the Apologetics, who are the defenders of the faith. Those are some things that I chose not to make comments on.

**Interviewer:** What kind of reaction did you have?

**Therapist:** The apologetic part was kind of a warm inner smile, kind of "I've been there, Kid, I know that place!" A found remembrance and back there for a moment.

**Interviewer:** What about the bible reading?

**Therapist:** Was there some annoyance? No, there was a sense of the theatricality of it. I found a little more on the amusing side.

**Interviewer:** There was something you said about that, I remember you did not stay silent.

**Therapist:** *(Laughter)* I said: "So, now we are going to hear the word from the world, the last word from the real world, the world of God" or something like that? I think my last statement was "Have you already put that to music?"

**Interviewer:** I felt your strong Family Therapy background in this session: When you explored all these relationships, how everybody in the family influences the other. You wondered about the presence or the absence of this or that relationship. I was aware of how this interested me. How you put that into context and in the presence of this very relationship making it more expansive, more situated in time. I don't know how purposeful it was, but you started asking questions about the past then the present and finally the future. It felt like the networks you created with your questions were finally broader than the room.

**Therapist:** Yes, I agree with you. In that regard, I believe that we are multi-voiced. Those multi-voices relate to our being in relation with others. That is who we are. Sometimes, even in developmental theories of adolescence and sometimes even in adulthood, people talk about people being more "I-centered" or less aware of how much they are in relations with others. I often think how much of that is about relationships and "being in relations with others". Although, this young man talked about using dope before his conversion with God, he discussed how much he was then: "I-focused". Now that he is expansive, I thought this might be helpful to talk about his real world of relationships, the one he is a part of. Sometimes my invitation to do that was accepted, sometimes it was not. At the beginning, I asked questions about who is it who was most upset about the past? He said: "mom", then I asked him: "Who else?" He did not show much interest in thinking more about these relationships so I did not pursue. *(Silence).* Another thought I have about therapy is more recent. I think about it now and I wasn't thinking about it then. I try to have a sense of what the client's "theory of change" is and what his "understanding of change" is. In relation to that: "Did they have a sense that our conversation was related to that *(his theory of change)*. "Did we have a conversation that was related to change or were they just coming in to... *(The therapist pauses)*?"

*Comment and analysis: The therapist presents a theoretical belief, rather than a RIA at this point. The therapist talks about his interest in exploring how the client's theory of change may be related to the kind of conversation that is created in therapy.*

**Interviewer:** To check-in?

**Therapist:** Yes, to check in.

**Therapist:** I think that with him and with his mother, their theories of change very much relate to their understandings of spirituality. That is something that it is beyond them and beyond us. They have no control over it. At least for him it was very clear that he has no control, except to cooperate with or not to cooperate with this sense of Grace. That's all.

There aren't a lot of theories of change that are in the textbooks of individual psychotherapy or Family Therapy. Well actually I take that back. *(Inaudible)* So, I want to respect the client's theory of change, unless there is some need expressed. By need I mean that they are telling me something that is going on in their life about their theory of change, that is not working for them. If they were telling me that, or saying that, then I may challenge their theory of change. I would talk with them about other possible theories of change. But neither of them was saying anything about their theory of change not working for them. Does that make sense?

**Interviewer:** It does make a lot of sense. I think even further as you said at the beginning there were no requests, no real work for a therapist expressed by client such as "I want to do that!" or "This is not working" or " I am in so much pain". Family Therapists have been involved with following what the client wants and doesn't want.

**Therapist:** Yes, certainly.

**Interviewer:** So, in some sense it is like: "Am I out of the job or what?" I think, as you said, maybe the only thing to do is just taking the position of a witness and exploring and expanding the conversation, waiting for an opportunity to jump in. I was very interested in what you did with what was there. I think that the way John presented himself in this interview was in some aspects very typical of a teenager. A teenager rarely presents with any request, and rarely wants to be in therapy to start with *(laughter).* Rarely a teenager has a clear sense of what he wants. So in that sense, he was very typical: the "I don't knows", "Whatever you want", and the constant shrugs of the shoulders...

**Therapist:** I am not dismissing that I could have started the session differently. I believe that what is said first by the therapist and the clients, initially in the meeting, may be the most important. These initial words have some strong influence in directing how the session goes. So I could have started by saying: "John, I am interested in what has been different since the last time we met four weeks ago? Or: "I was thinking about the session myself and I was wondering if we had a good meeting today and if this would be helpful for you, what might be different in our meeting today, what would you go away with?" Those kinds of statements I think can be very helpful to start with. I don't remember exactly how I started this session but I remember that they wanted to talk about or... I don't know exactly...

*Comment and analysis: The therapist questions how he started the session. He offers questions that he thinks could have brought more information, more engagement on the part of the teenager and the mother. He takes responsibility for his part and thinks that maybe he should have been more directive at the onset of the session with questions that might have directed the interview in a completely different direction.*

**Interviewer:** Well, I can tell you what I remember and I was very aware of the beginning. You mentioned the last discussion. You chose to make a liaison between the two discussions. You first asked: "Who is here today and who is missing?" You acknowledged that the father was absent and inquire about him. Then you said (and this really struck me): "I have some thoughts but, I am really curious about what you think about today?" At that moment I thought: "Why don't you say it (*therapist's name*)?" Then if I remember more or less John said: "Whatever you want. I do not have any specific agenda". You said: "I am very curious about your new direction. What is it that connects you with Christianity and Jesus-Christ? How has He been a part of your life, in the past?" I had the sense that you were inviting him to talk about Christianity before he had faith. You were inviting him to talk about his past. That surprised me I might have expected more questions like the one you just mentioned such as: "If we had a good meeting today and if this would be helpful for you, what might be different and what would you go away with?

**Therapist:** Yes. I was interested in his relationship to what he called "Christianity". Early on in his life, this "Christianity" influenced negatively. He was talking about how he really hated Christians and how, You know... double standards and other kinds of stuff...

**Interviewer:** This is a broader question linked to your work in general. Do you have a sense of yourself as leading the conversations with clients? What would you say? How do you find yourself shaping the conversations?

**Therapist:** I have problems with dichotomies. Someone is either theory-focused or client-focused. Either somebody is directive or non-directive. I think it has more to do with relationships. Again, it is more of a relationship focus and I am not talking about it.

*Comment and analysis: The therapist states that he does not define his style before the client, but rather in relationship to him. He is not directive or non-directive, following a model a-priori.*

**Interviewer:** Your answer helps me clarify what I wanted to ask next which is at the heart of reflection-in-action: Are you aware of what happens with you as you are doing therapy? What are you aware of that what happens in your mind, in your gut feeling as you are doing therapy? What is it that you know about the choices you make? How are you informing your next move? Maybe this is somewhat related to the words leading or non-leading but with some sense of moving along, informing your next step with the previous one with what happened in the room and within yourself? What is your level of awareness? How much of that can you share in words?

**Therapist:** Well, I can give you an example related to something I said earlier. I mentioned that, on some occasions, John was looking at this picture on the wall and one of the times that he looked at the picture, I thought about when he mentioned the move from Canada to the High Desert of Los Angeles. He was looking at a New Mexico desert on the wall. These are fleeting thoughts that came to mind, as mom was talking. I just put them aside. It is somehow a reference to what was in the conversation. It could have been included in there. I also have a belief and it is a theory-related belief. No! It is also from experience: If something is important to someone and if somehow I miss it. I am going to meet with them again, which does not always happen, but if I meet with them again. If a thing that I missed is still very important for them, it will come up again. So, hopefully the next time, I'll be able to do more than just acknowledge it. I will be able to stay with it.

*Comment and analysis: The therapist gives a specific example of an implicit knowledge that he chooses not to share. The therapist believes that if he misses something important the client will bring it back later.*

**Interviewer:** Now, if you were to qualify and describe your reflection-in-action in the therapy room, what would you say?

**Therapist:** Well, for me when it is the strongest is when it is also on "body-felt sensed" level. Sometimes, it is an emotion or sometimes it is a feeling that is different from the words. When that happens I usually pay attention to that. To reflect back on the session we had. I think two times I had an inner reaction. When mom was close to tears, very close to tears at one point when she was talking about this previous therapist. I felt a kind of serious grip here in my guts. I stayed with that for a moment. The other time was when he was talking about the defender of the faith thing there was in me kind of a warm *(laughter)*... a warm feeling... kind of a familiar feeling that brought a smile on my face... and I didn't share that with him. Maybe if we had an ongoing relationship and some kind of a contract for therapy, I might have shared that with him. I think it might have been an invitation to connect.

*Comment and analysis: The therapist talks about his RIA. His reflection-in-action appears more intense when linked to an emotional response. He talks about how he detects, in a session, moments of movement. The cues that lead to these moments of movement are his emotional reactions. He talks about the need to establish a therapeutic relationship before he is able to share this strong "body-felt sense".*

**Interviewer:** It is interesting. I believe sharing some of this physical and emotional information that you gather may really broaden the understanding of the relationship you create with somebody. The breathing, the signs of a therapist feeling touched or how can these be shared?

**Therapist:** And I have never thought of this before, but the reason I don't call that an internal monologue is that I believe that what happens internally is a dialogue. I call it dialogue because it has some relationship with whomever I am with. It is not some kind of psychotic space. *(Laughter)*

*Comment and analysis: The therapist believes that when he feels an emotion in the session with a client (joy, hope, fear, sadness, frustration, anger, irritation, boredom) that is usually related to something that exists in relationship with this client.*

**Therapist:** I have couple of other thoughts. My first thought is that I think that your research is important. Most people would frame it in terms of the process of therapy. I like to think in terms of process. I had some thought about the ending right at the beginning so to speak. When we all walked out of the room, I was wondering how this session might have an impact on their lives. Another related piece of research would be to have the client present and have some comments about what the therapist says. Although it is different, it has some similarities to that. In my early training with Carl *(Rogers)*, we were trained to listen to audiotapes. We were trying to do ratings on empathy and we had to say how empathic the therapists were, how genuine they were and how much positive regards. And it really did not matter in terms of outcome process. Therefore, the research you do is important.

**Interviewer:** I believe it is a slippery subject to include the patients in research. There are many complex ethical concerns. In whose interest of are we doing that? Are we helping, or disserving the clients? Where is the line between research and psychotherapy? I am not sure that the client is interested in that part of the therapy. I am not sure that showing what is behind therapy is helpful to the client. What I would have been interested in however is to present the reflection-in-action of therapist back to the client and notice his reaction. In other words, does the therapist's RIA match somewhat the client's response ? I thought long about these issues and I decided not to include that in my research.

*(We conclude this interview.)*

# Conclusion

The main theme of the therapist's RIA during these two interviews is the ongoing struggle to establish a therapeutic relationship. The reader should note the profoundly different context of this interview as opposed to the ones that follows, where the therapist has never met the client before. Contrary to the next two interviews with expert therapists as well who have chosen long-term clients (several years of psychotherapy). The focus of their work is necessarily different. The other observation I make is the tremendous importance of setting the boundaries and the frame for therapeutic conversation to occur. This is not new information. I find evidence of this theory with Freud (1921, 1922, 1930). It remains interesting to notice the application of this theory in practice.

The clear positioning of the therapist in his context appears to be conditional to the emergence of therapeutic conversation and the establishment of a therapeutic alliance. The corollary is that poor positioning and a poor clarification of the context may allow only a low therapeutic relationship. From the beginning of the interview on his reflection-in-action, the expert therapist reflects on the quality of the relationship that he initiates. The therapist defines his position as "a witness". The therapist acknowledges that there is little therapeutic relationship with this visitor (not quite a client, nor a patient). There is little ground to establish a working alliance. The therapist confirms that he is struggling with establishing a more personal connection with the teenager. The therapist also attempts to generate a sense of self-agency from the client. He elicits from the client a more personal stance.

The therapist is interested in his clients' theory of change. The therapist did not think about change until he was invited to discuss his RIA with the interviewer. This illustrates the importance of maintaining a reflexive practice. When two clinicians review an audiotape or videotape of their work, and engage in a reflexive practice there is much material for RIA and learning.

For the second interview, the therapist chooses the same client. Aware that the first session had not produced the effect he hoped, he invites the same client in and works on the area he previously struggled with. This is an example of using reflexivity about one's practice. The clinician's choice exemplifies the commitment toward his clients. In the second interview, the therapist changes his positioning. Instead of following a path that he is not interested in, a monologue that does not seem to include the therapist, he takes more of a directive stance: "Let me tell you what I am interested in". This comment initiates a stronger connection between John and the therapist. This is another illustration of how the positioning of the therapist may influence and transform the therapeutic alliance. The therapist does not define his style before the clients, but rather in relationship to them.

The therapist's reflection-in-action appears more intense when linked to an emotional response. He talks about how he detects, in a session, moments of movement. The cues that lead to these moments of movement are his emotional reactions. He talks about establishing a therapeutic relationship before he is able to share this strong "body felt sense".

The three expert therapists share a similar reaction at the end of the interviews. They remember shared found memories of early training, a sense of nostalgia, and regrets to have little space in their work for establishing truly reflexive practices.

# Thirteenth interview

## Context

This hour–long interview takes place in the expert therapist's office. The expert therapist chooses a long-term based on the following criteria: the insight of the client and the ongoing interest of the sessions he has with this client. The interview takes place just an hour after the session. Before the interview, I listen to the tape and familiarize myself with the content of the session.

**Interviewer:** I thought a lot about the questions I wanted to ask you. I don't want to come up with "ready-to-go" type of questions. I don't think it will fit what we are trying to explore here. I have some questions that I was curious about before the interview started such as: "How did you choose this client as opposed to another client?" Mostly, I would like to explore with you how a well-trained therapist thinks in action. So, anything that you can say about that would help me. If you could explain your thought process, your awareness and how you make sense of what happens in the session that will be interesting to me.

**Therapist:** Sure, OK.

**Interviewer:** As I listened to the audiotape, I had several questions that I wrote down. I will start with these preliminary questions: If you could rewind the tape and listen to it, if you think about the session that you just did, what would you like others to know about what you did and what you were thinking during this therapy session? Or... What would you qualify as being the highlights of the session? Or, even maybe...if you were to do this session all over again, is there anything that you would have done differently?

*Comment and analysis: The number of questions is an indication of my anxiety and the pressure to do a "good-enough" interview. However, this does not seem to bother the therapist, who directly focuses on what he considers as being the highlight of the session.*

**Therapist:** Hum.... For me the highlight happened just after she was writing the check, when I turned off the tape. What happened at that time is that we went back to the issue of boundaries and the fact that boundaries are a mutual responsibility. It is not just the responsibility of the person who once set those boundaries. It came up very naturally through her father, with whom she had to set boundaries, because he wouldn't set any. It came out at the beginning of the session, which, if you remember, had to do with boundaries and who is responsible for the boundaries. She was trying to claim responsibility for the boundaries.

**Interviewer:** I see.

*Comment and analysis: The clinician focuses on what he considers to be the most interesting part of the session, after the tape was turned off. The clinician has a theory on boundaries: they are mutually constructed. The clinician may think that he has something to do with it as well.*

**Therapist:** When in fact it is a mutual process. Once, a boundary is set by either person, it is the duty of both people to guard it, not just one person.

**Interviewer:** So, can you say a little more about what you thought after the tape went off?

**Therapist:** It came full circle. We ended up where we started.

**Interviewer:** Hum... OK… With you, in the relationship? So, it was not about somebody else? What are you trying to say?

**Therapist:** No. It was actually about her father. It started out being about me and ended up being about her father. And now that I am thinking about that, in retrospect, one another thing that is nice about it, that I did not think about at the time is that, it is the same process in different relationships.

*Comment and analysis: I am still unclear about the way the therapist makes sense of what happened after the tape went of. What was such a pivotal part of the session? I am still confused, but decide to move on to another question.*

**Interviewer:** Probably, it is obvious for you, but for somebody who listens to this tape for the first time: "How would you describe what you did in this session on the over whole?"

**Therapist:** The way I would describe what I was doing is: I was using every possible opportunity to make the things that happened just below awareness and the procedural memory, to bring them up to awareness. Both, in terms of what is happening at the moment and referring back and forth with other sessions, and within the session as well. I am using every possible opportunity to do that.

*Comment and analysis: The therapist explains his general theory of practice. He applies this process in most situations: using every possible opportunity to bring to awareness what has not yet been.*

**Interviewer:** And what is your intent?

**Therapist:** The intent is always to encourage awareness, so that people can have options. They can begin to look at things. They do not have to do things automatically, the same way again and again.

*Comment and analysis: The reader can see clearly the theoretical Gestalt background of this therapist. This is not a RIA but more a theoretical response.*

**Interviewer:** Yes.

**Therapist:** I am thinking back to an earlier question, that you asked me. I did not respond to it. It was: Would I do anything different in the session? I might do a little differently focusing on the anger, because it was clear to me that it was not really a foreground for her but one, which I created. It was a foreground, that I created, which I was aware at the time was not figural for her.

*Comment and analysis: The clinician is able to look back and review what he might have done differently. It is interesting that the clinician picks this question out of the all the questions I asked. This question involves clearly a reflexive ability.*

**Interviewer:** Hum.

**Therapist:** I knew it was ground, which is why I began to refer to it as ground. I would not have spent as much time on it. But, I would still have spent some time on it, even if there is not much excitement and liveliness in it.

*Comment and analysis: The clinician understands what is important for the client through her non-verbal attitude: excitement and liveliness. The therapist follows the lead of the client. He believes that the client knows where he needs to go.*

**Interviewer:** What do you mean? If you use words that everybody can refer to, even if they do not come from a background of Gestalt Therapy? What are you saying exactly?

**Therapist:** No, not that she might know, because it is pretty clear to me that she knows, at least, she is aware of how angry she is at that moment... The postulate that there is anything else for the therapist to begin to invent and imagine things that he can't read in imagination. But it was really ground for her. You could listen to the energy level. It is not there. I know that. I knew we had to go to something else, which is why I began to refer to it as ground. I would still stay with it a bit, because it is new for her. It's a new idea to consider and I want it to be simmering in the background over time. I am aware that it is something that for her is probably a pre-verbal experience, when she said, she had no language for it. She hasn't experienced talking about it. My guess is that it is something she experienced, before she could talk. Now, that is clearly a speculation. That would be something I have to verify later.

*Comment and analysis: The therapist continues to explain why, in his clinical judgment; the focus on the anger of the client is a mistake, because something more important is there. Then, the therapist refers probably to implicit knowledge. Despite the fact that this knowledge is implicit, it is a categorical knowledge. He refers to it as "It is not there. I know that". The clinician provides explanations to justify his clinical intuition, which he refers to as "the energy level". This is typically a concept that is assessed in the heart of the therapeutic relationship.*

*The second interesting idea is that there is a new "idea" for the client. In Bateson's term a "news of difference", or "a difference that makes a difference" (1972) occurs. The therapist knows that the client cannot integrate newness promptly. There is the notion of letting the idea "simmer" before it could be integrated by the client.*

*Last, there is a hypothesis that his client may refer to a pre-verbal experience. The client says and shows that she has no word for it. The clinician knows this only a speculation. He needs to verify it with the client. I did not ask how he would verify this hypothesis. This is an interesting hypothesis that seems to be also a focus of interest in the field of Neuropsychology, especially the latest research on memory and the procedural memory, where a whole field of experience has been experienced pre-language.*

*Another interesting notion is the idea that the therapist thinks in terms of "planting seeds". In other words, some material may not be relevant for this client right away but might be in the future.*

**Interviewer:** When you say: "I listen to the energy level". Again, you are assuming, that I know what you are talking about, but could you explain what you are referring to?

**Therapist:** Yes, if you listen to her voice, it usually has a lot of inflexions and modulations. It got flat. It got quiet. It's a thoughtful quiet. It is just quieter. It is flatter.

**Interviewer:** Which is an indication of what for you?

**Therapist:** It indicates to me that while what we are talking about may be valuable in the big picture, there is no emotional value for her at the moment. Knowing what I know about learning theories and how people learn, I know she will not learn anything from this conversation. It won't stick.

**Interviewer:** Are you saying it needs to be linked to some kind of excitement or some kind of arousal?

**Therapist:** It needs to be linked to an alert level of emotional arousal. If emotional arousal is too high in therapy, the client does not learn anything in therapy. If it is too low then they do not learn anything. This was too low.

*Comment and analysis: The therapist explains why the assessment of the "level of energy" is crucial. He includes in his RIA the learning theories. In order for a learning experience to take place, there need to be a sufficient level of emotional arousal. Beyond and above this level nothing happens.*

**Interviewer:** Could you perceive that by the sound of her voice?

**Therapist:** The sound of her voice, the look in her eyes, the fact that there is *(inaudible)*, and this is hard for me to check my memory on that, because obviously it is going to get contaminated with imagination. There seems to me that there was less eye contact. Just at the energy level, a sense for me of her not quite being present. It was like if she were speaking about somebody else.

**Interviewer:** What you are saying is interesting. It is rarely talked about these signs that you are referring to, these signs are para-language. I realize also the difficulty of finding words to talk about it. You are discussing it now. Are these para-verbal cues are informing your work a lot?

*Comment and analysis: The therapist discusses the importance of the para-verbal components in the therapy room. He highlights the importance of recognizing and integrating these elements into one's practice. We refer constantly to para-verbal elements to work on the therapeutic relationship and to inform our work.*

**Therapist:** Absolutely.

**Interviewer:** It's very difficult and interesting. We do not put these signs onto language. We do not know much about how they influence therapists. But, I think it is a big part of therapy.

**Therapist:** Absolutely. I put it in the language internally and I monitor it constantly throughout the session.

*Comment and analysis: The clinician describes that RIA is part of his daily practice. The clinician takes into account everything that is relevant for the therapy: a tone of a voice, a change of rhythm, an intonation of voice or a gesture.*

**Interviewer:** How do you do that? Can you say something about that?

**Therapist**: I just notice what their level of aliveness is, what their level of engagement is, and what the quality of the contact is. What their emotional investment in the topic is. The signs that I use are eye contact, voice inflexions, spontaneity levels, and things like that.

*Comment and analysis: The clinician further defines these para-verbal cues. These para-verbal cues reflect the quality of a therapeutic alliance. The clinician further refers to "spontaneity levels". I do not understand what he means by that. I should have asked.*

**Interviewer:** What happens if you are not interested in something that the client says? What are you doing? Does it ever happen to you? She was first talking about the stolen car; I was not very interested in that. That is what made me think about this question related to boredom.

**Therapist:** Sure, I get carried away with things that are not interesting to them. Yes. It happens!

**Interviewer:** Yes, and the other way around? If your client is interested in something that bores you?

**Therapist:** I have never had this experience, not that I can recall. If they are interested and really engaged in something, it draws my engagement. I use that knowledge, because when I am not interested usually they are not interested.

*Comment and analysis: This comment relates to the notion of intention. The therapist is able to maintain constant and unconditional curiosity toward the client, regardless of what happens. If the clinician is not interested, he takes that as an indication that maybe this is not where the client needs to be. The clinician shows us how he uses himself. He uses his own reaction to the client as cues to define and shape the therapeutic alliance.*

**Interviewer:** Hum...

**Therapist:** It is easy to interest me. I know that about me. I think that varies from person to person, but I am a sucker for interest *(Laughter.)*

**Interviewer:** It is a very interesting topic: boredom. My experience has been oftentimes that if I am not interested in what my clients say, they probably have lost contact with what they are saying as well they are probably not talking to me.

**Therapist:** Yes, I think that is right. They are giving you the news report, but they are not giving you the news. They are giving you the report. *(Silence).*

**Interviewer:** I was also wondering about something else: why did you choose this particular client? What do you have to say about her, about your relationship with her?

**Therapist:** I chose her because. *(Pause)* She is a good client. She is able to come in and open up immediately, as opposed to the client whom we might do next, which is somebody... Sometimes the whole hour goes by before something important occurs. With her, it is pretty constant. I made some choice there. There are other choices I could make with a moderately severe obsessive-compulsive case. This tends to be very boring work, you know because there is this reacting, the commenting, it is not very alive work, when you are working with these people.

*Comment and analysis: The clinician says that his work might not be always as interesting, but people always are. I am not sure to understand this comment.*

**Interviewer:** So you have a sense of interest when you work with her, a high interest. Is it what you are saying?

**Therapist:** I have a sense of interest in all of my clients, with two exceptions that I can think of, in my career. She is a good illustration of how I work.

*Comment and analysis: Of course, I am curious about the exceptions. Why did I not ask?*

**Interviewer:** Where you satisfied with this session?

**Therapist:** Yes. I thought it was a fairly good session. You know, once in a while, I do a really good session, which I think, is perfect. I think it should have been recorded forever *(Laughter).* I hate it, when I miss those. I would say this is a middling session. This is an OK session.

**Interviewer:** What would you like to say about the context of this session?

**Therapist:** She is the child of two inordinately selfish, self-absorbed people, whose only interest in her is what she can do for them. They are like not normal parents in that sense. Usually a parent has some sense of giving and wanting for their child, and making even a mild sacrifice. This did not happen in her family, not with her parents. You exist for us. That is it. That is fine.

**Interviewer:** Is her story connected with what you do in the session?

**Therapist:** Sure, the whole issue of boundaries, for example, the boundaries are not about her being responsible for looking after herself. It is also a parent's responsibility to look out for her and the partner's responsibility to look out for her. This is a concept that she is just beginning to grasp: you have a responsibility to me. That has come up in others ways. One of the delightful things about her is that if you work on something, she gets it, immediately.

*Context and analysis: The clinician gives an interesting context for the session: the type of relationship that this client had with her parents. In other words, the clinician thinks that what matters about this client is the type of relationship that she has had with her parents. The clinician highlights how these early relationships shape and change the way she is able to comprehend the concept of boundaries.*

**Interviewer:** Yes. She seems bright.

**Therapist:** Yes. She comes back the next session and something has changed.

**Interviewer:** She uses what you are saying. Actually, she referred to it in the session. I do not remember exactly how she puts it, but she said something in the relationship to her brother, daring to speak differently with her brother. She said that it had a very positive effect. I imagine how gratifying this can be. You witness something that comes back every session. She shows you that she uses what is talked about in therapy.

**Therapist:** I wouldn't call it gratifying. There is something esthetically pleasurable about it. I don't any longer take or am gratified by things that are somebody else's possessions. You know what I mean. That is really her work. There is something admirable about it, but not gratifying.

**Interviewer:** I am happy that you stopped me on this word. I am happy that you make this difference.

**Therapist:** What is clearer and clearer to me, through time, is that I am just a "consultant on process". I am pretty good at picking up on somebody else's phenomenology. That creates an atmosphere or a situation that they can work on. The learning and the changing are theirs, not mine.

*Comment and analysis: The therapist defines how he views his role as a therapist as "a consultant on the process". He has a theory of change where he encourages the client's awareness of what she is doing, as he understands it. The clinician is an expert in noticing how her client functions. The change is in the client's hands.*

**Interviewer:** Yes, actually I think you said that twice in the session, maybe in different ways.

**Therapist:** I was aware of that. I always try to make sure that that the credit is where it belongs. I don't mind taking credit, when I think it's mine, but I don't want to take credit for that which is theirs, because it creates or I imagine it creates, a situation in which I take on magical properties. You know, which I think is bad for them.

**Interviewer:** I share this opinion. You are right. We have to be careful about not taking credit that does not belong to us. *(Silence)*

**Interviewer:** When you gave her direct compliments, I was interested. Why did you do that? You might have tried instead to elicit that from her? *(The client talks about her car that has just been stolen, two days ago, as she was out to dinner. She notices that her reaction was quite different from the one she could have had few years ago: she took the upsetting event with "much philosophy". Looking back at her own reaction, she seems surprised and happy. Yet, she questions her reaction by asking: "Do you think it might be denial?" The therapist answers: "It sounds more like maturity to me!")*

**Therapist:** Actually, I first did that at the beginning. I asked her about denial and then it dawned on me that she had no way of discriminating. I was the one that was going to have to set the scale. So, that she would have a concept to think about. It would never occur to her, to think of anything she does as maturity. It wouldn't be a concept.

*Context and analysis: This comment goes back to a previous comment about the concept of boundaries. He refers to the client having no way of discriminating. The client has the intuition that her behavior is more mature, and controlled. She then immediately doubts it: "Do you think it might be denial?" She negates her progress. She cannot rely on her own judgment. The clinician refers to the need to "set the scale". At this point, the therapist provides the support that she is missing. This support further has been missing all of her life and she has not had a chance to internalize it. In other words, the therapist provides the frame of reference that the parents should have provided for her.*

**Interviewer:** She did not hear you at first. You had to repeat yourself twice.

**Therapist:** Yes, right. That was a concept that I was aware of introducing at the time and I sometimes use what people might call an "introject" like that. I put it out there for people to consider as a new way of thinking. I will not forget that I did that. I would watch to see what happens over the next few weeks or months with that concept, with her.

**Interviewer:** Yes. This is interesting.

**Therapist:** I would make sure that that did not get introjected. But, I am not afraid to put it out in the Vygotsky sense of the word: connecting something in the outside world, so that there is a possibility of connecting with the internal world.

**Interviewer:** It makes sense. It is not one or the other.

**Therapist:** Yes. That is why I tried the other one first. I realized that it was not working that given who she was, it wouldn't work. That is why I took the other direction.

**Interviewer:** When I think about the work of a clinician, I often have the same question, could you say something about what was very loud in your head and that you chose not to say at that time? Anything that you chose not to say during this session? We often talk about what we think and what we say in therapy. My question has more to do with the things that we might think and that we choose not to say.

**Therapist:** There is very little with this patient that I would not say. I may hold it back, because I think it is useless or misleading, or because I think it will interrupt the process. I think that will probably be the only reason where I would not say something. One of the things I was aware of doing that does not particularly have to do with psychotherapy but does fit my presence and my personality is using humor.

**Interviewer:** *(nodding)* Hum.

**Therapist:** We laugh at things that were in fact fairly serious and painful. But it didn't interfere, I thought, with her taking them in and assimilating them. One of the things I am aware of doing is; I want to give people a sense that it is OK to be human here. I think when therapists take things too seriously, they lose the sense that we are sometimes funny and ridiculous and that it is OK to be funny and ridiculous. That is part of being human. So, I use humor a lot in that way to minimize, not to minimize but normalize things and not allow them to get out of perspective but to keep them in perspective.

Therapists get too serious about their business. They take it too seriously.

*Comment and analysis: The clinician identifies another pattern in his practice: he frequently uses humor. He believes that humor conveys two helpful and important messages to clients. The first being that it is OK to be human and to make mistakes and the second is that humor allows people to put things into perspective and to look at them from a different angle.*

**Interviewer:** I agree with you, I have the greatest respect for therapists who can laugh in a session. It is so important. It heals lot of things especially if this is the right laughter. In larger context like with families or with couples, it can play an important role.

**Therapist:** Yes, that they can share a sense of humor, Yes I agree. Absolutely. It is much harder to do, though.

*Comment and analysis: Looking at my interaction with the clinician, I regret that my comments to him are not more interrogative, thought provoking; instead I often just agree and collude with the received answer, instead of maintaining a stance of curiosity.*

**Interviewer:** Would you say laughing may be a form of intimacy?

**Therapist:** Yes. You are right.

**Interviewer:** I am wondering when we were in the cafeteria an hour or so ago. You were overhearing the audiotape of your session, as I was listening to it and you came in the room. I was curious at the time about how it was for you to listen to yourself?

**Therapist:** I remember that I haven't listened to my work as often as I may have wanted to. I thought a great deal about my work but I haven't really seen videotapes of my work for a very long time or listened to it. For about four years, everything that I did was in front of a video camera, or if the video camera was not available in front of the audiotape. So, it felt very familiar. I have incidentally kept most of those tapes, although I have never listened to them again, after supervision. I liked what I heard.

*Comment and analysis: This question is linked to the ability to think reflexively about his practice. There is a touch of nostalgia about his early years of training, where he was using his reflexive ability by watching his work on videos or audiotape. This is a marked indication that the clinician likes reflecting on his practice and learns also from his own work. Jennings and Skovholt (1999) define master therapists as voracious learners. They have what the authors call "emotional receptivity" defined as self-awareness, reflexivity, non-defensiveness and openness to feedbacks.*

**Interviewer:** That is important.

**Therapist:** Yes.

**Interviewer:** If you were to do this exercise of comparing your own work, the work you do now as opposed to the one you did several years ago what would you have to say?

**Therapist:** What the difference would be?

**Interviewer:** Yes.

**Therapist:** I think I am much more natural. I am more able to do the therapy woven into conversations, rather than being too obvious about doing therapy. People would seldom identify a technique in what I am doing. It is just conversation between two human beings working on something. It is the direction, that I am heading toward. I don't know that I am there yet, but that is the direction.

*Comment and analysis: The clinician seems happy with the way he views the evolution of his practice in terms of skills. He defines his work as becoming more subtle, more embedded in conversation and less technical. He describes an evolution from a technician to a stage of mastery. The way he now practices is sometimes imperceptible. It holds an aesthetic quality.*

**Interviewer:** Would you say that you are mastering the techniques, so that they become less obvious?

**Therapist:** Well, I have always thought of Gestalt Therapy as a technique-less therapy, but sometimes people are stilted, if there are not using techniques. They have a formality, or a sense of self-consciousness. I try to let this be just a conversation. *(Silence)*

**Interviewer:** I have requested that you tape the session. I was curious. How it did affect your work?

**Therapist:** I think, at the beginning of the session, it made me a little more articulate. There are things that I may signal without saying. I was aware of the tape and then I lost consciousness of it, and quit doing that. So, it affected me at the beginning.

**Interviewer:** It is interesting. It is oftentimes how clients report that they are affected by the audiotape. At the beginning, they are aware of it and then they lose track of it. When you think about this interview: Is there anything you would like different? Fewer questions? More questions? Different kind of questions? Do you feel that I am giving you a chance to say what you want to say about this process? Am I asking you the right questions? Shall we go to more specifics?

**Therapist:** I think in the general sense: Yes. What I miss is... *(Silence)*. If they were a little closer together, if we could do something within the session. For example ask me: Why did you say this? Why did you use these words? Why these words instead of those words?

*Comment and analysis: The clinician rightly directs me back to his reflection-in-action.*

**Interviewer:** We can certainly go to more specifics. I have several questions. I will refer to the context. If you don't remember or need more information we can listen to the tape.

**Therapist:** OK.

**Interviewer:** She said something like: "Don't get attached to anything". She was referring to her car that was just stolen. Then she seemed to be establishing almost a theory. It was a kind of philosophy that she got out of that when she said "My mom would do the same thing to me". I was wondering how you made sense of this? Why didn't' you say something there? Would you like me to play the tape back? *(He nods. I play the tape back).*

**Therapist:** Actually, that is a reference to her mother, but you could not have known that without the context. I was making that very concrete. So your mother would steal your car, steal everything from you. Her mother would do that. Her mother would take anything from her.

**Interviewer:** I didn't get that. Thank you. Are you talking about procedural memory?

**Therapist:** Yes. That is right.

**Interviewer:** Out of that, she made meaning: I cannot attach to any object, because my mother would immediately steal that from me? Is it what you are saying?

**Therapist:** Yes. And so, I turned it into the present where she *(the client's mother)* would steal your car, steal your this, your that, steal everything. That is interesting. I have to think about that one, because there is a thought process behind this. The thought process is: I want you to see the similarity in this. It doesn't matter what the thing is: the process is the same. Things are being taken away from you. That is at one level. On the other level, it is the maturity of saying: It's done, now. It's over. There is nothing I can do about it. Being upset won't bring it back. It's an inconvenience. This is a very mature perspective. As opposed to somebody who feels like they have lost a part of themselves, if they have lost their car, you know...There is a little bit of a boundary problem in there...You lost your car, but it doesn't mean part of you is gone! *(Common laughter)*

*Comment and analysis: The clinician's RIA focuses on the sequential process of the client. What did she say first? What did she do then? How did she do that? The clinician places the behavior in a larger context for the client to be aware of the larger pattern. He puts the stolen car in the larger context of her family. Historically, in relationship with her mother everything was systematically taken away from her. The therapist points out the other part: her reaction to the current loss of her car, and the maturity she is able to show and how she has grown.*

**Therapist:** Exactly. It is terribly inconvenient. It is very upsetting that somebody would do that to you. But, you are still here. You are still OK. People who don't have good boundaries and who don't have good sense of identity sometimes get lost in that. They think: "It happened to me! No. It happened to your car!" *(Silence).*

*Comment and analysis: The therapist describes the good boundary that the client places with her environment. She does not take personal offense for things that do not have anything to do with her.*

**Interviewer:** Ok. Let me go to the next one, if it's all right?

**Therapist:** Let me say one another thing.

**Interviewer:** Yes. Please. Go ahead.

**Therapist:** For some people, you would have to reinforce that idea that that happened to them, because there is an acknowledgment there that is important. So, you wouldn't treat that same statement the same, in a different character structure or in a different maturity level. For some people you would say: Yes, it feels like somebody has moved in. Somebody has done something inside of you. So, you have to take into account their maturity level and their capacity to understand.

*Comment and analysis: The clinician states that his interventions are context-related and custom-designed to the client's needs, character structure and maturity level. He notes that this intervention only fit, because of the specific client's history and her character structure.*

**Interviewer:** OK. Let's move on. I like the comment you make here. I would like you to comment on that. Can you tell me what your thoughts were at this very moment? *(I play back the tape where the patient says: there is nothing in me wanting to call him (referring to her father) really nothing. The therapist says: What is in you?)*

**Therapist:** Please, rewind a little further.

**Interviewer:** Yes. Just before that, she was referring to the conversation she had with her brother. You kept trying to congratulate her for the courage it took from her to talk with her brother like that. You said: "Wow! What a conversation! Good for you! I would take the credit, if I were you". Then she kept going into this pattern of saying: "It is not me". Then she said "There is nothing in me" and then you said that comment: "What is in you?" *(I rewind the tape backward a little further).*

**Therapist:** In repeating all that, I am reinforcing the concept. I am not just repeating that to let her know that I know. I want her to hear that. In other words, I am building in new procedural memory, at the same time that you take the other one out.

*Comment and analysis: The therapist says that previously the client's response to encouragement was critical, self-demeaning. The therapist attempts to show her that in her present relationship with others, she reacts differently. The therapist highlights these new patterns of relationship and positively reflects on them. The therapist states his intent to assist the client build and store new procedural memories (i.e. new ways of knowing how to interact and how to be in relationship with others).*

**Interviewer:** Your reflection-in-action is important. I guess some therapists, who are doing the "repeating the client's statement" come from different intent. So, you are doing more than reframing or repeating?

**Therapist:** Right.

*(I stop the tape after the therapist's comment: What is in you?)*

**Therapist:** Oh! Yes! She says there is nothing in me willing to call him. *(Silence).* If you focus on that, what you are working from is a deficit model. There is something that ought to be there, that is not there, which I think is a serious mistake. What I need to do, is call her attention, not to what is not there, as if that would be helpful in some ways or teach her something, but: What is there? It is not an absence of something, but what is there? What is present? What is it that the organism wants to be and do at the moment? That is what I am asking.

*Comment and analysis: In this example, the therapist thinks that following the client where she is, would be a mistake. It would encourage her to follow a problematic view of herself. The clinician actively encourages her client in discovering what is there, instead of perceiving the absence of something.*

**Interviewer:** I was curious about your reaction and how you created humor? Can you say more?

*(I play back the audiotape.)*

*Client: "That I abandoned him"*
*Therapist: "What is that abandonment about?"*
*Client: "It was abandonment because… the bounding that we had was about body image. You know..."*
*Therapist: "It's a little bit like a flea leaving the dog and then feeling guilty for abandoning the dog" (laughter with the client)*
*Therapist: "What does it mean abandonment? That this man cannot take care of himself?"*
*Client: "It was abandonment because... You know... I mean … I imagine he can..."*
*Therapist: "Sorry. Because it left the dog?"*
*Client: "I mean… of course he can take care of himself. It was not up to me to..."*
*Therapist: "Yeah, with or without you.")*

**Therapist:** Hum... Abandonment is a buzzword for psychotherapists. They imagine that they know what it means. Therefore, when patients use it in a situation like this, it must be some kind of a projection or bullshit like that. Listen carefully to what she is saying. She is saying that she is not there for her parents. Therefore, she has abandoned them. What is the logic behind a child abandoning a parent? There is something very bizarre about that! It is the other way around! Parents abandon, if they are bad parents. They abandon their children. It is not the other way around. It just struck me. It was so ludicrous. Then I told her: It's a little bit like a flea leaving the dog and then feeling guilty for abandoning the dog *(Laughter)*. How could you say that the flea abandoned the dog? Poor dog, this flea left him! *(Laughter)*

*Comment and analysis: This is a perfect illustration of my definition of ethics-in-practice. The clinician demonstrates in the heart of the therapeutic relationship the ability to take a stance, to position himself when it touches an ethical dilemma. The clinician's RIA is focused on reestablishing the ethics: It is not the job of children to take care of their parents. The clinician takes a very clear position in front of the client to restore what is right. The therapist chooses humor to show her how she makes meaning. The therapist highlights the importance of listening to what the client is saying and how the client attributes meaning, rather than being carried away by largely overused theme such as abandonment.*

**Interviewer:** Why did you use humor? This is a serious matter after all. You could convey the same message being serious?

**Therapist:** Because if I am serious, I cannot convey the gap in logic.

**Interviewer:** Why not?

**Therapist:** It will then become a verbal problem, not a spatial and temporal problem.

**Interviewer:** Please, explain. I do not understand. Your comments reminded me of the Structural Family Therapists who highlighted the correct hierarchy and alliances in a Family System, but I do not understand your rationale for using humor.

**Therapist:** Just listen to this language. This comment gets to your limbic system. It does not get to your guts. It is understandable, but it doesn't hit you. It is not *experience-able.* Good therapy does not happen, if it is not experienced. Good therapy is not just a good explanation.

**Interviewer:** So you want her to have a strong metaphor, a shocking metaphor that she can remember.

**Therapist:** I want her to have an image. I want this to have an emotional impact. I want this to have a cognitive impact, all at the same time.

**Interviewer:** You were thinking about all that, just before you did your comment? Just before your intervention?

*Comment and analysis: The therapist purposefully uses humor, as opposed to a simple explanation. He thinks this will create an experience that will stay with the client longer. The therapist states his belief that good therapy is far more than a good explanation, it is the possibility of creating an experience that the client can assimilate, an experience that the client will carry outside of the therapy room.*

**Therapist:** I think about these things all the time. I have got to the point where I can do these things almost on procedural memory and just do it. I can quote where it comes from. Wagner says: "Learning is proportional to the difference between expectations, and what occurs". I have to make what occurs big enough, so that she will not lose it. If I just explain it, it will get lost. No matter how hard I try. If I hit her with it, it won't leave. It will stick with her. It will make a difference. It will be delivered. So, anytime I deliver something like that it has to be startling enough to be memorable.

*Comment and analysis: The therapist states that his reflection-in-action is constant. The therapist uses theoretical knowledge and information from research and applies this to his practice. He refers to learning theories and the need to create an impact, for knowledge to replace pre-existing learning.*

**Interviewer:** That is interesting. You know this client well enough to know she won't be hurt by such a comment? I imagine it could be shocking for some people.

**Therapist:** It is not only that I know her well, but I know me well enough. I know somehow that, because I have the personality that I have, I can get away with things like that. Somebody else may be offensive doing that. Somewhere, it is not offensive when I do it. If I were somebody else, I might have to find some other ways to surprise them.

*Comment and analysis: The therapist knows himself well and has a clear sense of how he will be experienced by his clients. Jennings and Skovholt (1999) refer to expert therapists as having a fine understanding about how they function and how they affect others.*

**Interviewer:** It makes sense. Thank you. The hour is almost over, so I would like to thank you very much for your comments and your time. It was interesting for me. I have learned a lot. Since you have generously offered me a second hour of interview: I will be interested in talking about your other session in the near future.

**Therapist**: That is fine. We shall do that.

*(This is the end of this interview)*

# Fourteenth interview

## Context

When I arrive at the expert therapist's office, he informs me that we will not have the hour in-between, for me to review the tape and prepare questions. I am forced to introduce a sudden change in my procedure. I do not have time to review the tape and prepare the interview. I will discover the session as I listen to it.

**Therapist:** Do you want to know something about the client, or about the session?

**Interviewer:** I guess both. Could you give me the context in which this conversation occurs?

*Comment and analysis: The therapist remembers from our last interview the questions I previously asked.*

**Therapist:** She was raised by people who did not fit with her. She is clever, sensitive, and intelligent. They could not follow. They meant well but they could not welcome so many talents in a person.

**Interviewer** What do you mean by the people who raised her? They were not the biological parents?

**Therapist**: She was adopted very early on. These people really loved her. Until I started seeing her, she did not think she was very bright. These people could not nurture this brightness. She felt a lot of insecurity around her mother. Maybe, the quite common thought that people who have been adopted have is: You are lucky enough to have found these people. Now you better show your gratitude. You better be what they want you to be. So that it won't happen to you again.

*Comment and analysis: The therapist explains the context of the session with historical elements of the client's childhood: her adoptive parents did not meet the emotional needs of this bright child.*

**Interviewer:** At what age was she adopted?

**Therapist:** Two days. This is a patient with whom sometimes nothing happens. After fifty minutes all of a sudden it all comes together. This is one of the sessions where something is happening all the way through. This has mostly to do with self-concepts. Introjects about who she ought to be. Discovering who she is, instead, and feeling uncomfortable with the extremes of who she ought to be and what she would be, if she doesn't pay attention to whom she ought to be. She is looking for a way to feel comfortable as herself. The concept of being somewhere in the middle is not easy for her. This is essentially what the session is about.

**Interviewer:** Interesting. Shall we listen to the tape? I will do this interview somewhat differently from the previous one, since I listen to this tape with you. I am discovering the tape now. I would like also for you to stop the tape, when you want to comment on something.

**Interviewer:** Yes. I have a question here. Do you have any purpose in mind, at the very beginning of the session other than explaining your trip to her? *(The therapist discloses to the client the following memory of his teaching trip to Ireland: He is invited to a female friend's house. He has some of his clothes washed by his female host and friend. Arriving in London, to do some more teaching on the way home, he tries on the clothes. They shrunk up to four inches! He wrote an electronic mail to his friend in Ireland saying: "What is wrong with the picture? Man goes to a woman's house, leaves in her husband's pants... (The client and the therapist are laughing)*

**Therapist:** Several. One knows that she enjoys traveling. She also enjoys stories. This particular story has fluid boundaries. It is a way of desensitizing her about it.

*Comment and analysis: No comment is randomly expressed. There are almost always thoughts behind any of the therapist's intervention.*

**Interviewer:** What do you mean by fluid boundaries?

**Therapist:** Whose pants are these? How did they get there? Do you know those kinds of things? *(Laughter)*

**Interviewer:** This is in relationship with her adoption?

**Therapist:** No. Not really.

*Comment and analysis: I should have asked more questions at this point. I do not understand what the clinician means by desensitizing the client to fluid boundaries.*

**Interviewer:** Why did she come to see you in the first place?

**Therapist:** Mostly, it had to do with confusion about who she is. Actually, let me look it up... *(The therapist consults his notes)* just a sense that therapy might be helpful to her.

**Interviewer:** She does not strike me as being a person in a stage of crisis.

**Therapist:** No. You are right. This is really a long-term therapy. Long-term, character-changing psychotherapy. What she said, when she started that she was just interested in psychotherapy. The sense of wanting to work something out in her life. She was having troubles with guys, losing interest in them, unless she cannot have them. If she could have them, then she is not very interested. We started the second session with the sense of being given away, because she was not enough. She was always trying to give her very best. So that she will not be given away again by others.

**Interviewer:** How do you think she made this meaning?

**Therapist:** It is pretty clear that everything she did was... *(Inaudible, an ambulance passed along the street).* It is just a life-long experience she had. She never felt any different from that. Therefore, a lot of the early work with her was just on learning to pay attention to what she felt. She was clueless about it.

*Comment and analysis: The therapist says that the focus of the therapeutic work with the client has been on how the client can learn to identify and trust what she feels. For years, she lost the way she felt, because she was too busy, making her adoptive parents like her.*

**Interviewer:** For how long have you been seeing this patient?

**Therapist:** Two and a half years.

**Interviewer:** Wow! Two and a half years! What about the previous client, in our previous interview?

**Therapist:** She had been my client for a couple of years also. *(The tape goes on. The client refers to a visit with a previous roommate. She shares her reaction to her life style. She sees her roommate's life as the one she "ought to have". She reports "It kind of freaked me out a little bit. I have been very comfortable with who I am, what I am pursuing, and all that, and suddenly I heard that and I am like... Oh gosh! This is so like not my life. Am I screwing up something or? But maybe I ought to be like this". The therapist says: What is the "ought"?)*

**Interviewer:** Can you explain your comment to her, when you said: "what is the ought"?

**Therapist:** She is using words about the way she ought to be. I don't want to ask her a precise question, which would be: How do you think you ought to be living? This would give me a concrete answer. I could ask about the "introject", the "ought". I am not very interested in that either, so I give her a question that is right in the middle. That will force her to create something, because there is no way to answer my question.

**Interviewer:** And so your intention is?

**Therapist:** It is to get her to stop there and to focus and see. So I can see what is there. If I give her a precise question, then the response I get has to do with my question. I don't want her response to have anything to do with my question.

*Comment and analysis: The therapist carefully pays attention to the way he frames his question. He intentionally delivers an unusual question so that the client would have to struggle. Not only does the therapist carefully pay attention to what he asks, but carefully explores how he asks the questions so that the client will have to react and reflect.*

*(The tape goes on. The client comes back to the theme of adoption : "I am so special because I have been adopted", she adds: "So if you are adopted you sort of owe your life to somebody". The therapist answers: "These are not the kind of thoughts that I usually have in mind, but the first thing that came to my mind when you spoke was: would I rather do that (do what I ought to) or would I rather die? Client answers (obviously surprised maybe a little shocked): Wow!)*

**Interviewer:** Why did you say that?

**Therapist:** Because, there are so many choices. My understanding of her "wow !" is that it is suddenly clear to her what the alternatives are. She has them on procedural memory. I need to exaggerate a little and turn them up a little, so that she can see them. Otherwise, it just slides, it won't stick with her.

**Interviewer:** So that she would see the extreme of what she is putting herself into?

**Therapist:** Not the extreme, the severity of what she is putting herself into. So I owed it as my projection, my thoughts, my response to what she is saying.

**Interviewer:** Yes. I see.

*(I continue to listen to the tape with the therapist. The client speaks about involving herself totally with God and how she gets a sense of wasting her life instead of giving it to God if she was to have a job and a family. The therapist asks: "And the purpose of what you would be doing would be what?"* )

**Therapist:** *(The therapist stops the audiotape at this point).* I used that question and I use it sometimes, because of what gets lost. Many times when people are talking about something, there is indeed a hidden intent. I want to know something about this intent, the purpose. So, I ask it.

**Interviewer:** *(I stop the tape).* You know this is an interesting topic. I have asked myself questions about spirituality. What is the place of spirituality in therapy? How do you address spirituality? I was wondering if you could say something about that.

**Therapist:** This is a question I have given a lot of thoughts to for many years. I am interested in how *she* refers to it and I keep following what she discusses. She sets it up as two sides: one is that there is this program for her, the way she sort of sacrifices her life, and the other one where she tosses the whole thing over. I know that neither of those can be right, so I have to find a way to find what is valuable to her, and keep my values out, as much as possible, which is what I want to do.

*Comment and analysis: Going back to the findings of Jennings and Skovholt (1999), expert therapists value cognitive complexity and the ambiguity of the human condition... The therapist thought for many years about the complex question of spirituality. He follows what feels right for the client and sets aside his own believes about spirituality as much as possible.*

*(I continue the tape. The therapist says: "This is the difference between what you prefer to do and what you do". After this sentence the therapist stops using words, as he refers to the "what you prefer to do" and the "what you do" and simply points at spaces to refer to them. This use of gestures instead of words raises my curiosity.)*

**Interviewer:** Why did you stop talking then? Is there any particular purpose for not using words at this point?

**Therapist:** Sure. As long as you use words, you are really limiting access to the brain to specific parts of the brain that work better and worse for different people. If I use space as well, it speaks to other parts of the brain in ways that are better understood emotionally.

*Comment and analysis: He refers to how a therapist can broaden access to a fuller knowing through the use of different channels of communication to convey the same information.*

**Interviewer:** So you broaden for her opportunities to comprehend?

**Therapist:** Right. So, I point out these places, so that I become identified with those words and feelings and all those kinds of things.

*(The therapist says: "And somehow this choice is taken away from you. So, if you are adopted it means that you, somehow, sort of sacrifice your life to someone?" After that comment, the therapist stops the tape and says...)*

**Therapist:** "That is a reference to several things. She used to be so out of touch with her feelings, partly because her adoptive mother would not allow her to do anything but feel good. When she was sad weepy or angry her mother would say: "Let's wipe up this face. Let's put on a happy face!" Her mother was like this. Then she became like this. She was like this for months, when she first came in.

**Interviewer:** Do you relate that to adoption? To make this child perfectly happy, because she could not have her own and this is such a gift, or be the perfect mother or both?

**Therapist:** Yes. Exactly.

*(I continue the audiotape. The therapist shares with the client his bodily experience, as he listens to the client. He feels breathless, as if something is frightening.)*

**Interviewer:** Your comment based on your bodily response is interesting. Even though that might be quite typical of Gestalt work. I am interested in what you did. You used, so to speak, your guts. Why did you choose to share that at this moment, what for?

**Therapist:** I noticed that I was tense. I felt out of breath. There is a way, in which I put myself in her world and I am feeling. There is the sense of "how she ought to be, because if she does not do that, she is going to hell!". I am feeling how impossible that is and how impossible this is. And not finding a place, but only panic. And I suspect that is a bit of what she is feeling. So, I want her to know what my reaction is. Just to see what it opens.

*Comment and analysis: The therapist uses his physical and sensory information. He uses a reflexive posture in trying to put himself in the shoes of the client without losing track of where he is as a therapist. The therapist uses reflexivity to access the capacity of having a sense of his client's mind and feelings thoughts. In other words he puts himself as Siegel (1999) states in "mental shoes", or emotional shoes, shall I say of his client. The means to deliver the intervention is important ; the therapist remains respectful and sensitive in sharing his emotional response rather than transforming it into an interpretation : This is how you feel.*

**Interviewer:** Is it an invitation for her to feel, as well?

**Therapist:** No, not an invitation. Rather normalizing and permission. Permission is different from inviting.

*(The client keeps referring to what she "ought to do" and how to get rid of the sense of "ought to". At this point, the therapist asks an unexpected question: "Is there anything in what you ought to do that you miss, that you would like to have?")*

**Interviewer:** Why did you ask this question?

**Therapist:** She now has two poles as a polarity. Obviously there is something valuable in each one. Otherwise, she would not hold on to them. I want to know what she values in the one she fears the most. If we don't bring that along, she is going to be stopping this process.

*Comment and analysis: The therapist focuses on the part that the client wants to avoid. The therapist asks what in this unwanted part she cherishes the most.*

**Interviewer:** I am aware of the time. I don't want to keep you too long. I really appreciate the time you have given me. I have a last question. I would like to know what was the clients' reaction when you invited them to participate to the research.

**Therapist:** Both of them said: "Oh yes! No problem, I'll have to bring you back that form". *(The therapist refers to consent to release information).* They signed, brought back the consent and that was the end of it!

**Interviewer:** Do you think that they were interested in participating in this research as soon as you asked?

**Therapist:** Yes, because we talked about it!

**Interviewer:** That is interesting. I would like to know more about how it happens that some patients say "Yes!" immediately and some others don't want to hear about it. This research does not involve any direct contact with the clients and the focus is really on the therapist's process. I am intrigued. I am wondering what gets in the way. Do you have any idea?

**Therapist:** I think that the therapist is usually the person who gets in the way. My experience is that if clients trust you, they will do almost anything. I can only think of one or two clients who might refuse and mostly that would have to do with my being uncomfortable with asking. I learned that, years ago. I was starting to do simple Gestalt work and I was asking people to put this part of them in this chair and that part of them in this chair, and people would absolutely refuse. It dawned on me that they were refusing because they felt my discomfort.

*Comment and analysis: The therapist thinks that clients will accept participating in this research if the clinician is interested and invested in it. They would refuse to participate in such a research, should they experience reticence in the therapist's reaction. The therapist seems aware of the power that he has over his clients and how much trust his clients develop in him.*

**Interviewer:** Hum! Interesting.

**Therapist:** When I worked that through. *(The therapist is referring to his discomfort using some interventions).* When I felt comfortable with this people no longer refused to me. So, I think it has something to do with the confidence with which the therapist asks, and the atmosphere that the therapist creates.

*Comment and analysis: Further, the therapist sees a link between how far, and how daring the client can be, and how comfortable the therapist is with his interventions and techniques.*

**Interviewer:** I tend to believe in your explanation. I don't know for how many years I have used the video camera and one-way mirrors and stuff. It was always an option for the client. I do not recall hearing a "no". Maybe three or four times but out of the number of times I requested, I must have had a really good argument for people to say "Sure I'll be happy to do that. I don't mind". Maybe I conveyed that by my attitude; this was important, this was what I was doing.

**Therapist:** Right. That is right.

**Interviewer**: *(Long silence).* Anything else that you would like to say about this process or this client or that I forgot to ask, before we finish?

**Therapist:** No. It is just that I think that the works goes on and deepens from here.

**Interviewer:** Why do you think it deepens?

*Comment and analysis: This is too bad that the hour is over. We may have missed the most interesting part of the interview. The therapist's comment is that at the point I stop the interview, the session becomes "deep". In the field of psychotherapy, the word "deep" is frequently associated with interesting. I notice that he said something similar in the first interview that the most interesting part of the session occurred after the tape went off.*

**Therapist:** Because we are starting here to pick up what is valuable with each. All we have so far is resistance. So now let's go beyond that and see if we can bring in what each of those have that is important to her. Then, she begins to integrate all that stuff. Maybe within the last ten to fifteen minutes, she integrates all that stuff and that becomes a much more solid place. For me, I am looking for the not-so-solid places, poking there until she feels comfortable. So there are a couple of cycles of that. I don't know if we have that on tape, or not.

*(The therapist forgot to turn the tape on side B. I guess this is a common experience of research ! I have only the first part of the interview on audiotape)*

**Interviewer:** Is it the experience you have of yourself in a session. You sort of wrap up toward the end of the session to help the person integrate what you did?

**Therapist:** Wrap up at the end?

**Interviewer:** Yes. Is this something you do?

**Therapist:** No. Sometimes, I do it at the beginning. Because you can never predict what is going to happen next.

*Comment and analysis: The therapist has not a predetermined strategy that he will apply with every client. Instead, he uses many strategies, depending on the contexts.*

**Interviewer:** How do you facilitate assimilation ?

**Therapist:** Yes, sometimes I give a piece of homework toward the end of therapy to make the work of the hour continue. So that the therapy doesn't stop, when the patient leaves the office. Sometimes, I do that to underscore things. If you have something where the patient sees all the concrete pieces, but doesn't see the whole. I give them a brief picture of the whole.

**Interviewer:** So to link the experience of the session with a broader part of their life?

**Therapist**: Yes. Yes.

**Interviewer:** Is this something you find yourself doing often?

**Therapist:** Almost every session.

*Comment and analysis: The therapist knows how limited his interventions are in the life of his clients. He finds ways to have the work continue in between sessions.*

**Interviewer:** Anything else that you would like to say? Or anything else you would like to say about how you know yourself as a therapist? Are there things that you often do, or things that you cherish about this reflection-in-action?

**Therapist:** No. I never know what is going to happen next. I always try my best to be prepared for nothing and everything at the same time. So, that I don't have anticipation or expectations. Unless somebody is fairly disturbed and I decide to make the session about this topic.

*Comment and analysis: The therapist does whatever it takes to maintain a sense of curiosity. He tries not to anticipate or create expectations for a session. The therapist makes a conscious effort not to set the agenda for the therapy session. The therapist makes a noticeable exception, when a client is "fairly disturbed". I should have asked more clarification on that.*

**Interviewer:** I was also wondering if you want to say something about how you know about yourself, as a therapist? What is it that you tend to focus on or pay attention to?

**Therapist**: I need to think about that. I guess, like all Gestalt Therapists, my goal is awareness. For me, it is awareness of how I do what I do, awareness of those processes that become so automatic that I do them without noticing them. Actually, she refers to that in the session later on where she comes up to something and she says: "Oh I see what happens. This was so emotional that I went back to old patterns, rather than to stay with the patterns that I know I have". What I said to her, was "There is something missing here for me and this is..." Because she was talking about being afraid that she could end up in one or the other poles, even after she integrated it. What she wanted from this pole and what she wanted from that pole, but what she was missing was a sense of confidence that she could carry through with that. So I said to her: "There is something missing and what is missing for me is that, over time, you know yourself to be a person of integrity. You know yourself to be a person who is persistent. You know yourself to be a person who doesn't give up when things are hard". She relaxed visibly, and said: "Yes, you are right. For a moment this was such an important issue to me, that I forgot those things that I have learned about myself". She said: "I really don't have to worry about how these things will turn out. They will turn out well. Whatever well means, they will turn well!"

*Comment and analysis: I ask the therapist to describe how he perceives generally his work. At first, the clinician taken by surprise reports that he would need some time to reflect on that. Indeed, this is a difficult and complex question. Then the clinician refers to his theory of reference: Gestalt Therapy. He discusses the focus on the clients' processes and how bringing that to awareness is central in his work. He gives an example about how therapy can generate awareness of new processes that can be more functional than old ones.*

**Interviewer:** I wanted to ask you one last thing. Let me recall. Oh yes! When you asked her: "What happened just before?" I was curious about this comment. Could you say something about that? Is it also along the lines of bringing onto awareness what was in her mind just before she did what she did?

**Therapist:** Yes, because there is a place in which the person loses awareness of the process. If you can go back to the moment just before. Then many times, the next moment will come to awareness. Some therapists try to go directly to the middle of the lack of awareness, and they get nothing from the client. If you go to the point just before and you just follow one step at the time, then, it will allow her to open up. You cannot just start in the middle of something where there is no anchor. There is nothing to go on.

*Comment and analysis: The therapist describes how he assists and encourages his client to retrieve procedural memories and to gain awareness of her own processes. He highlights the importance of setting the context in order to allow the memory back. The therapist states that the recollection and the awareness are easier to reach by bringing the client back just a few instants before she lost track of what happened, than if they have no "anchor".*

**Interviewer:** I have a question related to this client. This is one of my last questions: What sense do you make out of her silences?

**Therapist:** When she is silent, it means that she is assimilating. I try hard never to interfere with that. I wait until the person comes back with their eyes or I wait until there is some signal from their body that they are finished. Many times what will happen is ... *(the therapist mimes a person who would come back from concentration and breathes in deeply).* They shift their gaze when something is finished inside immediately.

*Comment and analysis: The therapist values and respects the silence in therapy. For him, it means that the client is assimilating what has just happened. He also highlights the efforts he consciously makes not to interrupt this assimilation process. Silence is a very important element of the therapeutic process.*

**Interviewer:** I guess you already have an answer to this one, but, when there is a silence, how do you know the difference between somebody who doesn't get what you are saying, versus this process of assimilation?

**Therapist:** Because, if they do not care what I am saying, they will come back to me immediately. Because they are searching for meaning there *(pointing himself, the therapist)* instead of for meaning here *(pointing to a chair, the invisible client).* Do you understand what I am saying? They are searching for meaning in the therapist rather than searching for meaning in themselves. If something just does not make sense to them, you can see it. Their attention and their awareness is moving from thing to thing in the room, so what you see is their eyes shifting, because they are not turned to the inside. You know you have lost them.

*Comment and analysis: The para-verbal cues measure the assimilation process of the clients. This assimilation process is an active search for meaning. Making something new with what happens outside and integrating it with something that happens inside.*

**Interviewer:** Thank you very much. I want to say I really enjoyed these interviews with you, they were rich and enlightening. I was highly interested by what you had to say. In terms of the process, I just wanted to let you know what my plans are. Once I transcribe the interviews and make my interpretations. I will give them back to you, for review. I would like you to add your comments, questions, disagreements, interests… whatever you wish to add. Then we can move on from there.

**Therapist**: Sure, no problem.

**Interviewer:** How was this interview for you? Interesting, frustrating, or something else?

**Therapist:** No, it was fun. It was *(long silence).* Interesting in a couple of ways. One was listening to the client's comment and getting a sense that I do not have the chance to pay attention to any hour. How much are they affected by what is going on? Because, I am in the middle of it like this, *(showing our interaction),* instead of just watching and listening. *(Long silence).* The other one is kind of embarrassing, the other reaction is a little bit arrogant... *(He laughs and seems uncomfortable).*

*Comment and analysis: The therapist reports how enjoyable, stimulating and interesting the reflexive activity of thinking about his sessions is.*

**Interviewer:** Would you like to share this reaction also or?

**Therapist:** A little bit arrogant...I found myself thinking: Wow! You really have this one well thought out, didn't you? Having it well thought out, most of the time all the way through.

*Comment and analysis: The therapist enjoys discovering his reflection-in-action. As his RIA progresses he realizes that he knows more than we he thought he knew. He wishes he could practice his RIA about his own work more frequently.*

**Interviewer**: But if I may, this is an interesting awareness.. That is exactly it. I guess you dismantle the idea that good therapy just happens. I believe therapy, good therapy, is well thought out. It is a process that requires intelligence, but much more than that at a lot of different levels and a different positioning. So, I am pleased to see how appealing the reflexive process can be. Because I would like to raise interest with students and interns about the process of reflection-in-action. I hope they will discover how satisfying this process can be. Eventually they will do it more often, which will make them, in return, I believe, better therapists. I believe that it is important to reflect on what makes us better therapists. So, I guess what I am saying it that I am very pleased with your reaction. The reflexive process for me is like a contagious disease: The more you think about that, and the more you to do it and the more you want to do it, the more interest you have in thinking about it. It is a self-feeding process that often goes in a good, generative direction. Of course, what is missing is the client's perspective. Even if your discourse always include the client it is still their voice through ours.

**Therapist**: *(Keeps nodding).*

**Interviewer:** I think my research lacks the client's response to this RIA. I want you to know that that has been in my thoughts. A further research may include seeking in details how therapists' RIA influence clients. Are there commonalties between how a therapist thinks in action and how the client thinks about his therapy session ?

**Therapist:** Yes. That is very interesting. That is your next study! You thought you were not going to be a scientist. *(Common laughter).*

**Interviewer:** Since you are talking about scientists, I meant to tell you, when I listen to your RIA, I realize with much admiration, how much of a scientist, in the pure sense of the word you are. In the room with a client you behave like a scientist, you never assume you know, you move a step, check out, come back, question. This is exciting for me.

**Therapist:** Yes. Good therapy, I think is research in the present.

**Interviewer:** I noticed that you often apply ideas from the field of research. You always apply them in a context, after checking them out. You have read much research. It is obvious and quite uncommon for a clinician. Of course, you are both a clinician and a researcher, it helps. *(Laughter).*

**Therapist:** Yes. That is right.

**Interviewer**: Many authors that have talked about this process of reflection-in-action. They have tried to categorize this thought process. I am still wondering if we can find some commonalties. I believe there might be some commonalties, but there might be much more than the one we suspect. Schön talks about creating a repertoire of practical knowing. It is a concept close to having experience and knowing "how to". You have been in so many clinical situations that you find yourself quiet and peaceful, because you know that in any situation you will be able to custom-design it with previous intervention. The knowledge can also be a constraint if it is not custom-designed for the client.

**Therapist:** That is really interesting … really interesting.

*(This is the end of the interview.)*

# Conclusion

In the first few questions of the first interview, the clinician seems to rely on what he knows best, his theoretical reference, rather than daring a reflection-in-action. He refers to key-concepts of psychotherapy such as the notion of boundaries and setting a therapeutic frame. He describes in general the way he practices psychotherapy. The therapist defines his role as "a consultant on the process". The clinician's interventions are context-related and custom-designed to the client's needs. The therapist has a clear awareness about how he relates to his clients. The clinician defines the evolution of his work reaching toward aestheticism. Techniques and interventions become more embedded in conversation and his work appears less technical.

In the two interviews, the therapist brings some elements of a theory of practice. First, the therapist states his intent to assist the client build and store new procedural memories (i.e. new ways of knowing how to interact and how to be in relationship with others). In order to do that the clinician focuses on the sequential processes of the client. What did she say first? What did she do then? How did she do that? The therapist describes how he assists and encourages his client to retrieve procedural memories and to gain awareness of her own processes. He highlights the importance of setting the context, in order to allow the memory back. The recollections of the procedural memory are easier by bringing the client just a few instants before she lost track of what happened, so there is an anchor. The clinician places the behavior in a larger context for the client to be aware of the larger pattern.

The second interesting idea is that the client cannot integrate newness promptly. There is the notion of letting the idea "simmer" before it can be integrated by the client. Last, there is a hypothesis that his client may refer to a pre-verbal experience. The rationale is that the client says and shows that she has no word for it. The clinician knows that his hypothesis is only a speculation and he needs to verify it with the client. Another highlight of the clinician's RIA: the notion of ethics in practice. When there is an ethical dilemma, the therapist takes a very clear position to reestablish what he believes is ethical.

Para-verbal elements are a central part of the therapist's RIA. The clinician understands what is important for the client through her para-verbal cues: a tone of voice, a change of rhythm, an intonation, or a gesture, or a silence. The therapist discusses the para-verbal components of therapy and how they inform his work. The therapist refers to para-verbal elements to discuss the therapeutic relationship. These para-verbal cues reflect the quality of a therapeutic alliance. The therapist carefully pays attention to the way he frames his question. He intentionally delivers an unusual question so that the client would have to struggle. Not only does the therapist carefully pay attention to what he asks, but carefully explores how he asks the questions so that the client will have to react and reflect.

The therapist' s RIA includes the reference to "learning theories". In order for a learning experience to take place, there needs to be a sufficient level of emotional arousal. Beyond and above this level nothing happens. The therapist assesses how he can broaden access to a fuller knowing. He refers to different channels of communication (voice, space, sounds,...) to convey the same information and to impact the brain more fully.

The therapist values and respects silence in therapy. It means that the client is assimilating what has just happened. He makes conscious efforts not to interrupt this assimilation process. This assimilation process is an active search for meaning, where the client uses something new from the outside and integrates it with something that happens inside. The para-verbal cues are indicators measuring the assimilation process of the clients. The therapist focuses much of his RIA on the importance of the assimilation process.

Another comment refers to the fundamental notion of intention. The therapist is able to maintain constant and unconditional curiosity toward the client, regardless of what happens. He tries not to anticipate or create expectations for a session. The therapist makes a conscious effort not to set the agenda for the therapy session. He uses his own reaction to the client as cues to define and shape the therapeutic alliance. The therapist recognizes individual differences and welcomes them.

The therapist defines his theory of change: change occurs when the therapist welcomes the patient just where he is rather than forcing him to change (by encouraging the patient to remain where he is). In this interview the therapist encourages the client's awareness of what she is doing so that it may facilitate change to occur. Change is in the clients' hands. The therapist positions himself in the therapeutic relationship as owning only what is his. The therapist refuses the invitation of being a healer or owning "magical properties". The therapist has a clear sense of how he impacts clients and constantly utilizes it. He welcomes his personality and uses it in therapy. The clinician uses theoretical knowledge and previous research in his work with client. Jennings and Skovholt (1999) refer to master therapists as having a fine and clear understanding about how they function and how they affect others. Jennings and Skovholt (1999) assert that expert therapists value cognitive complexity and the ambiguity of the human condition.

The therapist uses his physical and sensory information. He uses reflexivity to access the capacity of having a sense of his client's mind, feelings, and thoughts. In other words he puts himself as Siegel (1999) states in "mental shoes" of his client. The therapist seems aware of the power that he has over his clients and how much trust his clients develop in him. The therapist knows how limited his interventions are in the realm of life. He thinks about the importance of creating intervention that may affect the client past the session, in-between sessions.

Finally, the therapist reports how enjoyable, stimulating and interesting the reflexive activity generated by this interview has been. As his RIA progresses he realizes that he knows more than we he thought he knew. He wishes he could practice RIA about his own work more frequently.

# Fifteenth interview

## Context

This interview takes place an hour after the session to allow me the time to listen to the audiotape of the session and familiarize myself with the content of the session. The expert therapist chooses a female patient (in her early fifties), with whom he has a long-term relationship (the therapist has been working with her for close to ten years). The therapist describes the recovery the client has made in therapy, from severe functional impairments to being able to adapt quite well. The day before the interview, I receive an electronic mail from the expert therapist stating that he just heard that her client is in a lot of distress. He warns me of the possibility that the interview may not take place. This expert therapist was one of the most animated clinicians to reflect and respond after my transcription and analysis, mostly in terms of disagreements. These comments will be added to the interview as "therapist's reflection after my analysis and comments".

**Interviewer:** I just want to mention that, what is not part of this tape, is the discussion we had earlier today. In this discussion, I told you what I was hoping for this interview, and what my research is about. I told you about reflexive processes and reflexivity and my growing interest for reflection-in-action. You will have a chance afterwards, to review the transcript and my analysis. You will have a chance to add comments once you have my transcripts. You will be able to reflect on my reflections. You can also tell me if you want me to take something out of the transcript. So, as I was listening to your session, I had several questions: What do you have to say about this client? I wanted to have a little bit of the background history. I am landing in a context that I don't know much about. I am wondering if you can tell me something about this context.

**Therapist:** Sure, You were landing in a context, because I have been seeing her for almost ten years. When she came in originally, she was on disability. She was unable to work, she was unable to get out of bed most of the time. She was very depressed. She was suicidal at time. She was non-functional. She paid a minimal fee for therapy. She was like that for quite a while. Slowly, she has rebuilt herself. Two or three years ago, she got her first, as she calls, "real job" as an attorney again, for legal aid. Prior to that, she started with some clerical work and all kind of jobs, but she could not hold them very well. She couldn't follow through. She couldn't do the work. Also, she occasionally got into difficulties with people interpersonally, which is what this one is about. Do you want more on that?

**Interviewer:** No. I think this is enough. I just wanted to know something about the context. I guess what is confusing to me, as I think about it, is the e-mail you sent me before we started the interview. In this e-mail, you warned me that your client might be in high distress. I guess I was surprised, because I felt that she was doing rather well. Maybe that was the other reason why I asked you more about the context. To me, she seemed to be handling the situation remarkably, given the fact that she may be fired.

*Comment and analysis: The therapist chooses a long-term client for this interview. This choice may balance the unknown of the current experience on exploring one's reflection-in-action. It is also interesting to note that the clinician describes his area of specialization as being couple therapy, yet he chose a single client for this research project. When I ask about the context, the therapist describes in detail the healing process of his client moving from the almost complete incapacity to minimal functional impairment. The therapist picks this client by interest and for her insight.*

**Therapist:** Yes. When I wrote you the e-mail, she seemed very stressed, very upset, very scared. She said today that it took her about one day to get over it, meaning to get in touch with one side of the issue. This is what I noticed later, in the session. Usually, if something like that happened, either she would be completely self-deprecating, self-annihilating, or she would get righteously indignant about how wrong they were, or how bad they were, or how evil they were or, et cetera. She would then, even if she started being angry with them, end up being critical of herself. Then that would lay her out for months. So, one day only was incredible.

**Interviewer:** Yes, indeed. This is incredible. Thank you. Now, this morning I gave you a brief introduction of what my work is about. My hope is that, today, our conversation will be focused on how you can express, in words, what you do in a session. What is your recollection or reconstruction of the session? How is it that you think, as a psychotherapist? This is what I am interested in. So, I was wondering if you could go back to this session and talk about the process, and what you saw happening. What were your intentions? What did you see your client doing? How were you positioning yourself in response to her? How would you define the highlights of the session?

**Therapist:** Sure. Coming to the session, she and I share a long history. We have a really good connection, both serious as well as humorous. She is irreverent. She loves that. She likes that I am irreverent at times. The highlight to me is that typically she would go black or white. I don't think of it in these terms, but if one wanted to put it through theoretical lenses, you would either describe that part as hysterical, or you would describe it as borderline: splitting one or the other, all on one side or all on the other. I do not think often in diagnostic categories very much, never during the session. Sometimes when I think *about (verbal emphasis)* a client, it is sometimes useful, but not very often. The issue has always been to help her to hold on to both sides of an issue. It is actually even more that than the two sides. It is to help her hold on to the complexity and the range of an issue, rather than just one hand, or the other hand. To not cut it in half and not go just to ends, but to have the whole texture, so that she can hold it all in once. She had difficulties in the past doing that. The main theme for me was to notice how well she was doing that now. I was feeding that back to her. I was really impressed with that. I wanted her to take that in. Some of the times, she was aware of it, it seemed, and other times not. One other time when I fed it back to her, her voice dropped. She got very serious and a little teary. She just said quietly: Thank you. Because, the shorthand for that was: You really got it. You really got how important that was!

*Comment and analysis: This is a good example of what RIA is not. The therapist gives interesting and intelligent responses, but they are not integrating a reflexive activity of what happened in the room.*

*They are abstractions, theoretical constructs of the client and the client's processes, omitting to reflect on the participation of the therapist in the relationship. The therapist gives an interesting definition of a good connection, as a relationship that can be both humorous and serious, with irreverence. The therapist brings the diagnostic terminology ("borderline" and "hysterical") to describe the way his client functions. He adds on two occasions that he does not use diagnostic criteria, nor thinks in these terms, and certainly never refers to diagnosis during the session. He seems almost apologetic for bringing in the idea of diagnosis. The therapist describes the overall client's process and the objectives of treatment. He wants to help her to "hold on to the both sides of an issue". The therapist summarizes how he perceives the client's problematic process as "polarization". The therapist is interested in the progress that the client makes: the exceptions to the rules. At the end of his comments, the therapist makes an interpretation. He translated the client's statement: "Thank you" with "You really got it. You really got how important that was!"*

**Therapist's reflections after my comments:** No! I am not apologetic for bringing the concept of diagnosis. It is important to discriminate when it is problematic. It can be useful shorthand or a straightjacket for perceptions and responses. My interest is in the clarity of contexts.

*Comment and analysis: The therapist refuses part of my interpretation of his comments.*

**Interviewer:** Did you do the same parallel when she referred to her mother? Is it what you were trying to do? Please explain.

**Therapist:** No. It was not the opposite extreme. She only referred twice to her mother in this session. After she referred to herself as "bizarre". As soon as she talks about bizarre, then she refers to her mother. Her mother was quite crazy and quite bizarre in her behavior. As soon as she does something that does not fit very well socially, she immediately jumps to saying: I am bizarre. The next jump is: I am like my mother. Then, she starts talking about her crazy mother. What she did today, that I thought was really lovely, was that she could acknowledge ways that she was like her mother, that were positive. She didn't have to be either, like her mother, crazy and bizarre, or unlike her mother.

**Interviewer:** It is interesting to me that you say that, because as I was listening to the tape, just before my interview with you, I was taking notes. I wrote down a title for the session. The title was: "Working in the in between". So... *(Laughter).* It is reassuring to me to see that the way you read the session is similar to what I perceived.

**Therapist:** It was even more important that she could say something positive about her mother. Her mother abused her. She has a very long history of physical abuse. Some of it was pretty sadistic. So, being able to say something positive about her mother without either demonizing her mother as all bad, or saying: "It must have been my fault" which is the other side, was something.

*Comment and analysis: The therapist takes a clear position with his patient. He seems to share a traditional belief in the field of psychotherapy that may be summarized as: in order to achieve health, differentiation or maturity, grown-ups should be able to find*

*something good to say about their parents, regardless of the level of abuse that they endured. Tacitly, the modern tradition assumes that health and differentiation are reached through being able to recognize something positive in the most sadistic caregivers. Is it true? Is it untrue? The modern tradition asserts that it is true. For the postmodern critique, this belief is based upon a social consensus. For the modern tradition, it has been accepted as a foundation of health.*
*This is a subtle example of a modern versus a postmodern position toward knowledge. A postmodern stance may translate into a comment such as: "Traditionally, experts in the field of psychotherapy share the belief that it is ultimately healthier to be able to recognize goodness in one's own parents, even if they were abusive. What do you think about such a theory? How does this theory affect you? How does this theory fit?" The therapist who adopts a postmodern stance offers to his client an alternative theory. Better, he can offer alternative theories reflecting upon the variety of existing theories. Offering these contradicting and different theories is typical of a deconstructive practice. Open possible conversations (meta-conversations) about how theories mold and transform people, therapists and therapist's interventions with clients.*

*Specifically, this positioning requests that the psychotherapist unveils and discusses with his clients:*

1. *The source of knowledge.*

2. *The relativism of knowledge.*

3. *The possible effect of this knowledge on the clients and on the relationships with the clients.*

4. *Some alternatives to this knowledge.*

*A postmodern stance demands more parentheses, more contextual explanations, more carefulness, more hesitancy, and fewer certainties. It needs to introduce the fundamental doubt of the critique. It needs to add the nuances that will leave the other with reflexivity and unanswered questions.*

**Therapist's reflections after my comments***:* No! No! No! I am bothered by this comment. I am not talking about parents, good or bad and I am not even thinking of any barometer of mental health as you suggest. I am talking about being able to discriminate and see many sides of a person, issue, etc... For me, this is about clear and discriminating perceptions and not about mothers. And Yes! There are many ideas of clear discriminations and perceptions. All of the above is the standard postmodern point of view about these things and I agree. However, please present them as postmodern biases and not as an alleged polarity to what you interpreted me to say which I did not.

*Interviewer's reflections and comments: The therapist is annoyed by my comments. I am surprised by his reaction. It is an important comment that shows that interpretation does not always fit the other's perception of himself. It is interesting to me to see how interpretation can be misunderstood. It is an important comment and a strong reaction that made me think. Maybe we shall wonder about extending this comment to our work with clients since we are so fond of interpretations.*

*I still wonder: Could it be that, even if we do not think that we refer to any preconceived ideas about health our comments still convey implicit references? Is it possible to discuss perceptions (or any other thing) without its inherent relation to context "being also a mother"? Is it further possible that we convey through what we say more than we intend? Sometimes by the way we say something, we may carry implicit and unwanted reference. I still wonder.*

**Interviewer:** Yes. *(Silence).* I am intrigued. When you answered my previous question; you said: "I rarely think diagnostically". This is very much the trend nowadays not to think diagnostically. What surprised me more was when you made this distinction: "I don't ever think diagnostically in the session". I am curious about this comment "not in the session". Can you say more?

**Therapist:** As soon as I, or any other therapist, start thinking diagnostically, it begins to limit. It begins to limit both sides. It begins to limit what you see and what you hear. You take it in through the prism, through the stencil of a diagnostic category. You begin to limit. It also works the other way. You keep in some of your own responses. You are not supposed to respond that way to someone with that diagnosis. You are not bracketing off, so that you could really have an involvement and an engagement between where you are, and where the other person is. It does not mean to throw away your clinical judgment. The judgment still has to be there about what the relationship can support, and continue to a deeper contact, and what might lead to a diminution of contact or withdraw. So, that kind of clinical judgment is important, but not through the lens of a diagnosis, more through the lens of the contact support level.

*Comment and analysis: This is again a good example of what reflection-in-action is not. This is an interesting reflection on the function and the effect of diagnosis. Diagnosis constrains and limits the possible relationship we may have with a client. Diagnosis can limit the domain of possible interventions. The therapist did not explore the positive and maybe structuring effect of diagnosis.*

*The therapist presents an interesting theory of psychotherapy but not what I would call a RIA since he does not reflect on his presence in the relationship nor on the specific clinical situation that occurred with this client. He discusses the notion of "contact" and how to assess whether the relationship with a client may be deepened. He defines clinical judgment as the ability to discern between a response that will lead to a "deeper contact" and a non-helpful intervention that may lead to a withdrawal or diminution of contact.*

**Interviewer:** I think that I understand your point. It makes sense to me. A focus on diagnosis can constrain the possible relationship that you may have with a client. My question is then: How do you get that away from the session (i.e. your knowledge of diagnosis)? At other times, do you think about your client diagnostically? The reason, I am asking you this question is that I have in mind some trainees, I just spoke with last week, and I can hear them say: "It seems easy to say, but how do you do that?"

**Therapist:** First, I do not think diagnostically frequently at all, even outside of the session. It doesn't mean I don't think about what happened, or that I don't think about the person. I am much more likely to think about it in terms of repetitive processes, in terms of, from my orientation, repetitive Gestalts or fixed Gestalts. I am looking at it in process terms and not in a cluster that forms a label. The main problem with thinking about someone in diagnostic categories is that: then you begin to relate to the category and not to the person. You miss things, because it doesn't fit the box.

*Comment and analysis: The therapist offers a metaphor to escape the dilemma of diagnosis versus non-diagnosis. He would rather think about "repetitive processes" as a way of defining what is unhealthy. Rigidity, repetitiveness, lack of adaptability errs on the side of disorder and adaptability; context sensitivity errs on the side of health. The therapist further asserts that he prefers to find a functional way of defining a person, rather than a static, structural definition.*

**Interviewer:** So, in other words, when you were talking about polarities before, could this be thinking diagnostically? If we stretch the word diagnosis? I mean, your intention was much broader than just defining the person in a static way, then you have a self-explanatory system that you have created. Is that what you are saying?

*Comment and analysis: My questions are not leading the therapist back to a reflection-in-action. This is a mistake. Instead I am arguing with him. I suggest that the therapist think diagnostic in functional terms, rather than in a structural way.*

**Therapist:** Yes. An example is, in ten years until today, I have never thought of or used the term: "Borderline" in association with this client. I only use it with you, as shorthand. That becomes the only foreground and the background fades away. One of my favorite expressions is: "If you put a thumb in front of your eye, the whole world looks like a thumb!" I have never thought of her in that language, because that language changes how you see and changes what comes out of you. So,

I have thought of her as someone who tends to only see one part of the picture. She tends to blow up one part of the picture at the expense of any other parts of the picture. One who has difficulties holding on to polarities, holding on to a continuum of feelings, or implications of a piece of behavior.

**Interviewer:** Would you say that it is a functional or process diagnosis as opposed to a structural one?

**Therapist:** Yes. Exactly.

**Interviewer:** What was your general impression of this session? In regard to how you usually experience yourself as a clinician. What was your feedback of this session? If you were to look back and reflect upon your style, if you were to observe the way you usually know yourself as a therapist, what would you say?

**Therapist:** I am not sure that I understand the question, but let me try. I have to try to reframe the question a little bit. If I took a meta-view, I would say that it reflects who I am as a therapist fairly well. However, I could have a whole different session, that looked very different, that I would also say reflected me, as a therapist. The difference is that, what happens in the therapy is co-created. It has to be appropriate to that context, to that person and where they are that time, that day. Her session today was, to a large extent, self-confirmatory of her own ability to hold on to both the bad parts and the good parts and to neither be all against herself, nor all against the other. It was confirmatory, because most of that she has done already. It took years to work on it. So, today's session was self-confirmatory. I added to that confirmation, as an important person whose opinion she values. We could have had a wholly different session that could have been, for instance, very emotional, or one of very little words and I will still say: This is very much like me. Because the phenotype, the outside, may look very different but the genotype, the core, is still the same. It is meeting the person, where they are with who I am, but deferring more to where they are. Does that answer your question?

*Comment and analysis: The therapist's style depends on the context.*

**Interviewer:** Yes. It does. If you were to do the session all over again, are there things that you would like to do differently?

**Therapist:** Yes. I think some fine points. A couple of times, I told her what stood out for me. I might do that a little more incrementally, by just pointing out what happened and asking her: What strikes you about that? Does this have any meaning for you?

**Interviewer:** Instead of presenting your reaction, first?

**Therapist:** Yes. Exactly. So, I think I would have done that. I am just trying to think... (Silence). With a client, whom I did not know very well I very probably would have been doing more of that, instead of telling her what stood out for me. With this client, since we share shorthand. We have known each other for a long time. We have a good connection, I think, I may not do as much of that. I think it may be a good idea for me to look at that. I was also pleased when she shook her head and disagreed with me. It is important. At one point during our work, she was confluent with everything I said. We looked at that for quite a while. There, she immediately shook her head and had a different experience. She even started the session, as I remember now, it refreshes me, that she had taken something I said, at the last session and it turned out not to be accurate. She stated that her own sense of what was going on was accurate. That is how she started the session. The history on that is that, whenever somebody tells her something, she typically thinks the worst of herself. This has happened hundred times, in the last ten years. Most of the time, the worst scenario was possible, but her evidence is very thin. This time, evidently, she was accurate. It is not that the guy did not have a job. It is just that he did not want to give it to her. She thought that already, when he said: "I don't have a job!" and he did not add the other part "I have a job but not for you!". She was right this time. Importantly, she noticed that. She was able to articulate (that is my take on it) that she had swallowed too quickly my own saying. She didn't stay with her own long enough.

*Comment and analysis: The therapist starts a reflection-in-action. When looking back at his work he starts wishing he might have done something else. If he could do the session all over again, the therapist would elicit more from the patient by using more open questions, rather than stating his opinion. He explains then the context and the long history supporting the relationship between him and his client that allows him to use this "shorthand". He then wonders about the comment he just made. He does not seem so sure. He adds: "It may be a good idea for me to look at that". The therapist finally highlights how pleased he is with his client being able to disagree with the therapist.*

**Interviewer:** (Silence). I had a different question. So if I may… (The therapist is nodding) I was wondering about the tape and its presence during your session. How was it for you to know that you were taped and that the session was taped? How do you think it did affect the client? You have a long history of being taped for the purpose of training.

**Therapist:** I only thought about it a couple of times. I haven't been audio-taped in a long time, but videotape is far more vulnerable or noticeable than an audiotape. I did have some thoughts about the client. I was wondering, whether she was putting on a show at some point, but I had no real… It wasn't very strong. If it got any stronger, I probably would have said something to her about it being my concern, because that may have been all me.

*Comment and analysis: I ask the therapist if he is bothered by the presence of the tape, he answers that this process is familiar to him. He then makes an interpretation that the client "was putting on a show".*

**Interviewer:** What made you think that?

**Therapist:** She was a little more animated, through most of the session. She usually is a very animated woman, but she is animated and then she is quiet. This was a bigger percentage of animated. That was the only thing. She always is talkative, but not always so animated.

**Interviewer:** What were you aware of doing when she was talking, when she was telling her story?

**Therapist:** Sometimes, I was just listening. Sometimes smiling, both outside and inside, because I was so pleased that she could deal with some adversity, real adversity in real life, without going overboard one way or the other. She neither fell apart, nor went into righteous stuff. So, I felt pleased with that.

**Interviewer:** How did you let her know that? I could not hear, by smiling?

**Therapist:** Yes, but again that wasn't planned like that. A smile is what came up. Because, I was pleased and she could read that, I would bet. Again, had she been a client whom I did not know that well or who didn't know me that well, I probably would have said more.

**Interviewer:** Since I listened to the tape, I missed the part about smiling and nodding.

**Therapist:** I had a thought. I just remembered. As you said some of the time, when I was nodding and smiling, I thought: This won't come up on the tape. On the other hand, I don't want to say anything for the tape.

**Interviewer:** That is right. (Laughter).

**Therapist:** So, I didn't say. (Laughter).

*Comment and analysis: The therapist discusses his awareness of the audiotape. The therapist is aware of the para-verbal communication he holds with his client.*

**Interviewer:** I noticed a few things you said… my interpretation of it was, that there were ways to let her know that you understood the context. At some point, you referred to conversations that you had with her, earlier in a previous session, in another context. I don't know how consciously aware you were of doing that, or if it is just the effect of a long practice. Can you say something about how you do that?

**Therapist:** Yes. Some of them are pivotal, like the stuff about her mother. She is intelligent like her mother. She does many things like her mother. Even though her mother was not educated and didn't work. She wasn't a professional woman. She was generalizing being like her mother. She talked about friendships and not being able to maintain friendships very long and not having a partner. I know from history that her mother was nuts. Most people would not want to have anything to do with her mother. I know that it is not what happens with her. With this woman, when a friendship ends, sometimes it is the other person, but usually it's her. She loses interest or something like that. She was likening herself to her mother because the result had some similarities. The way to that end result was totally different.

*Comment and analysis: The therapist defines some moments of the therapeutic process, as pivotal. I should have asked more about what he would define as "pivotal moments" in therapy. I may have missed an important question here. He discusses the larger context of what he previously calls "repetitive processes".*

**Interviewer:** Did you pick up on her anxiety? I heard that. At one point, she said: "If I don't find a job, I don't know what I am going to do?". She had a very different voice, almost a trembling voice. (I review and listen to this part of the session with the therapist). What do you think about that?

*Comment and analysis: I make a comment that is not "politically correct" for an interviewer. Far from neutral, I share my own clinical judgment with this therapist.*

**Therapist:** The choice was for me not to go with this anxiety. I agree with you, this comment had some anxiety in it. My choice was to go with helping her to get it, and assimilate that. She handled this difficulty very well. Much differently than what she has done in the past.

**Interviewer:** So, that was what you meant when you told her: "You did it well"? If I want to play the devil's advocate, you did not really respond to her comment: "What am I going to do?" You went back to a previous topic, without addressing this one.

**Therapist:** That is right.

**Interviewer:** Do you think it would take away her anxiety?
**Therapist:** It will certainly run the risk of deflecting her comment. But at that point, my foreground was to let her sharpen her comment on how differently she dealt with that this time, even if it deflected some of the anxiety.

*Comment and analysis: The therapist highlights an important subject of clinical practice. There are so many different venues, so many choices to be made during a therapy session. What should we focus on? What should we track? What should we emphasize? That is a typical example of two therapists thinking about the same moment of a session and choosing two different venues. Different clinical choices may have similar benefits for the client. This is a very distinctive quality of expert therapists. They make choices and clinical judgments on an ongoing basis. Each choice can be discussed and criticized. However, the therapist's expertise is highlighted by the ongoing awareness of the possible effects of the choices he makes. The therapist highlights the importance of the process of assimilation for a client. He shows that he is able to stand on firm ground, justify the reason for his choice, and envision the possible effect of his intervention. The therapist clearly identifies the intent behind an intervention.*

**Interviewer:** When you decided to set the next appointment. Suppose you come from a background informed by something like: this woman is very fragile; she is currently under a lot of distress. You may tell her: Come back tomorrow! Call me if there is a need! Or: I will call you between now and the next session. When you asked her to set the appointment date herself, you conveyed a whole different message that might activate her anxiety. So, when you set the next appointment and let her choose, she chose an appointment that was more than a month from today: What were your thoughts?

**Therapist:** This is not strategic. There have been times, when I was working with her, that I have been concerned. I said: "I am concerned. I would like us to meet in a couple of days, just to check in briefly by telephone!" I haven't done that with her in a long time. This is just being respectful of her concern about her job and the money. For the past few months, we have only been seeing each other every two weeks. Before that, it was down to once a month. *(Silence).* There is a similar thing here with her fee. Her fee is quite low. When I first saw her, she was on disability insurance. I think I have raised it a few dollars, but it is a very low fee. When she got the first job in legal aid for the first time, she got a real salary. It was not a big salary because she was in a non-profit agency. It wasn't even a good salary. So, I did not raise her fee. When she got this job, her salary now is respectable. She could afford to pay a higher fee and we talked about that. She was afraid because these jobs are filling jobs. They usually are for young lawyers on maternity leave. So, we left it at a lower fee and agreed that, if her job became permanent, we would renegotiate.

*Comment and analysis: The therapist explains his intent behind an intervention. Every decision he makes in therapy is well thought out, even rescheduling an appointment. The therapist discusses how sensitive he is to his patient's income.*

**Interviewer:** Do you do that with all of your clients? You adjust the fee with them?

**Therapist:** Yes, yes. But, this is not a negotiation, which gets confusing. It is not a negotiation about how much they want to pay. I don't care what they want to pay! It is about what is equitable for their financial resources and my scale. I have a range.

**Interviewer:** Why do you choose to do that? May I ask?

**Therapist:** Yes. One reason is a form of giving back. People helped me when I couldn't afford to pay regular price for therapy and for training. So, I want to give back. I can't give back to the same people because they are dead. I can give back to the next generation, both of clients and trainees. That is part of it. The other part is the concern to have a practice, with only people who can afford the going top rate. If you do that, I would guess within five to ten years you don't have a clue what is going on in the real world. You rule out single mothers, students, and people who are not on a fixed income. You rule out the working class people. You end up with Beverly Hills' housewives, intellectuals…you lose connection. You become an ivory tower. You lose the range with what real people deal with all the time. So, that is the second reason. If there was a third reason, I feel better about myself doing that.

*Comment and analysis: I ask the therapist to explain his motivation for this philanthropic gesture to adjust the fee to clients. I invite the therapist into a difficult and interesting topic "money in therapy". The therapist presents a well thought response. Money, he says is not a negotiation. He pre-establishes a sliding scale and adjusts the fee based on what the client can afford.*

*One interesting topic leading to another, the psychotherapist thinks that this profession should be concerned with helping. Part of his practice should be available to "lower income clients". Therapy should be accessible to anyone regardless of his budget. The therapist considers important to "give back". The therapist explores the benefit of low-fee clients. They bring a more realistic diversity of the population in the therapist's office. The therapist alludes to an awareness of social inequalities. He seems to say that a therapist is also a "political animal".*

**Interviewer:** I know it is an uncommon question. Maybe you need more time to answer this question, but I would like to know: Why did you choose this profession?

**Therapist:** I have always been fascinated by relationships of all kinds. Therapy is essentially about relationships, which is why my area of specialization is couple. But, individual therapy is about relationships as well. If you think about that, if nobody had relationships with parents, children, bosses, lovers, husbands, wives, students, and teachers. If we did not have relationships, what the hell would we ever talk about in therapy? It is almost always about relationships. Sometimes, even when you are talking about your own internal process, that is related to out there as well. That has been a fascination to me. As far back as I can remember, the only other thing I ever had any interest in, were, there were actually two of these: one was pediatrics, and the other was in a whole different area architecture. Those were the two other areas that I had interest in. I think pediatrics was there before I even knew there was such a thing as psychotherapy.

*Comment and analysis: I ask the therapist to explain his motivation to doing this profession. The therapist describes an ongoing "fascination" for relationship. This fascination goes back in time to "as far back" as he can remember.*

**Interviewer:** Thank you very much I think that our time is up. Is there anything that you would have liked me to ask you? Is there anything else that you would like to discuss?

**Therapist:** Only, that I think it is important for this research to realize what is foreground. For any therapist working with a client, it is not only a function of who that therapist is, versus who another therapist is. They have different backgrounds, different lenses. Different things will stand out, different meanings. Also, having a history with a client changes who you are in that relationship. A therapist who doesn't share that history could not have the same reaction, because he does not have the same connection.

*Comment and analysis: This important comment refers directly to his grounding theories. What he would call "field theory" and what I would call second-order cybernetic is a direct reference to the continual importance of the context. Relationships, he asserts, change and modify people all the time. Therefore, a therapist cannot have one single style. This goes back to a notion, so brilliantly discussed by Gergen (1991, 1992, 1993a). The notion of multiple selves shaped and transformed moment-by-moment by a multitude of relationships is also discussed by Shotter (1993).*

**Interviewer:** It is good that you add that. I wanted to come back to this question. I know it can be a constraining question. You probably cannot fully answer it. If you could portray yourself as a clinician, what would you highlight? What do you think are your strengths, and your weaknesses?

*Comment and analysis: I did not give up on this question. I asked again what qualities he perceives in himself as a clinician.*

**Therapist:** I think, I am quite good at noticing the process, and noticing patterns of process and noticing patterns of patterns. I think, I am also good at noticing the two different kinds of processes, the one that is happening right here, right now, that I would call the "fresh fish" and the one that happens over time that I would call "the big fish". The fresh fish is a manifestation of the big fish. They are related. The judgment is when to stay with the fresh fish and when to go for the big fish: the larger one.

*Comment and analysis: This expert therapist knows he excels at noticing processes and pattern of processes and pattern of patterns, what he called earlier repetitive processes.*

**Interviewer:** You said earlier that one of the reasons that Gestalt therapy had such an impact on you is that it encouraged you to be yourself. So, what are the traits of your personality that you value, that you think make a good therapist?

**Therapist:** Some personal qualities: humor, I don't have to stay serious all day long. My willingness to be authentic is important. But not to use authenticity as an excuse to not modulate, to not be appropriate, to the support that is there.

*Comment and analysis: The therapist, as the previous one, uses humor in therapy. He also adds his: "willingness to be authentic". The therapist does not say: "I am authentic". This nuance seems honest and humbling.*

**Interviewer:** Two words that are often used in describing you: clarity and sharpness? What do you think?

**Therapist:** Yes. I think I do have a good way to communicate clearly in crisp and simple ways, sometimes fairly complex things that still do justice to the complexity of the issue. I get the same comment about training. I am able to connect the work to the theory in ways that are very clear. Some of that is just a lot of practice, but this is something that is effortless now.

**Interviewer:** What about the conversation we just had? Is it something you feel is effortless? Is it something you feel you do often? Is it something that is familiar to you?

**Therapist:** Yes, very much so, quite effortless and simple.

*Comment and analysis: I invite the therapist to reflect on reflexivity. The therapist shares that this is a familiar territory for him that is effortless and simple.*

**Interviewer:** What is the effect for you of doing this reflection-in-action right now?

**Therapist:** I am not sure at this point. Probably, it has made clearer for me some of the issues that I was focusing on with the client. The importance of prioritizing the foreground in my jargon, like how she handles anxiety is not as important as how well she handled the situation. She did not go off on one way, or the other. That edged it in my mind. The other issue that was important to me is what I could have done differently.

*Comment and analysis: I invite the therapist to reflect upon his reflection-in-action. The therapist shows an ongoing commitment to being challenged and to revisit his knowledge. He likes the question: "What could I have done differently?"*

**Interviewer:** Do you feel this kind of exchange, this kind of interviews and I am is: clarifying, generative, stimulating, helpful, useful, non-helpful, boring, useless?

**Therapist:** I think it is generative and clarifying. It might have been challenging, if the session was less clear to me.

*Comment and analysis: The therapist chooses the qualifiers of "generative and clarifying" to define an interview that seeks to explore reflection-in-action.*

**Interviewer:** Thank you so much. I recall Polanyi, the father of practical knowledge. He says: "We know more than we can tell". When we start talking about our practice, I think we should do that much more often, for the sake of training, our own training and our own reflection. We realize how much more we know, than what we assume we know, without saying. It is a kind of knowledge in discovery that is interesting to me. Before you say something, and that is one of Vygotsky's ideas you do not always know what you are about to say. Ideas evolve through language and are formed through language. Before each interview there is always anxiety and excitement for me. There is anxiety because I feel slightly intimidated by your knowledge. There is anxiety because I move into an arena that is never known. That is both scary and exciting. The questions I ask are generated after the context, which means I cannot prepare. That is scary as well. Thank you for your patience and kindness. Moreover, mostly thank you for your time and your interest in my project.

## Conclusion

At the beginning of the interview, the therapist does not attempt directly a reflection-in-action. He holds on to theoretical concepts. Several attempts on my part to welcome a reflection-in-action remain unsuccessful (How do you think? If you could go back to this session and talk about the process, what did you see happening? What were your intentions? What did you see your client doing? ). Out of the four expert therapists' interviews, this is where *the least RIA is presented.* It is also interesting to note that the therapist refers to RIA as being "effortless and simple". There are several good illustrations of what RIA is not and will bring a tighter focus to our definition. The interview clearly demonstrates professional expertise. The therapist refers to professional examples, has a large repertoire of practice, uses his theory of reference that he has well integrated, uses interpretations, professional examples, favorite expressions. The therapist gives interesting responses, but they are not frequently integrating the reflexive activity of what happened in the room with the clinician and the client. They are abstractions, theoretical constructs of the client and the client's process, omitting any discussion of the participation of the therapist in the relationship. Let me give several examples of what I do not consider to be a reflection-in-action: (*"You take it in through the prism, through the stencil of a diagnostic category. You begin to limit. It also works the other way. You keep in some of your own responses". "One of my favorite expressions is: If you put a thumb in front of your eye, the whole world looks like a thumb! I have never thought of her in that language, because that language changes how you see and changes what comes out of you. So, I have thought of her, as someone who tends to only see one part of the picture. She tends to blow up one part of the picture at the expense of any other parts of the picture."*) The therapist is good at describing his professional experience. The therapist presents an interesting *theory of psychotherapy,* but not a RIA since he does not reflect on his presence in the relationship, nor on the specific clinical situation that occurred with this client.

I was surprised when analyzing this interview by how many times I was asking the same questions. This is an interesting interview also in that most of my interpretations do not match the therapist's interpretation of his work. The therapist has a negative response to my analysis. He is sometimes annoyed by my comments ("*No! No! No! I am bothered by this comment!"*). It is an important comment that shows that interpretation does not always connect with the other's perception of his sayings and actions. Some examples of RIA are presented here and illustrated by statements such as (*"I am just trying to think... (Silence) (...) I think, I may not do as much of that...I think it may be a good idea for me to look at that".)*

The therapist defines clinical judgment as the ability to discern an intervention that will lead to a deeper contact, from a non-helpful intervention that might lead to a withdrawn, or a diminution of contact. The therapist would rather think about "repetitive processes" than about diagnostic categories. Rigidity, repetitiveness, and lack of adaptability err on the side of disorder and adaptability; context sensitivity errs on the side of health. The therapist further asserts that he finds a functional way of defining a person, rather than a static and structural definition. The expert therapist knows he excels at noticing processes and pattern of processes and pattern of patterns, what he called earlier repetitive processes. The therapist's style adjusts to the relationships he builds and creates with clients. The therapist highlights an important subject of clinical practice: there are different venues, multiple choices to be made during a therapy session. What should we focus on? What should we emphasize? Different clinical choices may have similar benefits for the client. Each choice can be discussed and criticized. This is a very distinctive quality of expert therapists: their expertise is highlighted by the ongoing awareness of the possible effects of the choices they make. The therapist envisions the possible effect of his interventions. The therapist clearly identifies the intent behind an intervention.

The therapist highlights the importance of the process of assimilation for a client. The therapist enters a difficult and interesting topic of therapy: money. The therapist has evidently though a lot about the discourse on and about money and its management in clinical practice. The psychotherapist thinks that this profession should be concerned with helping "real problems" and that a therapist should also be a "political animal" engaged in social issues. The therapist brings in an awareness of social inequalities.

To define an interview that seeks to explore reflection-in-action, the therapist chooses the qualifiers of "generative and clarifying", he adds that it could have been challenging if the session had been less clear to him.

# Chapter XIV

## Conclusion

### Toward a theory of reflection-in-action

I have expanded a definition of reflection-in-action (how therapists think while they practice) throughout this present research. RIA is an evolving definition based upon the growing repertoire of therapists' narratives. I select the most interesting concepts that have come from the analysis of the interviews. I link them with the theoretical elements of my research. My findings help me to move toward a theory of reflection-in-action that is in motion, and based on the information and the narratives I have gathered.

### What is a reflection-in-action?

RIA is a discourse forming and clarifying through language (Vygotsky, 1986). In the interviews, I find the pure enactment of Vygotsky's thesis that ideas form and emerge through language: "I think it was more felt sense stuff, before we talked together. Then, when I talked with you about it, ... I ... you know... I started to see more patterns". Reflection-in-action is a thought in process, which grounds itself in the theoretical background of the psychotherapist. RIA is deepened and enhanced by its very practice. Implicit knowledge is broader than what is disclosed through RIA. The therapist's RIA refers to previous sessions and establishes patterns within the sessions. From an initial confusion, ("Daaah... a big daah... (Laughter)...(Long sigh) to: "I am not sure. Part of it is... I guess... there is something about that, that seems a little familiar to the last time we worked together, she and I. About wanting to have something and not having it, and feeling some sadness about that. I just feel like it is an exploratory stage. I don't feel like I can say that I am anywhere or go anywhere, or I make any definitive statement about anything"). Along with my questions, the therapist's RIA becomes more articulate illustrating Polanyi's idea: "we can know more than we can tell" (1966, p.4). RIA brings, through language, elements that were previously implicit and inchoate in the domain of the explicit, while some implicit knowing stays in the implicit. In the interviews, several therapists highlight the importance of building first a therapeutic alliance before anything else can happen. RIA seems to frequently sharpen the focus of the session.

Sometimes RIA contrasts with what is obvious in the session. In other words, the therapist's RIA may be more sophisticated than what we witness in the session. There is an example in the fifth interview at the training institute where the therapist has much information about her client, about her relationship to the client, about herself as a therapist, and about the impasse reached that she was not sharing. The intervention remained sterile before the reflection-in-action was shared. One of the most interesting findings is to highlight that some interventions, when using RIA, may hold a relational purpose. The example provided here is: "I need you to slow down so that I can pay more attention to you" as opposed to "Slow down, so that you will feel more connected to your feelings."

In several examples through the interviews, the therapist's disclosure of his RIA strengthens the therapeutic alliance. It means that the sharing of the therapist's RIA may have a positive effect on the therapeutic relationship. We should not confuse sharing a reflection-in-action with the therapist's self-disclosure. It is not; it is a sharing of the understanding of the process of therapy. The language used in front of the client is inviting and inclusive, as opposed to an objectifying language, which would have probably cut off the client.

In order to produce RIA, the therapist uses his physical and sensory information. He uses reflexivity to access the capacity of having a sense of his client's mind, feelings, and thoughts. He puts himself as Siegel (1999) states in the "mental shoes" of his client(s). Practicing reflection-in-action involves an intention. It involves a pause in the process: taking a break and thinking outside of the box. The pre-requisite to practicing RIA is a reflexive attitude toward knowledge and toward oneself. RIA is a moving concept. It is not a tool. One therapeutic intervention can be a success in one context and useless in a different one. A therapeutic intervention is sustained by a therapeutic alliance and happens in a context.

RIA is not a statement of one's theoretical position. Practicing RIA involves an effort from the therapist who explores his own responses and processes and, at times, shares them. In order to be a reflection-in-action the therapist needs to integrate the reflexive activity of what happened in the room with himself and the client, and to discuss the participation of the therapist in the relationship. Therapists can engage their clients in a reflexive posture by statements such as: "So let's talk about what we just did!" In the interviews, several therapists highlight the relational and contextual nature of RIA. A therapist's response depends on the response of the client, not only the words but also the affect, the tone and the volume of the voice, the body movements, and the facial expression.

RIA can be a methodology for learning. By its regular practice, a clinician will become more aware of how he learns, functions, and relate. RIA permits a deepening of clinical practices. For example, RIA may be applied to the process of supervision and should be used to enhance training. In the interviews, I note several times that a clear positioning of the therapist in his context appears to be conditional to the emergence of therapeutic conversation and the establishment of a therapeutic alliance. The corollary is that poor positioning and a poor clarification of the context may allow only a less solid therapeutic relationship. RIA may be an interesting methodological instrument for approaching the unsettling concept of the "therapeutic relationship". This is worth looking into with further research.

Therapists' RIA parallels a therapeutic process. I could have shortened these three interviews with the expert therapists and only keep "la crème de la crème". This would be a mistake. Therapy is not only made of moments of movement, and brilliant therapists' interventions, but also hesitancies, floating moments, repetitions, and at times confusing interactions. When these moments of movement occur, it is important to emphasize them and to materialize our response in helpful intervention.

## Why should a clinician invite reflexivity in the therapy room?

As in a chess game, by taking a step back, we may learn more about how to make the next move. Reflexivity may broaden the therapist's understanding, allowing him to see more clearly the possibility of making the next intervention. The reflexive process can also paralyze a therapist. The therapist's reflexivity can become only a mirroring act, omitting its object (the clients) and its purpose (the therapeutic process); he may lose contact with his client. Reflexivity is a difficult equilibrium to maintain. Shotter (1993) talks about "temporary essentialism" to qualify this position in between dogma and relativity.

RIA is a powerful instrument to refine our professional practice. It reviews, corrects, and redirects. By practicing RIA, a psychotherapist creates a theory in motion, a theory of practice. By bringing into awareness what just happened in the session, the clinician may change whatever does not suit the context. The more a therapist trains and uses RIA as a central element of his work the more skilled and articulate he will become.

Building a repertoire of RIA may be the leading narratives that will inspire clinicians to understand how we create, maintain, strengthen, suffocate, damage, repair, and terminate these relationships that we want therapeutic. RIA is not only a clarifying instrument for the psychotherapist, but may also have a positive clinical impact when shared with clients. The sharing of RIA with our clients may be an essential element in the construction and solidification of a therapeutic alliance with clients. It is probably when the therapeutic is the least solid that the sharing of the therapist's RIA is the most powerful. It is a difficult exercise, since the art resides in the way the message is delivered.

A session of therapy is a work in progress. It can always be ameliorated. The use of RIA highlights an important subject of clinical practice. There are so many different venues, so many choices to be made during a therapy session. RIA will bring to our awareness the rationale behind our choices.

Reflexivity invites reflexivity. The practice of RIA appears to be generative. Once a clinician becomes familiar with reflexivity, this process is difficult to stop. If the therapist is able to maintain a reflexive position while doing therapy, he may be more attuned to emotional content of the client. The practice of reflexivity in a session may produce a generative effect on the clients as well, assisting the clients to become more aware and to use RIA themselves to define, correct and strengthen relationships outside of the therapy session.

Reflexivity may prevent reification. It may prevent dogmatism. It encourages us, clinicians, to keep questioning our daily practice, and to keep questioning what we think is obvious.

At times, our knowledge of theories of psychotherapy can constrain and limit our practices, if it is not custom-built to the clients. RIA has links to the practice itself and the theories of psychotherapy, making knowledge relevant and context-sensitive.

The effects of RIA may be multiple. Practicing RIA invites the therapist to position himself in the system he is engaged in, and this almost moment-by-moment. The practice of RIA during the session can be utilized as an intervention for the client. Sharing the therapist's RIA may produce a therapeutic effect.

## From novices to expert therapists

The first observation is that the RIA from less trained therapists carries hesitancies. RIA resembles much a thought creating sense through its elocution. The less trained therapist's RIA is less coherent, less consistent, and less formalized. For fear of displeasing or hurting the client, he puts himself on hold. He holds on to what he knows best: the theories that he has learned to make sense of the complex reality he encounters without always knowing how to connect this knowledge with what happens in the room. Another interesting point is the difficulty that the non-expert therapists have finding a clear focus to the work. They often seem to wander around, unsure where to go and which direction to take. The RIA of a non-expert therapist may reflect a unilateral focus on the client, or else on himself. It rarely encompasses the three founding polarities of RIA: the therapist, his theories, and the client.

The therapist in training appears reticent to share his dilemma with his clients. It is possible that he attributes that to a weakness, when it is possibly a core element of building a stronger therapeutic relationship. The novice therapist has probably a very limited understanding that an intervention may serve a relational purpose. It appears challenging for the less expert therapists to discuss their emotional response as a part of their RIA, even when asked. Yet these same therapists may encourage, or even push, their patients for an expression of emotions. There seems to be little awareness of the intent behind an intervention.

Some interviews with non-expert therapists demonstrate the fine line that reflexivity imposes, requiring the clinician to be present in the interaction and to think and reflect upon his interaction. Running this dual track of doing the work and thinking about the work at the same time is demanding. Some interviews highlight the difficulty of practicing reflection-in-action when one is not trained to do so. It shows the damaging effect of stress, anxiety or self-inflicting critiques on the process of reflection-in-action. I should probably add that the length of the training is not a warranty of the level of expertise of the therapist nor is it necessary indicative of the quality of reflection-in-action.

## What are the qualities of expert therapists?

RIA seems to increase in length and in sophistication, along with the level of expertise of the therapist. The more skilled the clinicians become the less noticeable their theoretical influence seems to be. This may mean that talented clinicians transcend the different theoretical orientations to describe their works in a language almost free of jargon. Over the years, their work has become subtle, more embedded in conversation and less "technicky". One describes his career as an evolution from a technician to a stage of mastery. The way they practice is sometimes almost imperceptible because it holds an aesthetic quality.

Expert therapists almost never seem to operate on automatic pilot. The expert therapists whom I have interviewed are able, moment-by-moment, to explain, justify, and anticipate the reason and the choice of their intervention(s) and response(s). With expert therapists random does not constitute a justification for an intervention. They are able to maintain reflexivity in their work and question what they do at all time. Expert therapists are able to repetitively think outside of the "nine dots' square". They move past the content to identify pattern. They move past the patterns to identify patterns of patterns, and processes of processes.

Expert therapists use their physical and sensory information as a guide in the therapeutic process. Para-verbal elements (facial expression, posture, eye contact, body movement, walk, tone of voice, volume, rhythm…) seem to be an essential component of the RIA of expert therapists. The expert clinicians I have interviewed seem to reach a consensus that frequently what is felt in the session with a client (joy, hope, fear, sadness, frustration, anger, irritation, boredom, anxiety) is related to something that exists in relationship with this client. Expert therapists relate para-verbal cues to the level of aliveness or excitement. The para-verbal cues may sometimes be stronger indicators of the quality of the therapeutic alliance than the content of what is said.

Expert therapists are interested in silence. Silence is as important an element of the therapeutic process, as are words. Silence may mean that the client is assimilating what has just happened. The interviewed expert therapists highlight the efforts that they consciously make not to interrupt this assimilation process. By the client's response, the expert therapist can distinguish whether or not the client is assimilating what just happened. Silence may be an active search for meaning. Expert therapists, each with his own style, apply the concept of assimilation of Piaget (1970, 1974) to psychotherapy. This assimilation process needs to start happening in the session. Assimilation produces two important effects:

- It will ensure that the client understands and is able to make something of what happens in the session, after the session, and not only obtain a cathartic effect. Assimilation implies that in some ways the client has learned, and is changed by this learning. This change remains outside of the session. This learning is most frequently both emotional and cognitive.

- It will help the client to make generalizations and parallels what happens in and out of the therapy room.

In the interviews, expert clinicians highlight the importance of aiming toward coherence between the methods used in therapy and the ends of therapy. It is important to have a continuum between the interventions, the goals and the procedures, rather than a rupture. Expert therapists are strong-willed. They are masterminds. They do not give up easily. Should they not understand what is happening in a session, they trust that they will, if they try hard enough. Their strong emotional support leads them to stay with the data until it makes sense. They are committed to learn. Expert therapists have a vivid interest in the evolving notion of therapeutic relationship. They recognize the uniqueness of each relationship.

Expert therapists seem to practice reflexivity with ease. They have mastered this difficult ability of not losing track of who they are while being closely connected to a client. They have an incredible talent for putting themselves in the shoes of their clients without losing track of who they are[8]. They are able to access a sense of the other's mind.

Expert therapists use daily the categories suggested by Schön (1983). They identify with ease a problem and place it in the sub-category of a known phenomenon (frame analysis). They are able to create a micro-theory to fit the unknown situation (fundamental methods of inquiry or overarching theories). Moreover, since they have a large repertoire of practice, the identification of a frame analysis is probably easier for them. They are then able to connect their overarching theories to both the frame analysis they have just done, and their repertoire building. Expert therapists seem to

[8] I do not like to use the word of empathy. Empathy has been overused as a technique of therapy. Reflexivity is not a technique, but a process. It is a complex movement: in order to feel with our clients, we need to stay who we are. Empathy has been sometimes confused with this enmeshed sort of feeling, emerging from a fantasy that if we tried hard enough, we could feel *for* our clients.

have a clear and precise overarching theory of change and what changes people. They refer to this theory often during the course of their work. Finally, the psychotherapists whom I have observed follow the fourth category of Schön (1983): they are at ease reflecting on their theories of action and modify them when necessary. Expert therapists seem well able to detect and work with what Rogers (1942) called "moments of movement" in psychotherapy.

Finally, expert therapists know that they practice in a field of knowledge that is always evolving. Expert therapists are not trying to simplify the immense complexity of humanness and relationships. On the contrary, they seem to worship this complexity. Their discourse reflects that interventions are context-related and custom-designed to the client's needs, and that relationships are co-created. The therapist's style may change with these evolving contexts. Most of the psychotherapists I have interviewed wish they would have more time in their day to reflect on their practice, whereas some non-expert therapists may feel threatened and unprepared for the task. Good therapy is research in the present with a constant and active attitude of raising questions and hypotheses and trying to confirm, or infirm them.

## What are the implications of RIA for training?

The interviews with less expert clinicians suggest that a therapist under the pressure to perform (stress, anxiety) is likely to lose his ability to generate RIA. The novice therapist may have a hard time formalizing his thoughts and generating a theory of practice, while immobilizing himself with sterile conflict such as: "Should I follow my gut feeling or should I be analytical?". RIA encompasses both. This is an interesting finding for the field of training. Trainers may use this information to understand the importance of creating a safe and welcoming context, accepting of mistakes and hesitancies, in order to encourage clinicians to practice RIA.

An interesting comment emerging from the interviews is to notice that when the therapist shares his RIA in front of his clients, his anxiety may be reduced. The therapist simply shares his confusion in front of the patient; that apparently clarifies his RIA, and reduces the therapist's anxiety. After the interview, I notice that the therapist uses his RIA to produce a clear and effective intervention. RIA could allow the therapist to sharpen his previous ideas in one single intervention for the client, bringing clarity, focus and redirecting the work.

Another expert therapist asserts that RIA is trainable. Sharing one's RIA will lead the client to become reflexive. Reflection-in-action should frequently be made explicit for the client, so that the client may learn and integrate this process. The practice of reflexivity should be an integrated part of the therapy session.

RIA is a powerful medium to enhance the quality of training. RIA can ameliorate our current clinical practices. Reflection-in-action and its exercise teach us, clinicians, to describe and formalize our practice and create ongoing narratives about "how do we do what we do". These theories of practice are moving, evolving, sometimes, unsettling, and exciting since they stand at the heart of an essential element of psychotherapy: the therapeutic alliance. RIA is also a theorization of the evolving relationship forming between the therapist and his patients. RIA may possibly be one of the highways in ameliorating our understanding of the therapeutic alliance. Accordingly, clinicians and researchers seem to have acknowledged the central role of the therapeutic relationship in the process of change. Beutler (1990), Butler and Strupp (1993), Bordin (1979) Beutler, Machado & Neufeldt (1994), Lambert (1989) Lambert and Bergin (1994) and Bachelor and Horvath (1999) show that the therapeutic relationship in psychotherapy is the most significant determinant of positive outcome in psychotherapy. Given what we know on the importance of the therapeutic relationship and the secondary importance of the therapeutic model, we can wonder about the efficacy of current training.

For years, we have just accepted that therapeutic relationship is the single best predictor of successful therapeutic outcome. We have tacitly agreed that we know what a therapeutic alliance is *(We are psychologists after all!)*. Further, clinicians are usually able to detect a therapeutic relationship from a non-therapeutic one, but we are still rather ignorant of how we may strengthen a therapeutic alliance. Training should focus also on learning how to develop a strong alliance with clients. An effective training should include helping trainees to adapt their style and personality to deal with different sort of client. RIA can be a useful medium to explore this domain.

Practically, RIA can be taught with interviews, as in my research, questioning trainees on their RIA. I recommend carefully preparing the trainees for the difficult and stressful task of discovering their RIA. I recommend performing RIA in front of trainees. The use of the one-way mirror is an excellent means of provoking reflexivity, since the observation of live sessions, places trainees in a reflexive posture where they may say "why did this clinician make this move, use this word?" "What could I have done instead, if I were in his shoes?" The use of reflecting teams may also be an excellent way to promote RIA (Anderson 1987, 1991, 1995) and may promote a supportive climate for learning and practicing RIA.

I have a recommendation for therapists-in-training, who may wonder where to learn the practice of RIA, and which school would be best able to promote this essential skill. I would say to them: go to two different schools. I would even say to them: go to two conflicting orientations of psychotherapy. Why am I recommending that? Trainees need to develop the art of respectful irreverence (Cecchin, 1993). At the heart of reflexivity, lie doubts and the ability to expose our thoughts to critique. If you enter one school, you may become a disciple. At the worst, you may lose your soul. If you enter two schools, you will maintain a critical stance toward your two "parents", because you will remember what theories of psychotherapies are: helpful guidelines and not truths.

The last recommendation I have for clinicians who want to develop their reflection-in-action and practice reflexivity is nothing new: "Know yourself enough so that you practice reflexivity and not projection of your unfinished issues on others". The therapist's psychotherapy is a very controversial chapter. Yet, therapists need to know their own issues, their blind spots, their sore points, their strengths, their limits, so that they work ethically, so that they do not impose their unresolved issues on patients. We therapists should never assume that our therapy is over. We may have to go back and revisit psychotherapy. I would give the same advice for supervision. Supervision should be a life long commitment even for the expert therapists.

## Why should reflection-in-action be used with clients?

I have noted on several occasions that the sharing of our RIA seems to have a therapeutic effect on clients. This domain needs further exploration. RIA encourages procedural awareness. In other words, it helps clients to understand how they do what they do. RIA may bring to awareness the different steps a client takes toward achieving a goal. In order to bring procedural knowledge into awareness, the psychotherapist deconstructs the process in front of the client showing, step-by-step, what has just happened, so that the client starts to understand how he does what he does. The idea is that procedural knowledge is trainable and eventually, the client can do it on his own. The intent is to assist clients in creating new ways of knowing how to interact, and how to be-in-relationship with others, in ways that are different, more satisfying.

## What clients should look for in a therapist?

If I had one piece of advice to give clients searching for a psychotherapist, it would be first to allow this search. It is evident that one therapist does not fit all. If the first therapist does not seem to fit the needs of a patient, there may be a variety of reasons. It may be worth finding an easier relationship with a therapist, a relationship that appears to find its mark easily, since a therapeutic relationship is so crucial for the positive outcome of treatment. I recommend finding a therapist who is reflexive and may not only provide answers, but generate useful questions. I would recommend a therapist who is able to question his own stance. So that ultimately, this therapist joins the client in learning "how he does the things he has done for so long that has made him miserable, but still cannot help but doing the same things".

## Where therapy should go? A reflexive theory of practice: Reflexivity, Positioning, and Ethics-in-practice

Our field is packed with countless theories of psychotherapy. Yet, clinicians are still struggling with the same issue: there is very little theory of the practice. The expanding narratives of RIA and the interviews that I have completed provide some elements of a theory of the practice of psychotherapy. This theory of practice, namely reflection-in-action, should maintain a constant movement, inserting doubts in our practice. RIA guides a practice, which grounds, transforms, and shifts rapidly. RIA reviews, redirects, and reflects upon a developing alliance with clients. The three postures that I suggest as a ground for a reflexive theory of practice are:

1. REFLEXIVITY is about maintaining a reflexive posture. Each clinician shall strive for making reflection-in-action more explicit. Maintaining a reflexive posture means to practice RIA, creating theories in motion as they emerge from the practice and refer back to it. RIA links theory to practice. We clinician should establish a self-feeding dialectic between theory and practice. RIA reminds the clinician to question continually what informs his next moves in the therapy process and where ideas and interventions are informed (reflexive loop).

2. POSITIONING is about redefining the therapist's position in context. RIA assists the clinician in modifying its intervention and responses depending on a constant moving context. The clinician takes into account each emerging concept and positions himself toward the essential topics of power and knowledge in therapy.

3. ETHICS-IN-PRACTICE will enable the therapist to maintain an ethical stance at all times. A fundamental application of reflection-in-action is in the domain of ethics. In other words, it is the ability of the clinician in the heart of the therapeutic relationship, to take a stance, to position himself when it touches an ethical dilemma. RIA is an excellent instrument to define, question and assess the notion of ethics-in-practice.

The three concepts of reflexivity, positioning and ethics-in-practice are the core elements of a theory of practice. This could be a bridging theory overarching the existing theories of psychotherapy. The reflexive theory may guide the practice of psychotherapy. This reflexive theory may assist the therapist in practicing his profession with his chosen theory(ies) of reference in a manner that nurture and build therapeutic relationships. Practicing RIA comes first, along with the positioning of the therapist and the use of ethics applied to practice. In the therapy room, knowledge has a fluid status. I have illustrated in the interviews the importance of the positioning of the clinician. I want to go back to an example that illustrates a postmodern position. For the postmodern critique, beliefs are based upon social consensus. A postmodern stance toward knowledge would contain most of the following elements:

1. The therapist will engage the client in a discussion of the source of knowledge. He will raise the awareness that this knowledge is socially constructed. In other words, that this theory is not the truth, but a social construct (Lyotard, 1979).

2. The therapist has the ability to convey to the client that this knowledge is a theory, and not the truth (Derrida, 1978).

3. The ability to communicate to the client, that, should he not adhere to this belief, nor follow this theory, it does not make him crazy or unfit. It just would be a way to attest that this is only a theory that does not fit all clients at all times.

4. The therapist who adopts a postmodern stance offers to his client an *alternative theory*. Even better, he can offer alternative theories that will account for the variety of existing theories. Offering these contradicting and different theories may help the client to understand that this is just one lens, among others.

5. Open possible conversations (meta-conversations) about how theories mold and transform people, therapists and therapist's interventions with clients.

The difference between a modern and a postmodern position has finally very little to do with the content of the message. It has everything to do with the "how" it is conveyed. A postmodern psychotherapist invites a certain positioning toward knowledge. It is easy to see how a postmodern stance can become verbose. Indeed, by definition, a postmodern stance demands more parentheses, more contextual explanations, more carefulness, more hesitancies, and less certainties. It needs to introduce the fundamental doubts of the critique. It needs to add the nuances that will leave the other with reflexivity and unanswered questions. It is what indeed a question truly should be, a rising of a doubt, a matter to be discussed or a problem requiring a collaborative solution. Unfortunately, we clinicians have often forgotten to ask questions. Maybe we try to forget how uncertain we are of our certainties. Learning to ask real questions is one of the hardest challenges of the profession. We have learned to think that we know; that we understand our patients' realities. We may even think that we can mind-read them. Our profession has fooled us into believing that we have some kind of psychic abilities. Let us face it: we cannot know for sure how our patients think, feel, comprehend, and respond unless we ask. Making assumptions and interpretation without checking them out, or without recognizing that they are assumptions or interpretations, often hurt our clients. It is highly unfortunate most of our interventions should be client-informed (Kuenzli, 2001).

In the face of moving knowledge, a constant re-positioning of oneself in the system becomes essential. Even if I choose to redefine my position, it does not give me the right to escape a position. In this field of uncertainty, where nothing stands still, one notion stands out and takes a profound importance: the positioning of the psychotherapist. Moment-by-moment, in an evolving context, reflexivity allows the psychotherapist to position himself in the system, in which he evolves.

Each relation is context-dependent, flexible, and fluctuant. In return, my constant positioning allows clients to position themselves. That is of crucial importance in the fast-speed world of today, realities evolve quickly and we need to be able to find our place in each context. The positioning questions the choice of the therapist to position himself toward power, toward a wanted or less wanted hierarchy, and also invites the clinician to position himself toward knowledge. These are complex issues. I suspect that a successful positioning toward knowledge is essential when sharing the therapist's RIA. A sensitive, respectful, uncertain, and tentative positioning will invite our client to "want" to understand the "therapist's point of view". Suggesting, rather than imposing is typically a position inviting reflexivity and inserting the doubts that prevent the reification of therapist's and client's position, reification that is likely to lead to therapeutic impasse.

RIA invites the notion of ethics-in-practice in the therapy room. For too long, ethics has been posted as an external locus of control. Ethics *should be* profoundly internal. Ethics is *not* something we should practice in order to avoid trouble with the law or for fear of losing our clientele, or our license to practice. We need to stay as psychotherapists in constant dialogue with ethics. We do so practicing reflexivity. Moment-by-moment, in a therapy session we are invited to make judgments, choices, and to decide on interventions. Ethics overrule any other issues. When ethics is involved, it becomes the priority in the therapy session. RIA allows the psychotherapist to think about his own relationship to ethics. Using reflection-in-action, the clinician positions himself toward the "right thing to do, regardless of the consequences". Consequently, RIA allows the clinician to think about the way to convey such information, to make it a useful intervention.

In order for ethics to be invited in the therapy room as an ethics-in-practice, Kearney (1988) encourages the therapist to invite, along with ethics-in-practice, the notion of play:

> "Ethics without play shrinks into a posture of cheerless moralizing. The ethical imagination needs the poetry of play to ensure that it is ethical, in a liberating way, one that opens possibilities for the other and enlarges our own response to the other and to the world beyond"(1988, p.5).

These three postures are the core of what I call a reflexive theory of practice. They are interdependent. They are related to the ability and the desire to practice reflexivity. I believe that these core and moving postures, that are reflexivity (i.e. practicing RIA), the positioning of a therapist and ethics-in-practice, move the therapist closer to a success in building a therapeutic alliance.

In our profession, we too often try to reduce the immense complexity of our work, too afraid to realize how little we finally know. We create guidelines, cookbooks to attempt to reduce the complexity we face. We get frustrated with their inability to account for the complexity of the work we chose. Facing an increasing complexity, our tendency remains to categorize, to generalize, and to compartmentalize. We forget that this reduction may also mean losing the possible essence of what we do.

Like psychotherapy, or an analysis, the criteria that define the completion of this book are multiple. A book is the beginning of a larger project. I am about to conclude this book, but I am continuing my reflexive process. For that reflexivity is the process that keeps me alive, that protects me from ignorance and certainty. It allows me to change and ameliorate my work. If you have read my work as an invitation to do more research, to ask yourself questions about your evolving practices, to develop interest in the domain of reflection-in-action, if you are willing to venture into the fascinating domain of reflection-in-action and have gathered a better understanding of this way of constructing a theory of practices. I shall be content. Would my work instill in you the incurable disease of reflexivity? Have you invited reflexivity in your therapy room? What difference has it made in your daily practice?

# Part three:

# Addendum

# Chapter XV

## The researcher's journal: A personal journey

*"The creation of an integral self is a work of a lifetime and although that work can never be completed, it is nonetheless an ethical responsibility (...) Dishonesty may result not from a motive, but quite often, form the failure to undertake the project of responsibility" (Bakhtin, 1990, p. 31).*

In the tradition of qualitative research, it is widely accepted that elements of the researcher's experience may add relevant information to the qualitative inquiry (Gale, 1991; Rennie, 1992, 1994, 1996; Seidman, 1991). It would be dishonest to escape a reflective practice on my own processes. I give an extract of my experience of completing this research process. The journal I have written has been the motor for my work. It has been a way to keep my sanity, a motivation to continue this project. I have documented elements in my journal that I then considered futile. They later became relevant.

This research has been a transforming experience. Before I started several doctors in Psychology scared me. They warned me that I could lose my marriage over that work. They warned me of the possibly destructive effect of this research haunting your mind like a spider. I never took these warnings seriously. It did not happen to me. What they meant maybe is that a research of this amplitude is perhaps a micro life lesson, perhaps even closer than we think to good psychotherapy. For me, this research process has been for the most part a passionate and fascinating endeavor. Throughout the whole process, I have managed to maintain, and even to enhance my growing interest and fascination for reflexivity and the subject of reflection-in-action.

I have used RIA in my daily practice. It has become contagious to many colleagues. Clinicians who have read my drafts gave me the best compliments and the most validation for this research. They shared the positive effect it had on their practice. They shared the contagious effect of their growing reflexivity. I have loved and cherished this process, more than I have ever hated it. It has been an enriching path. It took me a hundred miles away from where I thought I might go.

The journey into this qualitative inquiry has not been a picnic party. The pain I experience divorcing the good method, I was taught. I have had much difficulty of distancing myself from the "should" (also called introjects in the jargon) these implicit or explicit "ought to, should" that guide and frame the way I think. I spend a long time asking myself whether I could even start to question some of the assumptions about science that I took in as "reality". I want to challenge these "realities", so that they keep their status of approximation, theoretical construction of the reality.

I freeze. I have often faced painful inaction. I experience anguish, in front of the blank paper. This frozen stage looks like depression. I torture myself with ideas that keep freezing and constraining me. I imagine myself plagued by a critical audience. The most critical dissertation committee resides in my head. It judges everything I am about to think and say. Within the field of qualitative research, there is a tradition of reporting directly on these feelings (Kvale, 1996; Mc Leod, 1994; Toukmanian, 1992; Yin, 1989; Wolcott, 1990). Along with these authors, I have certainly experienced the unpleasant part of qualitative research:

> "Several of the symposium contributors document the anguish, conflict, anxiety, despair, and other varieties of personal turmoil that can accompany research of this kind: the personal challenge of qualitative research can be substantial." (Mc Leod, 1996, p. 312)

## "Legal alien unauthorized to work"

Before I start writing, a massive anxiety, which is one of my strongest features under stress, literally freezes me when I think about this dissertation. The anxiety increases with other external factors of uncertainty, following my thesis's choice: changing countries, home, habits, language. In Houston, Texas, I stay in the anguish. I avoid writing. I avoid my computer. I excel at convincing myself that it is way beyond what I am able to do. I repeat like a litany: "I cannot do that." I blush every time, a colleague, learning that I am a doctoral student, shows interest about conducting a "European" dissertation. I feel shame and self-blame often when I think about this dissertation. I blame myself for freezing. I mock this whole neurotic labyrinth. I have come to the USA especially for this dissertation. I am not doing it. I can already imagine the complete disappointment of my friends and the one that I am projecting onto my director. He has given me a fantastic opportunity and I waste it. I cannot stand the thought of it. What a complete failure! Welcome into the so-much-hated land of procrastination. I judge myself hard and abusively.

Following the well-known principle of the paradoxical theory of change (Beisser, 1970) these critiques and intrusive thoughts fade away as I allow them to appear on this piece of paper. They are in the back seat now. I breathe more freely. They do not govern me. I am more in charge. I just shut them down by allowing them to be. I am amazed. I am relieved. I have made one more attempt to shut down the destructive critique. I know by now I never will. Self-doubts and self-critiques will always be a part of me wherever I go, whatever I do. This is a fine feature, I guess, that keeps me within the boundaries of reflexivity. Self-doubts are the drive that brought me this far. I learn to tame them so that they do not become destructive. They always haunt me at the core of my vulnerabilities. That is fine.

What I do not see at that time is that I am planting the seeds of my research. Looking back, the research project started before. The seeds mature slowly. They create roots for strong ideas to emerge later. In Houston, I complete a research project in the field of Family Therapy with Harlene Anderson. I observe the process and learn what I like and what I do not want to reproduce. I learn. Then, I move back to California in September of 1999. In Santa Monica, California, I am back on a very restricted budget. I live on the few savings accumulated during my three years back in Switzerland. I am reminded of uncertainty, daily, physically, I feel the lack of safety, the vulnerability of my position: "legal alien unauthorized to work". I am allowed to stay only at the boundaries, not to participate. I long for belonging. Yet, I get so used to being an outsider. I live in a dark, smaller than small humid and rather insalubrious single apartment, in the middle of a paradisiacal city. That is what my husband and I can afford at this time. Without an income or a working visa, I feel like a pariah. I am immobilized and gagged. I feel hopeless.

I console myself with the close access to a spectacular beach. The financial and acculturation issues have a tremendous impact on my mood. My sense of basic safety is shaken. What is the space in which I can freely allow myself to study? What is the space left in my brain, as I constantly obsess on: "how I am going to make it to the end of this research"? How am I going to avoid the invitation of insanity in this tiny and dark studio for two doctoral students? How do I make sense? How do I belong? Where do I belong? In that financial constraint, the choice of the United States adds a significant problem. I cannot fight. I do not hold the keys to change my current situation. I cannot even wait tables because of the visa. My non-immigrant visa proudly announces my desperate status of a "legal alien unauthorized to work" (*sic*).

Again, I find, I have resilience. Instead of sinking in the abyss of depression, I start writing, like a maniac. I write with my earplugs in, most of the day, to isolate myself from any noise annoyances since the building is not insulated at all. I write. I write and I run. Running is almost like an incantation. It is has a long history of success, of a forbidden, impossible activity. I started running at the age of twenty-five. Before, I thought I *could* not run, not even a few steps. It was an impossibility. I suffered from asthma during my childhood. That narrative of a sick and rather overweight child has defined me. I knew that I could not run.

At twenty-five, I suddenly feel the urge to try the forbidden and dangerous activity, to run against all predictions. It was the day, I found myself for the first time in the mystic megalopolis of L.A. I ran. I remember the feeling of flying. I can still re-live today this sense of exhilaration, power, and mastery. This was my little miracle. I did something I never thought I could. Now, I can. With the dissertation process, I start talking myself into running again. I want to run more. I want to run past my limit. The equation is simple: If I can train for the impossible a full marathon, I stand a chance to complete this dissertation.

So I write and I run. My stamina is high. My brain is clear. It is easy to focus. I feel alive. I drug myself with endorphin. I feel young, beautiful, energetic, and strong. I challenge myself, physically, emotionally, and intellectually. I complete the marathon on March 5th 2000. I shall remember this day forever. It was the day of my thirty-third birthday. I run the marathon, under pouring rain. The news says: "That is the worst storm of the year, for the LA marathon's runner". Never, have I seen that much rain in Los Angeles. I do not care about the rain. All I care about for that day is running. So I run. One foot after the other, I keep running to the final line. That is it. I have completed this marathon. All it took was putting one step at a time, one in front of the other and a lot of strong will and commitment. Discipline and commitment are the best allies of success. I discover again that my mind is strong. I can succeed great things. Now I can move on with the dissertation.

## Rite of Passage

Trying to belong to academic community and to be recognized as "intellectually fit" is a challenge. Becoming part of the academy is like joining a family. More or less functional, but a family with rites, loyalties, hierarchies, traditions, and rules (explicit and implicit ones). It is not familiar for me to belong. It is something I have longed for. I have run away from it too as it scares me. I have a history of being an outsider. I now cherish this status that allows me much freedom and flexibility. Through my immigration process, in my personal life, in my professional life, I have been familiar with this status of an outsider. I joke about where I belong. In Los Angeles, I belong to different professional communities: the Gestalt Therapist, I proudly announce: "I am a Family Therapist" and claim my love for the work of Milton Erickson (Erickson 1962; Erickson, Rossi & Rossi 1976; Erickson & Rossi, 1979). To the Family Therapists, I am known as having an extensive training in Gestalt Therapy. Belonging has been an alien concept for me. This doctorate is a rite of passage. The doctorate represents a long accomplishment. It is then evaluated to see if it is acceptable to the academy, if it belongs there. I am worried and scared. Of course, I chose a qualitative inquiry, which is still largely an uncommon way of doing research. I have the extra "handicap" of my femininity. The institution of knowledge has been for centuries a masculine sanctuary. To this date, the University of Lausanne only reports a few women in all its Faculties.

In the frozen stage of my research, I constrain myself with questions such as: What should research look like? What creates scientific knowledge? What are the criteria for scientificity? The answers I then give to these questions are constantly in my disfavor. These questions keep me from being in a creative place. I project expectation outside instead of taking a stance, where I claim: "This is what I know. This is what I believe in. This is what I am searching for. This is what I am interested in. This is the method I choose to use to explore this subject". I need to thank Polkinghorne (1991a) for a particularly illuminating quote that keep me going:

> "Doing science does not mean a different way of thinking or the use of special cognitive skill. (...) What differentiates scientific knowing from ordinary knowing is its deliberate and communal dimensions. Doing science is a purposeful and self-conscious activity: science involves a methodical effort to correct and refine the initial understanding until it clearly fits experience" (p. 175).

I relate to this notion of doing science, as an "extension of an ordinary process" (Polkinghorne, 1991a) with an addition of rigor, and methodical effort, until I approach a "good-enough" definition (Sterlin, 1987). In that process of divorcing the introjects of science, I would never find the courage to question such a powerful institution on my own. I want to thank the authors who helped me on this path. My voice discovered some echo with Polkinghorne, Kvale, Danzinger, and Bakan. I felt less isolated. I owe a lot to those who taught me how to be respectfully irreverent toward science and knowledge.

I find it difficult to be an outsider in the institution of knowledge. It feels less lonely to be part of a group of outsiders. The outsider position is not an incensed, counter-political, and deliberate choice on my part. Some questions are best addressed by qualitative methodologies. I remember a Jungian psychoanalyst telling me one day: "Whatever you research, you bring forth your life questions to the front stage". It made much sense. I find this statement to be true. Infusing reflexivity in my dissertation is a never-ending story. I welcome reflexivity in the process, and the reflexive process of this process and the reflexive process of this reflexive process and so on, until a bad headache stops me. I cherish almost like a mantra this fantastic quote of Bakhtin (1990) during my dissertation's process:

> "Relativism and dogmatism are two sides of the same coin."(p. 26)

Let me reflect on reflexivity. I can prudently say something about the importance of reflexivity in my life. As far as I can remember I have always wanted to comprehend why people behave the way they do. What could prevent somebody from falling into the chains of dogma, or into the abyss of relativism? Will I be able to keep learning and changing without being trapped by the questions? How will I be able to hold this balance? What will it take to continue to question the obvious? I can say something about how reflexivity keeps me alive. Early on in my life, I discover the taste for the uncertain, the questions, the complex and the ambiguous. I fear dogma and its unwearying righteousness. Reflexivity, I believe is a strong instrument that prevents all forms of dogma, because it inserts doubts. Doubt is movement and aliveness. There is no faith without doubt. Doubt and uncertainty are powerful forces maintaining movement and discovering. This human capacity to remove oneself while in action and to have a broader access to awareness and choices is one of my life interests. Reflexivity is, I believe one of the most powerful tools to approach difference.

Banister (1981) shares the importance and the personal relevance of the subject in the process of writing a thesis:

> "The quality of reflexivity has many implications for research method. It implies the questions involved in the research should have personal meaning and significance for you. Thus, because so-called scientific issues cannot ultimately be separated from personal issues since, as they are manifest within you, they are part of your *personal* construct system. It makes no more sense to inquire into trivial, conventional and institutionally provided issues in your work as psychologist that it would make sense to inquire into such issues in your personal life. If a question has no seriousness for you, why should you expect other people to take seriously the answers you provide for it? Thus, in turn, implies that personal experience is a rich and relevant source from which to derive, and in terms of which to argue psychological issues. Personal experience is no more a subjective, chaotic, anecdotal nonsense in relation to science, than it is in relation to life"
> (p. 194).

# Nothing stands still…

When I look back at my former interest, early on, as a pre-graduate student at the University of Lausanne, Switzerland, I can trace back this interest. There is nothing that has provoked more enjoyment and distress than traveling from the class of Anthropology to the one of Sociology, and back to the class of Psychology. I was facing different truths. Learning about different cultures, tastes, looks, values, ways of approaching reality caught my interest very early on. Learning to tolerate, to stand uncertainty has been a challenge. My childhood did not teach me to live in uncertainty. I have a whole culture, a set of prejudices to challenge. I continuously wonder about what is the effect of my questions, attitudes, role, statement, absence of statement, and position, on others. I modulate my being to approach the other according to the way I would want to be approached. That method works well. It even was formalized through religion: "Do unto others, what you would like others to do unto you". It is in this very insecure, doubtful stage of uncertainty, where nothing stands still that knowledge really moves and advances. The challenge is to keep the balance. It is important to maintain the equilibrium between an extreme form of relativism, where no stance is taken and a dogmatic posture. In a dogmatic posture, there is no possibility to transgress, question, challenge, and move beyond, because every statement and idea is rigidified.

The exercise of a dissertation, a painful and structuring discipline influences my sense of being in the world. I learn to enjoy the journey, rather than to long for the end result. I learn to love and live in the ever-changing moment of my life. Anxiety comes in when I start projecting myself to the final product, without ever having a sense of what this product may look like. When I lose my ground, it is frequently because I project myself into the future. Therefore, I lose track of where I am. This has been a grounding exercise. I learned to live the process day-by-day, as a process, for the sake of researching and exploring, rather than for the sake of achieving something. This discovery of a journey rather than a goal has an immense value to me, intellectually and affectively. It has been a powerful life lesson.

The hardest part of the process has been to continually give up the idea of discovering truth, or uncovering the covered. I reflect on how often this invitation has nagged me, throughout the research. The hard part was to give up the control I want to have over this research process, I have to accept (sometimes "bear with" would be more appropriate) never knowing what the final box will look like. The challenge and the excitement lie in tolerating and taming the uncertainty, and the unknown. I have the same struggle with daring to construct a methodology that fits my object. I read Danzinger (1990) and feel inspired:

> "Investigative practice therefore constitutes an area of considerable anxiety within the discipline of psychology. Concern with questions of methodological orthodoxy often takes the place of concern about theoretical orthodoxy when research or its results are discussed and evaluated. These preoccupations with the purity of method frequently deteriorate to a kind of method fetishism, or "methodolatry". From this point of view there may be something profoundly subversive about the

> suggestion that the sphere of methodology is not a realm of pure reason, but an area of human social activity governed by mundane circumstances like any social activity." (p. 5)

I am often surprised at the force that draws me (maybe most of us?) to certainty. I am sometimes discouraged by how little I can stand uncertainty. That makes me think about the people who sink into Fundamentalism or Dogmatism. The not-knowing position (Anderson 1993a, 1993b, 1997, Goolishian & Anderson 1988b, 1990b, 1988b) is a scary place to be. Western individuals have less tolerance for ambiguity:

> "Thinking about the legitimacy of what I think I know and what others think they know is never far from my mind. It may be ethical, but it is often exhausting. A little certainty sometimes would be such a relief!" (Speed, 1999, p.137)

If I nourish the fantasy of overcoming positivism, I still operate often under a positivist paradigm. Thinking that I was going to discover "something" indicates this influence. To the findings of truths, I prefer the notion of co-creating knowledge. Knowledge is defined by several as a "social consensus" (Gergen, 1991a 1991b, 1994; Lyotard, 1979; Kvale 1993; Mc Namee & Gergen, 1999). Defining knowledge as a social consensus challenges the restricted scientific notion of knowledge. This choice has profound implications: It changes the dialectic between researcher and research. I look at "the other" (previously called the "subject" of research) as a co-researcher. If reality is created in the social interchange, I then question the notions of research such as: neutrality, distance, dualism subject-object, databases, objectivity, validity, variables.

## To whom I owe what

My ideas do not emerge from a vacuum. During the course of my thesis, my ideas have been co-constructed with others friends, colleagues, patients. My ideas are challenged and transformed by others in conversations. These conversations create a slight difference within my ideas and create "a difference that makes a difference" (Bateson, 1972). Ideas start forming as I speak, an utterance becomes an idea (Vygotsky, 1986). As large as my awareness permits, I give credit to those who influenced my ideas. I hope my awareness is broad enough. A dissertation is always a collaborative effort among scholars. I sign this book as the author and I take responsibility for these ideas, but the emergence of these ideas was created in a relational context that is broader than me.

## About the personal relevance of writing

I used to claim repeatedly that I would not do a thesis. It is too much work and I feared not to be able to sustain my focus on the same subject for that long. I did not want to waste the splendid years of my life working on a project that may never be accepted. I also know myself as a "doer". I like to work from project to project and have professionally a sense of accomplishment. I like to see the effect of my project. The idea of a thesis initially did not appeal to me for these reasons. I hated the idea having to sit in front of a computer or in Libraries for hours and days, for such an obscure outcome. I was wrong. This process has been one of the most exciting journeys I have ever made. It has been a life-transforming process. I have pushed myself to and beyond my limits. I have brought meaning into my life. I have reached mastery instead of sinking in what Erick Erickson refers to as stagnation. I have learned to rely on and to trust myself, even in the hardest doubts, even in the heart of anguish. I have always enjoyed the creative act of writing. Writing has a therapeutic function for me. As I think about it, writing is by essence a reflexive activity. I have always enjoyed writing. Writing as the action of speech has a clarifying function. From blurred and inchoate my ideas become clearer through writing.

I started thinking about this project of a thesis, when I start thinking about reflection-in-action. I do not recall exactly how this concept dawned on me. I remember the excitement and the liveliness linked to the topic. I remember so many clinicians discouraging me. The project is too ambitious, too vast, too poorly defined. This is not a good-enough topic for a dissertation project or for that matter for a book. My rebellious side was just more interested and wanting to go forward. I started developing a true fascination for the present subject. How do clinicians think in action? What is in their mind as they work? How do they formalize their work? I knew at that time, that with this subject I could maintain this fascination for long enough to finish the thesis and much longer.

Mentoring is another essential part of a dissertation process. This has been emotionally a strong component of my decision to complete this present book. My professor plays the role of a mentor for me. I feel that this work would be a nice form of "giving back". I feel privileged to have a professor who let me be free. Freedom creates anxiety. Looking back, I would never have done this research project with a controlling professor. If I had to give a strict plan of my dissertation at the onset I would never been able to do the work I did. I chose the subject of my research and most of my journey was a solitary one. At times, I have hated that freedom. I have resented my professor for the absence of support. I have felt anxious and vulnerable. I felt often, I was going crazy. Overall, I feel profoundly thankful for this distant mentoring. It takes trust to rely on students like that. I want to honor this trust. On my own, I have learned to trust my judgment enough to be able to set the boundaries around my work on my own. I have learned to tolerate the tension of the anxiety to move forward in knowledge, through further questioning. I also know that this work is mine. I have leaned that I am able to correct, edit, and modify on my own.

When I start anticipating cross-references and authors citations I rejoice. I realize that I am becoming an insider in the field of qualitative research. From the stuckness that I have described earlier, I now experience passion, and an intense creativity. My ground is more solid. My ideas take form. I start making sense in the over all organization of my text.

I remember the first stages. They frightened me. I frightened myself. When I try to gather information and reactions from clinicians at social gatherings to prepare myself for the interview process. I remember the embarrassing hesitancies. I remember the strength and courage it took to try repeatedly to explore this subject. I certainly remember the constant struggle with my inner doubts and panics: the subject is too ambitious, too poorly defined, and not "scientific" enough. I remember also the immense passion and involvement for the RIA. The feeling that it is worth introducing this concept to our field has kept me going. The struggle is worth it. The confusion, the pain and the constant uncertainty has gently transformed into a comfortable stage of not knowing. I now have a clear sense of what I am looking for and what is outside of the scope of this research. I move on with ease and eagerly look forward to having several hours ahead of me to pursue my project. I am confident. I know I will follow through with this project. It is worth the effort.

Until very late in the process, I have felt unstable and insecure. When I find my ground, I discover it is one in perpetual movement. I have learned to live with the dizziness and excitement created by an evolving and moving ground.

# Appendix 1

I have gathered over the years of my practice of psychotherapy a list of helpful guidelines that assist me in respecting an honoring clients/patients and the sacredness of our clients' story. I wish to offer here my list of « mantra » for therapist. They address the three concepts I have explained in the conclusion chapter and illustrate them in action: Reflexivity, positioning and ethics-in-practice.

## MANTRA FOR THERAPISTS

1) Honor the client' s pace, rhythm and timing.

2) Do not go faster than the client.

3) Do not assume that the client has understood or agreed check it out.

4) Avoid intentionally or unwittingly disqualifying client's stories by premature understanding.

5) Check with the client to see if they had an opportunity to say what they wanted to say at least one time per session.

6) Use outcome-measure to control the quality of your work with clients. (Boss scale, Helping alliance questionnaire, Miller's scale of therapeutic alliance, 2004…)

7) Check with the client to see if you have heard and not misunderstood what they have said.

8) Give to the clients a chance to correct any misunderstandings that they may have developed, and to clarify and expand on what they have told you.

9) Avoid premature assumptions.

10) Prefer lateral interactions to hierarchical ones.

11) Learn the unique sense that each client makes of his or her own illness and its circumstances.

12) Be willing to let go of early assumptions and stereotyping thoughts.

13) Be willing to challenge yourself and be challenged.

14) Maintain coherence with the language, vocabulary and metaphors of clients.

15) Use cooperative and positive language, a language that invites client into a conversation with you.

16) Remember your questions always have an intent they communicate something about you and what you think (Tomm, 1988).

17) Remember your questions will shape the future conversations.

18) The questions you ask and the ones you do not ask influence the construction of the clients' answer and their narratives.

19) Use a cooperative and positive language that invites clients into a conversation.

20) There are many possible versions of a patient's illness and wellness; circumstance, context, and you, the listener, influence the telling.

21) Try to interact and respond to when the client asks for your response. If not you create resistance.

22) Actions speak sometimes louder than words, as the proverb says.

23) Invites clients to tell about their inner concerns, what it is like for them.

24) Think of yourself (as a therapist) as a momentary guest in the life of my clients. I am not familiar with them, with their lifestyles, or their context and the history of their pain and turmoil.

# Informed Consent for the Clients

## *(Interviews with the expert therapists)*

August 9, 2000

Dear client,

This study is part of a doctoral dissertation with the University of Lausanne, Switzerland. The goal of the study is to enhance and deepen the understanding of how professionals think "in action". In other words, how a therapist chooses to intervene. How can I therefore, as a researcher, approach what one calls in the profession "the clinical judgment"? Ultimately, this research aims at two major goals:

- To improve the services and the quality of psychotherapy by refining its understanding.

- To improve the training of the beginners therapists by helping them understand how expert therapist thinks.

I am also a psychologist and a psychotherapist. (In my country, Switzerland, one becomes a licensed psychologist before completing a Doctorate in Psychology).

The tape of the session will be used as a support for interviewing your therapist. The research interview will be conducted in your therapist's office right after your therapy session. Your therapist and I shall review the content of the tape (after your session) and I will stop the audiotape at some points to ask your therapist "what just happened?"

<u>Your Rights</u>

a) If you choose to participate voluntarily to this research, I wish to thank you.

b) I want you to know that you are free to decline being part of the study and to withdraw at any time. After the session, if you change your mind you can always ask your therapist to give you back the tape or to destroy it. Your decision will in no way affect your status as a client.

c) The tape will only be recorded one time. The focus of the research will not be on your comment it will be essentially on the therapist's interventions.

d) Your comments will be used to respect confidentiality. Any names, places or identifiable data will be transformed in order to maintain your privacy, they will not appear in the final publication.

e) The tapes are kept in a safe place in my home. After the dissertation, I will destroy them as well as any file, or computer disk containing this information.

f) I will be the only person to access those data, listen to the tape, and transcribe part of them.

If you would like to meet or talk with me before making your final decision, or even after, you are more than welcome to do so. You don't have to. If you have questions or comments, you are welcome to reach me at the following addresses.

I also welcome further comments on your part after the end of the process.

I have read the consent form and discussed the content and any concern that I have with the researcher.

| ______________________ | ______________ |
|---|---|
| (Client's signature) | (Date) |
| ______________________ | ______________ |
| (Therapist's signature) | (Date) |
| ______________________ | ______________ |
| (Researcher's signature) | (Date) |

<u>Researcher:</u>

Fabienne Kuenzli
Valley Child Guidance Clinic
310 E. Palmdale Blvd., Suite G
Palmdale, CA 93550

Phone (office):
Phone (home):

Facsimile:

Thank you again.

____________________
Researcher's signature

# Informed Consent
## *(Interviews at the Training Institute)*

May 9, 2000

Dear Colleague,

First of all, I would like to thank you. This year of training with you has been an enriching experience. I thank you for being open to participate with me in this ongoing inquiry, which is to approach and thicken the definition of reflection-in-action. This study is part of a doctoral dissertation with the University of Lausanne, Switzerland. The goal of the study is to enhance and deepen the understanding of how professionals think "in action". How a therapist chooses to intervene? How can I therefore, as a researcher, approach what one calls in the profession "the clinical judgment"? Ultimately, this research aims at two major goals

- To improve the services and the quality of psychotherapy by refining its understanding.

- To improve the training of beginning therapists by helping them understand how expert therapists think.

I have recorded the audiotape, with your permission will be used as a support to show how reflection-in-action takes place, while doing therapy. The quasi simultaneity of this exercise was made unique, thanks to your willingness to open up and to collaborate in this inquiry, as well as for the courage it takes to show your thinking and your work in action. I also thank the trainers for offering this very unique setting and being willing to participate to this research project.

You have options regarding how you wish to have your information used. If there are any options, I am not thinking of, please, add them below.

**Please underline the proposition(s) that fit(s) for you.**

a) I would like the information I have shared as a therapist to be used for the purpose of the qualitative inquiry.

b) I would like my name as a therapist to be mentioned as well as my background:
(Please write down how you would like to be introduced if you have any specific wish)

c) I don't mind that you use the information I have shared as a therapist, but I do **not** want my name to be mentioned. (If this is the case all therapist's names will be removed from the text).

In any case, the name of the clients will be changed.

## Your Rights.

a) If you choose to participate voluntarily to this research, I first wish to thank you.

b) I want you to know that you are free to decline being part of the study and to withdraw at any time. If you change your mind, you can always ask the researcher to remove the information you've given.

c) The focus of the research will be essentially on the therapist's interventions.

d) **Your comments, as a client will be used to respect confidentiality.** Any names and most possible identifiable data will be transformed in order to maintain your privacy, they will not appear in the final dissertation. Even though, given the context it is impossible to remove all the identifiable data, since the group is not a large size group.

e) The tapes are kept in a safe place in my home. After the dissertation, I will destroy them as well as any file, or computer disk containing this information.

f) I will be the only person to access those data and listen to the tape and transcribe part of them.

I would enjoy very much your feedback on your participation to my research, if you have any. (Please use the back of this form to add any additional comments.

<u>My reaction to this research is:</u>

<u>My advice to you is:</u>

a) I have feedback and I would rather them **not to be added** the research

b) I have feedback and comments and am happy for them to be added in the research.

If you would like to meet or talk with me before making your final decision, or even after, you are more than welcome to do so. You don't have to. If you have questions or comments, you are welcome to reach me at the following addresses.

I also welcome further comments on your part after the end of the process. If you wish to receive a summary of the final research please write here your name and address or e-mail address.

I have read the consent form and discussed the content and any concern that I have with the researcher.

________________________ _______________

(Interviewee's signature) (Date)

________________________ _______________

(Researcher's signature) (Date)

# Bibliography

Agar, M. (1980). The professional stranger: an informal introduction to ethnography. New York: Academy Press.

Allman, L. (1982). The aesthetic preference. Family Process. Vol. 21, pp. 43-56.

Andersen, T. (1995). Reflecting processes acts if informing and forming: You can borrow my eyes, but you must not take them away from me! In Friedman, S. (Ed.) The reflecting team in action. New York: Guilford.

Andersen, T. (Ed.) (1987). The reflecting team: Dialogues and meta-dialogue in clinical work. Family Process. Vol. 26, pp. 415-428.

Andersen, T. (Ed.) (1991). The reflecting team: Dialogues and dialogues about dialogues. New York: Norton.

Anderson, H & Goolishian, H. A. (1988a). Les systèmes humains comme systèmes linguistiques: implications pour une théorie clinique. (Vander Borgh, C.& Goldbeter, E. Trans). Cahiers critiques de thérapies et de pratiques de réseaux. Constructivisme et constructionisme social. Vol. 19, pp. 99-132.

Anderson, H. & Goolishian, H. (1988b). Human systems as linguistic systems: preliminary and evolving ideas about the implications of clinical theory. Family Process. Vol. 23, pp. 371-394.

Anderson, H. & Goolishian, H. A. (1990). Supervision as collaborative conversation: questions and reflections. Von der supervision zur systemischen vision. Salzburg: Otto Muller Verlag. (Unpublished document).

Anderson, H. & Goolishian, H. A. (1991a). Thinking about multi-agency work with substance abusers and their families: A language systems approach. Journal of Strategic and Systemic Therapies. Vol. 10, no 1, pp. 20-36.

Anderson, H. (1993a). A collaborative language system approach to therapy: toward a postmodern systems therapy. In Mikesell, R., Lusterman, D. D. & Mc Daniel, C. (Eds.) Family Psychology and System Theory. Washington: American Psychological Association Press.

Anderson, H. (1993b). On a roller coaster: a collaborative language system approach to therapy. In Friedman, S. (Ed.) The new language of change. New York: Guilford.

Anderson, H. (1996). A reflection on client-professional collaboration. Families, systems & Health. Vol. 14, no 2, pp. 193-206.

Anderson, H. (1997). Conversations, language and possibilities. A postmodern approach to therapy. Basic Books.

Anderson, H. (1998). Collaborative learning communities. In Mc Namee, S. & Gergen, K. J. (Eds.) Realities and relationships, soundings in social construction. Newbury Park: Sage, pp. 65-70.

Anderson, H. (1999). Reimagining Family Therapy: reflections on Minuchin's invisible Family. Journal of Marital and Family Therapy. Vol. 25, no 1, pp. 521-528.

Anderson, T., Ogles, B. M., & Weis, A. (1999). Creative Use of Interpersonal Skills in Building a Therapeutic Alliance. Journal of Constructivist Psychology. Vol. 12, pp. 313-330.

Argyris, C. & Schön, D. A. (1974). Theory in practice. Increasing professional effectiveness. San Francisco: Jossey-Bass.

Atkinson, B. Heath, A. (1990). Further thoughts on second-order Family Therapy. Family Process. Vol. 29, no 2, pp. 145-155.

Atkinson, B. Heath, A. (1990). The limits of explanation and evaluation. Family Process. Vol. 29, no 2, pp. 164-167.

Atkinson, B., Heath, A. & Chenail, R. (1991). Qualitative research and the legitimization of knowledge. Journal of Marital and Family Therapy. Vol. 17, no 2, pp. 175-180.

Bachelor, A. & Horvath, A. (1999). In Hubble, M. Mark, L., Duncan, A. et al. (Eds.) The heart and soul of change. What works in therapy? American Psychological Association, pp. 133-178.

Baddeley, A. (1997). Human Memory: Theory and practice. (Revised Edition). Boston: Allyn and Bacon.

Bakan, D. (1967). On method: Toward a reconstruction of psychological investigation. San Francisco: Jossey-Bass.

Bakhtin, M. (1981). The dialogic imagination. (Emerson, C. & Holquist, M. Trans.). Austin: University of Texas Press.

Bakhtin, M. (1990). Creation of prosaic. (Morson, G. S. & Emerson, C. Trans.). Stanford: University Press.

Baldwin, M. & Satir, V. (1987). The use of the self in therapy. New York, London: Hayworth Press.

Bannister, D. (1981). Personal construct theory and research method. In Reason, P. and Rowan, J. (Eds.) Human inquiry. New York: Wiley and Sons, pp. 191-225.

Baron-Cohen, S. Tager-Flusberg, H. & Cohen, D. J. (2000). (Eds.) Understanding other minds: perspectives from developmental cognitive neuroscience. New York: Oxford University Press.

Bateson, G. (1972). Steps to an ecology of mind. New York: Ballantine Books.

Baudrillard, J. (1970). La société de consommation, ses mythes, ses structures. Paris: Gallimard, (SGPP, Série: Le Point de la question).

Baudrillard, J. (1986). Amérique. Paris: Grasset.

Baudrillard, J. (1998). Car l'illusion ne s'oppose pas à la réalité. Paris: Descartes et Cie.

Baudrillard. J. (1977). Oublier Foucault. Paris: Galillée. (Série: Collection: L' espace critique).

Beisser, A. R. (1970). The paradoxical theory of change. In Fagan, S. A. & Shepherd, I. L. (Eds.) Gestalt Therapy Now. Science and Behavior Books, pp. 77-80.

Bennett-Levy, J. (2003). Reflection: a blind spot in psychology? Clinical Psychology. Vol. 27, July, pp. 16-19.

Berg, I. K. & Miller, S. (1993). Working with the problem drinker. New York: Norton.

Berg, I. K. & Miller, S. (1995). The miracle method. A radically new approach to problem drinking. New York: Norton.

Bernstein, R. J. (1983). Beyond objectivism and relativism. Science, hermeneutics, and praxis. Philadelphia: University of Pennsylvania Press.

Bertalanffy, L. von (1968). General system theory: Foundations, developments, and applications. New York: Braziller.

Best, S. & Kellner, D. (1991). Postmodern theory. critical interrogations. New York: Guilford Press.

Beutler, L. E. (1990). Introduction to the special series on advances in psychotherapy process research. Journal of Consulting and Clinical Psychology. Vol. 58, no 3, pp. 263-264.

Beutler, L. E., Machado, P. P. & Neufeldt, S. A. (1994). Therapists' variables. In Bergin, A. E. & Garfield, S. L. (Eds.) Handbook of psychotherapy and behavior change. New York: Wiley & Sons, (4th ed.), pp. 229-269.

Bogdan, R. C. & Biklen, S. K. (1982). Qualitative research for education: An introduction to theory and methods. Boston: Allyn & Bacon.

Bograd, M. (1992). Values in conflict: Challenges to family therapist's thinking. Journal of Marital and Family Therapy. Vol. 18, no 3, pp. 245-256.

Bohart, A. C. (1999). Intuition and creativity in Psychotherapy. Journal of Constructivist Psychology. Vol. 12, pp. 287-311.

Bolton, G. (2001). Reflective Practice. Writing and professional development. London: Sage.

Bolton, G. (2003). Lift the box lid: reflective writing for professional development. Clinical Psychology. Vol. 27, July, pp. 34-38.

Bordin, E. S. (1979). The generalizability of the psychoanalytic concept of the working alliance. Psychotherapy, Research and Practice. Vol. 16, pp. 252-260.

Bordin, E. S. (1983). Supervision in counseling: Contemporary models of supervision: a working alliance based model of supervision. The Counseling Psychologist. Vol. 11, pp. 35-42.

Boscolo, L & Cornwell, M. (1989). Interview: Falling in Love with ideas, an interview with Luigi Boscolo. A. N. Z. Journal of Family Therapy. Vol. 10, pp. 97-103.

Boscolo, L. & Bertrando, P. (1992). The Reflexive loop of the past. present and future in systemic therapy and consultation. Family Process. Vol. 31, no 2, pp. 119-131.

Boyle, J. S. (1994). Styles of Ethnography. In Morse, J. M. (Ed.) Issues in qualitative research methods. Thousand Oaks, CA: Sage, pp. 159-201.

Breunlin, D. C., Schwarz, R. C., Krause, M. S. et al. (1983). Evaluating family therapist training: The Development of an instrument. Journal of Marital and Family Therapy. Vol. 9, no 1, pp. 37-47.

Brown, J. (1996). The I in science: Training to utilize subjectivity in research. Cambridge, MA: Scandinavian University Press.

Bruner, J. (1986). Actual minds, possible worlds. Cambridge: Harvard University Press.

Bruner, J. (1990). Acts of meaning. Cambridge: Harvard University Press.

Bryman, A. (1992). Quantitative & Qualitative Research: further reflections on their integration. In Brannen, J. (Ed.) Mixing methods: qualitative and quantitative methods. Avebury: Aldershot, pp. 57-78.

Burley, T. (1998). Minds and Brains for Gestalt Therapists. Gestalt Review. Vol. 2, no 2, pp. 131-142.

Burley, T. (2000). Awareness as an instrument. Gestalt Review. Vol. 4, no 1, pp. 46-63.

Butler, S. F. & Stupp, H. H. (1993). Effects of training experienced dynamic therapists to use a psychotherapy manual. In Miller, N. E. Luborsky, J. B., Barber, J. P. et al. (Eds.) Psychodynamic treatment research: A handbook for clinical practice. New York: Basic Books, pp. 191-210.

Byng-Hall, J. (1998). Evolving ideas about narrative: re-editing the re-editing about family mythology. Journal of Family Therapy. Vol. 20, pp. 133-141.

Cade, B. (1998). Honesty is still the best policy. Journal of Family Therapy. Vol. 20, no 2, pp. 143-152.

Cantwell, P. & Holmes, S. (1994). Social Construction: A paradigm shift for systemic therapy and training. Journal of Family Therapy. Vol. 15, no 1, pp. 17-26.

Carey, M. A. (1994). The Group effect in focus groups: Planning implementing, and interpreting focus group research. In Morse, J. M. (Ed.) Issues in qualitative research methods. Thousand Oaks, CA: Sage, pp. 225-241.

Casement, P. (1985). On learning from our patient. London: Tavistock.

Cavell, T. A. & Snyder, D. K. (1991). Iconoclasm versus innovation building a science of Family Therapy. Comments on Moon, Dillon, and Sprenkle. Journal of Marital and Family Therapy. Vol. 17, no 2, pp. 181-185.

Cecchin, G. (1987). Hypothesizing, circularity, and neutrality revisited: an invitation to curiosity. Family Process. Vol. 26, no 4, pp. 405-å413.

Cecchin, G. (1993). From strategizing to nonintervention: toward irreverence in systemic practice. Journal of Marital and Family Therapy. Vol. 32, no 2, p. 125-136.

Chenitz, W. C. & Swanson, J. M. (1986). From practice to grounded theory: Qualitative research in nursing. Menlo Park: Addison-Wesley.

Coltard, N. (1993). How to survive as a psychotherapist. London: Sheldon Press.

Comte, A. (1789-1857). Choix de textes et d'études du système philosophique, Hubert R. Paris: Louis Michaud (1927).

Comte, A. (1789-1857). La philosophie positive. (1911), 4 vol.

Comte, A. (1789-1857). Philosophie de Sciences. Auguste Comte. Textes choisis par Jean Laubier (1ère Ed.) Paris: Presses Universitaires de France, (1974).

Coyne, J. C. (1982). A brief introduction to epistobabble. Family Therapy Networker. Vol. 6, pp. 27-28.

Cozolino, L. (2002). The neuroscience of psychotherapy. Building and rebuilding the human brain. New York: Norton.

Creswell, J. W. (1998). Qualitative inquiry and research design: Choosing among five traditions. Thousands Oaks: Sage.

Damasio, A. (1994). Descartes' error: Emotion, reason and the human brain. New York: Avon Books.

Damasio, A. (1999). The feeling of what happens. San Diego: Harcourt Brace & Company.

Danziger, K. (1979). The social origin of modern psychology. In Buss, A. R. (Ed.) Psychology in a social context. New York: Irvington, pp. 26-45.

Danziger, K. (1990). Constructing the Subject: Historical Origins of Psychological Research. Cambridge, UK: Cambridge University Press.

Dell, P. & Goolishian, H. (1981). "Order through fluctuation": An evolutionary epistemology for human systems. Australian Journal of Family Therapy. Vol. 2, no 4, pp. 175-184.

Dell, P. (1982a). Beyond homeostasis. Toward a concept of coherence. Family Process. Vol. 21, pp. 21-41.

Dell, P. (1982b). Family theory and the epistemology of Humberto Maturana. Family Therapy Networker. July-August, pp. 23-40

Dell, P. (1985). Understanding Bateson and Maturana: Toward a biological foundation for the social sciences. Journal of Marital and Family Therapy. Vol. 11, pp. 1-20.

Dell, P. (1986). In defense of "lineal causality". Family Process. Vol. 25, pp. 513-521.

Dell, P. (1989). Violence and the systemic view: the problem of power. Family Process. Vol. 28, no 1, pp. 1-14.

Denzin, N. K. & Lincoln, Y. (1994) (Eds.) The handbook of qualitative research. Thousand Oaks, CA: Sage.

Denzin, N. K. (1978). The research act: A theoretical introduction to sociological method. (2nd ed.). New York: Mc Graw-Hill.

Derrida, J. (1967). L'écriture et la différence. Paris: Seuil.

De Shazer, S. (1991a). Putting difference to work. New York: Norton.

De Shazer, S. (1994b). Words were originally magic. New York: Norton.

Doherty, W. J. (1991). Family Therapy goes postmodern. Networker. September-October, pp. 37-42.

Dreyfus, H. L. & Dreyfus, S. E. (1988). Minds over Machine. New York: Free Press.

Drucquer, H. (2003). Lift the box lid: reflective practice writing, an example. Clinical Psychology. Vol. 27, July, pp. 39-41.

Duncan, B. L. Miller, S. D. & Sparks, J. A. (2004). The heroic client. San Francisco: Wiley & Sons.

Duriez, S. (1997). L'art d'échapper à Procuste ou la pratique du constructivisme. Constructivisme, mythologie et management. Cahiers critiques de thérapies et de pratiques de réseaux. Constructivisme et constructionisme social. Vol. 19, pp. 261-274.

Efran, J.S. & Clarfield, C.E. (1992). Constructionist therapy: Sense and nonsense. In McNamee, S. & Gergen, K. J. (Eds.) Therapy as Social Construction. London: Sage.

Eliott, R. (1986). Interpersonal process recall (IPR) as a psychotherapy process research method. In Greenberg, L. S. & Pinsof, W. M (Eds.) The psychotherapeutic process: a research handbook. New York: Guilford, pp. 503-527.

Elkaïm, M. (1997). Du constructivisme au constructionisme social: Un rappel historique. Cahiers critiques de thérapies et de pratiques de réseaux. Constructivisme et constructionisme social. Vol. 19, pp. 13-26.

Elkaïm, M., Prirogène, I., Stengers, I. & Denenbourg, J-L. (1982). Openness: A round-table discussion. Family Process. Vol. 21, no 1, pp. 57-70.

Epstein, E. K. (1993). From irreverence to irrelevance? The growing disjuncture of family therapy theories from social realities. Journal of Systemic Therapies. Vol. 12, no 3, pp. 15-27.

Erickson, G.D. (1988). Against the Grain: Decentering Family Therapy. Journal of Marital and Family Therapy. Vol. 14, no 3, pp. 225-236.

Erickson, M. H. (1962). The identification of a secure reality. Family Process. Vol. 1, no 2, pp. 294-303.

Erickson, M. H., Rossi, E. L. (1979). Hypnotherapy. An exploratory casebook. New York: Irvington.

Erickson, M. H., Rossi, E. L., Rossi, S. (1976). Hypnotic realities. An introduction of clinical hypnosis and forms of indirect suggestion. New York: Irvington.

Fisch, R., Weakland, J. H & Segal, L. (1982). The tactics of change. San Francisco: Jossey-Bass.

Flaskas, C. & Humphires, C. (1993). Theorizing about power: Intersecting the ideas of Foucault with the "problem" of power in family therapy. Family Process. Vol. 32, no 1, pp. 35-48.

Foucault, M. (1980). Power and knowledge: Selected interviews and other writings (1972-1977). (Gordon, C. et al. Trans). Brighton Sussex

Foucault. M. (1969). L'archéologie du savoir. Paris: Gallimard.

Foucault. M. (1972). L'histoire de la folie à l'âge classique. Paris: Gallimard.

Freud, S. (1856-1939). 1930. Cinq leçons sur la psychanalyse. (Lelay, Y. Trans.) Paris: Payot.

Friedman, S. (Ed.) (1995). The reflecting team in action: collaborative practice in family therapy. New York: Guilford.

Frosh, G. (1995). Postmodernism vs. psychotherapy. Journal of Family Therapy. Vol. 17, no 3, pp. 175-190.

Gadamer, H. G. (1975). Truth and method. New York: Seabury.

Gale, J. E. (1991). Conversation analysis of therapeutic discourse. The pursue of a therapeutic agenda. Norwood, NJ: Ablex.

Galley, F. & Droz, R. (1999). L'abandon des études universitaires. Des difficultés du métier d'étudiant. Suisse, FR: Editions Universitaires Programme National de Recherche, No 33.

Garfinkel, H. (1967). Studies in ethnomethodology. Englewood Cliffs, NJ: Prentice Hall.

Geertz, C. (1983). Local Knowledge. New York: Basic Books.

Gelso, C. J. (Ed.) (1984). Philosophy of science and counseling Research. Journal of Counseling Psychology. Vol. 31, pp. 415-476.

Gelso, C. J., Betz, N. E., Friedlander, M. L. et al. (1988). Research in counseling psychology: prospects and recommendations. The Counseling Psychologist. Vol. 16, pp. 385-406.

Gergen, K. J. & Kaye, J. (1992). Au-delà de la narration: la négociation du sens thérapeutique. (Trad. Fr. 1997). Cahiers critiques de thérapies et de pratiques de réseaux. Constructivisme et constructionisme social. Vol. 19, pp. 77-97.

Gergen, K. J. (1982). Toward transformation in social knowledge. New York: Springer-Verlag.

Gergen, K. J. (1985a). Theory of self: impasses and evolution. In Berkowitz, L. (Ed.) Advances in experimental social psychology. New York: Academic Press

Gergen, K. J. (1985b). The social constructionist movement in modern psychology. American Psychologist, Vol. 40, pp. 266-275.

Gergen, K. J. (1991a). The Saturated Self. New York: Basic Books.

Gergen, K. J. (1991b). The Saturated Family. Networker, September/October, pp. 26-45.

Gergen, K. J. (1994b). Realities and Relationships, soundings in social construction. Cambridge, MA: Harvard University Press.

Giddens, A. (1984). Hermeneutic and social theory. In Shapiro, G. & Sica, A. (Eds.) Hermeneutics: Questions and prospects. Amherst, MA: University of Masachusett Press.

Giddens, A. (1991). Modernity and self-identity. Self and society in the late modern age. Stanford, CA: Stanford University Press.

Gillmer, B. & Marckus, R. (2003). Personal professional development in clinical psychology training: surveying reflective practice. Clinical Psychology. Vol. 27, July, pp. 20-23.

Giorgi, A. (Ed.) (1985). Phenomenology and psychological research. Pittsburgh, PA: Duquesne University Press.

Goetz, J. P. & LeCompte, M. D. (1984). Ethnography and qualitative design in educational research. San Diego: Academic Press.

Golann, S. (1987). On description of family fherapy. Family Process. Vol. 26, no 3, pp. 331-340.

Golann, S. (1988). On second-order family therapy. Family Process. Vol. 27, pp. 51-65.

Goldbeter-Merinfeld, E. (1998) (Eds.) Constructivisme et constructionisme social: aux limites de la systémique. Cahiers critiques de la thérapie familiale et de pratique de réseaux. Vol. 19, no 2.

Goldner, V. (1985). Warning: Family therapy may be hazardous to your health. The Family Therapy Networker. Vol. 9, no 6, pp. 19-23.

Goodyear, R. K. & Nelson, M. L. (1997). The major formats of psychotherapy supervision. In Watkins, C. E. (Ed.) Handbook of psychotherapy supervision. New York: Wiley & Sons.

Goolishian, H & Anderson, H. (1992). Strategy and intervention versus nonintervention: a matter of theory. Journal of Marital and Family Therapy. Vol. 18, pp. 5-16.

Goolishian, H. (1991). The dis-diseasing of mental health. Plenary address presented at the Houston-Galveston Institute's Conference II. (Unpublished paper) San Antonio, Texas.

Grafanaki, S. (1996). How research can change the researcher: The need for sensitivity, flexibility and ethical boundaries in conducing qualitative research in counseling/psychotherapy. British Journal of Guidance and Counseling. Vol. 24, no 3, pp. 329-337.

Greenberg, L. S & Pinsof, W. M. (1986). Process research: Current trends and future perspectives. In Greenberg, L. S. & Pinsof, W. M. (Eds.) The psychotherapeutic Process. A Research handbook. New York: Guilford, pp. 3-20.

Greenberg, L. S. (1984a). A task analysis of interpersonal conflict resolution. In Rice, L. N. & Greenberg, L. S. (Eds.) Patterns of change: Intensive analysis of psychotherapy process. New York: Guilford, pp. 67-123.

Greenberg, L. S. (1984b). Task analysis: The general approach. In Rice, L. N. & Greenberg, L. S. (Eds.) Patterns of change: Intensive analysis of psychotherapy process. New York: Guilford, pp. 124-148.

Greenberg, L., Rice, L. & Elliott, R. (1993). Facilitating emotional change and the moment by moment process. New York: Guilford.

Guba, E. & Lincoln Y. S. (1981). Effective evaluation: Improving the usefulness of evaluation results through responsive and naturalistic approaches. San Francisco: Jossey-Bass.

Guba, E. & Lincoln Y. S. (1988). Do inquiry paradigms imply inquiry methodologies? In Fetterman, D. M. (Ed.) Qualitative approaches to evaluation in education. New York: Praeger, pp. 89-115.

Guba, E. & Lincoln Y. S. (1994). Competing paradigms in qualitative research. In Denzin, N. K. & Lincoln, Y. S. (Eds.) Handbook of qualitative research. Thousand Oaks, CA: Sage, pp. 105-117.

Gurman, A. S. & Kniskern, D. P. (1978). Technolatry, methodolatry, and the result of family therapy. Family Process. Vol. 17, no 4, pp. 275-281.

Gurman, A. S. (1983). Family therapy and the "new epistemology". Journal of Marital and Family Therapy. Vol. 9, no 3, pp. 227-234.

Haley, J. (1971). Family therapy: a radical change. In Haley, J. (Ed.) Changing families: a family therapy leader. New York: Grune & Stratton, pp. 272-284.

Haley, J. (1973). Uncommon therapy. New York: Norton.

Harré, R. (1981). The positivist-empiricist approach and its alternative. In Reason, P. & Rowan, J. (Eds.) Human inquiry. A sourcebook of new paradigm research. New York: Wiley & Sons, pp. 3-18.

Harré, R. (Ed.) (1986). The social construction of emotion. New York: Blackwell.

Heath, A. W., Mc Kenna, B. C. & Atkinson, B. J. (1988). Toward the identification of variables for evaluating family therapy workshops. Journal of Marital and Family Therapy. Vol. 14, no 3, pp. 267-276.

Heidegger, M. (1962). Being and Time. (Macquarrie, J. & Robinson, C. Trans.) New York: Harper and Row.

Held, B. & Pols, E. (1985). The confusion about epistemology and "Epistemology"- and what to do about it. Family Process. Vol. 24, no 4, pp. 507-522.

Held, B. (1990). What is in a name? Some confusions and concerns about constructivism. Journal of Marital and Family Therapy. Vol. 16, no 2, pp. 179-186.

Helmeke, K. B. & Sprenkle, D. H. (2000). Client's Perceptions of pivotal moments in couples therapy: A qualitative study of change in therapy. Journal of Marital and Family Therapy. Vol. 26, no 4, pp. 469-485.

Heritage, (1994). Garfinkel and ethnomethodology. London: Polity Press.

Heron, J. (1981). Philosophical basis for a new paradigm. In Reason, P. & Rowan, J. (Eds.) Human inquiry. A sourcebook of new paradigm research. New York: Wiley & Sons, pp. 19-35.

Hill, C. E. & Rhodes, R. H. & Thompson, B. J. (1996). Therapist Retrospective Recall of Impasses in Long-term Psychotherapy: a Qualitative Analysis. Journal of Counseling Psychology. Vol. 43, no 2, pp. 207-217.

Hill, C. E. (1984). A personal account of the process of becoming a counseling process researcher. The Counseling Psychologist. Vol. 12, no 3, pp. 99-109.

Hill, C. E. (1990). Exploratory in-session process research in individual psychotherapy: A review. Journal of Consulting and Clinical Psychology. Vol. 58, no 3, pp. 288-294.

Hill, C. E. (1991). Almost everything you ever wanted to know about how to do process research on counseling and psychotherapy but you didn't know whom to ask. In Watkins, E. C. & Schneider, J. (Eds.) Research in Counseling. Hillsdale, NJ: Erlbaum, pp. 85-118.

Hoffman, L (1990). Constructing realities. An Art of lenses. Family Process. Vol. 29, pp. 1-12.

Hoffman, L (1991). A Reflexive Stance for Family Therapy. Journal of Strategic and Systemic Therapy. Vol. 10, no 3-4, pp. 4-17.

Hoffman, L. (1981). Foundations of Family Therapy. New York: Basic Books.

Hoffman, L. (1997). La thérapie familiale sans modèle: retour vers la pratique. Cahiers critiques de thérapies et de pratiques de réseaux. Constructivisme et constructionisme social. Vol. 19, pp. 57-76.

Horvath, A. O. & Simons, B. D. (1991). Relation between working alliance and outcome in psychotherapy: a meta-analysis. Journal of Counseling Psychology, Vol. 38, pp. 139-149.

Horvath, A. O. (2001). The alliance. Psychotherapy. Vol. 38, no 4, pp. 365-372.

Hoshmand, L. T. & Polkinghorne, D. E. (1992). Redefining the Science-Practice relationship and Professional Training. American Psychologist. Vol. 47, no 1, pp. 55-66.

Hoshmand, L. T. (1989). Alternative research paradigms: a Review and Teaching Proposal. The Counseling Psychologist. Vol. 17, no 1, pp. 3-79.

Hoshmand, L. T. (1993). The personal narrative in the communal construction of self and life issues. In Neimeyer, G. J. (Ed.) Constructivist assessment: a casebook. (Counseling Psychologist Casebook Series). Thousand Oaks, CA: Sage, pp. 179-205.

Hoshmand, L. T. (1994). Supervision of a predoctoral graduate research: a practice-oriented approach. The Counseling Psychologist. Vol. 22, pp. 147-161.

Hubble, M. Mark, L. Duncan, A. et al. (1999). The heart and soul of change: What works in Therapy? American Psychological Association.

Husserl, E. (1913). Ideas: A general introduction to pure phenomenology. (Boyce Gibson, W. R. Trans. 1931) New York: Humanities Press.

Hutchinson, S. & Wilson, H. (1994). Research and therapeutic interviews: a poststructuralist perspective. In Morse, J. M. (Ed.) Issues in qualitative research methods. Thousand Oaks, CA: Sage, pp. 310-317.

Iacoboni, M., Woods R. P. Brass, M. et al. (1999). Cortical mechanism of human imitation. Science. Vol. 286, pp. 2526-2528.

Imber-Black, E. (1986). Maybe "lineal causality" needs another defense lawyer: A feminist response to Dell. Family Process. Vol. 25, no 4, pp. 523-525.

James, K. & Mac Intyre, D. (1983). The Reproduction of families: the social role of family therapy? Journal of Marital and Family Therapy. Vol. 9, no 2, pp. 119-129.

Jennings, L. & Skovholt, T. M. (1999). The cognitive, emotional, and relational characteristics of master therapists. Journal of Counseling Psychology. Vol. 46, no 1, pp. 3-12.

Johnson, S. M. & Greenberg, L. S. (1988). Relating process to outcome in marital therapy. Journal of Marital and Family Therapy. Vol. 14, no 2, pp. 175-183.

Kearney, R. (1988). The wake of imagination: ideas of creativity in western culture. London: Hutchinson.

Keeney, B. P. & Sprenkle, D. H. (1982). Eco-systemic epistemology: critical implications for the aesthetics or pragmatics of family therapy. Family Process. Vol. 21, no 1, pp. 1-19.

Keeney, B. P. (1983). Aesthetics of change. New York: Guilford.

Kelly, G. A. (1955). The Psychology of personal construct. (Vol. 1-2). New York: Norton.

Kniskern, D. P. (1983). The new Wave is all wet. Networker. July-August, pp. 56-60.

Kottler, J. A. & Carlson, J. (2003) The mommy at the dining room table. Emminent therapists reveal their most unusual cases. San Francisco: Jossey-Bass.

Kuenzli, A. (1996 b). Nothing stands still... Une introduction aux psychothérapies postmodernes. Mémoire de troisième cycle, Suisse: Université de Lausanne. (Unpublished paper).

Kuenzli, A. (2002). La critique postmoderne en action: Une orientation professionnelle au-delà de la négativité. Thérapie Familiale. Vol. 23, no 1, pp. 81-93.

Kuenzli-Monard, F. & Kuenzli, A. (1996 a). Postmodernism and psychotherapy. (Professional paper for the obtention of the Master of Art's Degree in the field of Marriage, Family and Child Therapy). Los Angeles, CA, (Unpublished paper).

Kuenzli-Monard, F. A. (1998). La violence domestique: On s'en sort. Un guide pas comme les autres, pour comprendre, mais surtout pour agir. (Unpublished paper).

Kuenzli-Monard, F. A. & Kuenzli, A. (1999). Une différence fait-elle la différence? Le reflecting team comme partie intégrante d'une pratique thérapeutique. Thérapie Familiale. Vol. 10, no 1, pp. 23-39.

Kuenzli-Monard, F. A. & Kuenzli, A. (2000). Aux confins de la systémique: Les points forts d'une approche collaborative. Thérapie Familiale. Vol. 21, no 1, pp. 33-41.

Kuenzli-Monard, F. A. & Kuenzli, A. (2000b). La psychothérapie de famille à la recherche d'une famille: Une crise d'identité aux Etats-Unis. Psychoscope. Vol. 4, no 1.

Kuenzli-Monard, F. (2001). Déconstruction des idées reçues sur la violence: Une alternative. Thérapie Familiale. Vol. 22, no 4, pp. 397-412.

Kuenzli-Monard, F. A. (2001b). "One only understand the things that one tames" Inviting reflexivity in the Therapy room. Copyrighted article Published on line. *Internet* http://www.hal-pc.org/~boha/oneonly.html

Kuenzli-Monard, F. (2005). Comment inviter la réflexivité ; en thérapie : la pensée pratique du psychothérapeute. *Submitted to Press.*

Kuenzli, F. (2005). Postmodernity and existencial based therapies toward a possible dialogue ? Copyrighted article Published on line.
*Internet* **http://www.hal-pc.org/~boha/postm.html**

Kvale, S. (1993). Postmodern Psychology: a contradiction in terms? In Kvale, S. (Ed.) Psychology and Postmodernism. Newbury Park, CA: Sage, pp. 31-57.

Kvale, S. (1996). Inter-Views: An introduction to qualitative research interviewing. Thousands Oaks, CA: Sage.

Lakoff, G. & Johnson, M. (1988). Metaphors we live by. Chicago: University of Chicago Press.

Lamb, B. & Huttlinger, K. (1989). Reflexivity in nursing research. Western Journal of Nursing Research. Vol. 11, no 6, pp. 765-772.

Lambert, M. J. & Bergin, A. E. (1994). The effectiveness of psychotherapy. In Bergin, A. E. & Garfield, S. L. (Eds.) Handbook of psychotherapy and behavior change. (4th ed.) New York: Wiley & Sons, pp. 664-700.

Lambert, M. J. (1989). The individual therapist's contribution to psychotherapy process and outcome. Clinical Psychology Review. Vol. 9, pp. 469-485.

Larner, G (1994). Para-modern family therapy: Deconstructing post-modernism. A. N. Z. Journal of Family Therapy. Vol. 15, no 1, pp. 11-16.

Larner, G (1995). The real as illusion: deconstructing power in Family Therapy. Journal of Family Therapy. Vol. 17, no 3, pp. 191-217.

Lask, B. (1987). Cybernetico-epistobabble, the emperor's new clothes and other sacred cows. Journal of Family Therapy. Vol. 9, pp. 207-215.

Lask, B. (1987). Jargon, ambiguity, pomposity, and other pests. Family Process. Vol. 26, no 3, pp. 396-397.

Lavender, T. (2003). Redressing the balance: the place, history and future of reflective practice in clinical training. Clinical Psychology. Vol. 27, July, pp. 11-15.

Lawson, H. (1985). Reflexivity: a postmodern predicament. La Salle, Il: Open Court.

Lax, W. D. (1992). Postmodern thinking in a clinical practice. In Mc Namee, S. & Gergen, K. J. (Eds.) Therapy as Social Construction. Thousand Oaks, CA: Sage, pp. 69-85.

Lax, W. D. (1996). Offering reflections: some theoretical and practical considerations. In Friedman, S. (Ed.) The reflecting process in action. New York: Guilford.

Leiper, R. & Kent, R. (2001). Working through setbacks in psychotherapy. Crisis, impasse, relapse. London: Sage.

Leitner, L. M. & Faidley, A. J. (1999). Creativity in experiential personal construct psychotherapy. Journal of constructivist psychology. Vol. 12, pp. 273-286.

Lincoln, Y. S. & Guba, E.G. (1990). Judging the quality of case study reports. International journal of qualitative studies in education. Vol. 3, pp. 53-59.

Lincoln, Y.S. & Guba, E.G. (1985). Naturalistic inquiry. Newbury Park, CA: Sage.

Lipson, J. G. (1994). Ethical issues in ethnography. In Morse, J. M. (Ed.) Issues in qualitative research methods. Thousand Oaks, CA: Sage, pp. 333-355.

Lowe, R. (1990). Re-imagining family therapy. Choosing the metaphors we live by. Australian & New Zealand Journal of Family Therapy. Vol. 11, pp. 1-9.

Lyotard, J. -F. (1979). La condition postmoderne: Rapport sur le savoir. Paris: Editions de Minuit. Série: Collection Critique.

Lyotard, J. -F. (1988). Jean-François Lyotard: Réecrire la modernité. Lille: Les Cahiers de la philosophie.

Mahrer, A. R. (1988). Discovery-oriented psychotherapy research: rationale, aims, and methods. American Psychologist. Vol. 43, no 9, pp. 694-702.

Maine de Biran, (1804/1929). The influence of habit on the faculty of thinking. Baltimore: Williams and Wilkins.

Manicas, P. T. & Second, P. F. (1983). Implications for psychology of the new philosophy of science. American Psychologist. Vol. 39, pp. 399-413.

Margolis, J. (1971). Values and conduct. New York: Oxford University Press.

Margolis, J. (1973). Knowledge and existence. New York: Oxford University Press.

Margolis, J. (1984). Philosophy of psychology. New York: Basil Blackwell.

Margolis, J. (1987). Science without unity: reconciling the human and the natural sciences. New York: Prentice-Hall.

Margolis, J. (1989). Texts without referents: reconciling science and narrative. New York: Basil Blackwell.

Marmar, C. R. (1990). Psychotherapy process research: Progress, dilemmas and future directions. Journal of Consulting and Clinical Psychology. Vol. 58, no 3, pp. 265-272.

Marshall, C. & Rossman, G. B. (1999). Designing qualitative research. 3rd Edition. Thousand Oaks, CA: Sage.

Maruyama, M. (1963). The second cybernetics: deviation-amplifying mutual causal processes. American Scientist. Vol. 51, pp. 164-179.

Maruyama, M. (1981). Endogenous research: rationale. In Reason, P. & Rowan, J. (Eds.) Human inquiry. A sourcebook of new paradigm research. New York: Wiley & Sons, pp. 227-238.

Masters, J. C. (1984). Psychology, research, and social policy. American Psychologist. Vol. 39, no 8, pp. 851-862.

Maturana, H & Varela, F. (1987). The tree of knowledge. Boston: New Science Library.

Mc Cracken, G. (1988). The long interview. Newbury Park, CA: Sage.

Mc Kinnon, K. L. & Miller, D. (1987). The new epistemology and the Milan approach: feminist and sociopolitical considerations. Journal of Marital and Family Therapy. Vol. 13, no 2, pp. 139-155.

Mc Leod, J. (1994). Doing counseling research. London: Sage.

Mc Leod, J. (1996). Qualitative approach to research in counseling and psychotherapy: issues and challenges. British of Journal Guidance and Counseling. Vol. 24, no 3, pp. 309-316.

Mc Leod, J. (1996). Qualitative research In Counseling Psychology. In Woolfe, R. & Dryden, W. (Eds.) Handbook of Counseling Psychology. pp. 65-86.

Mc Namee, S. & Gergen, K. J. (1992). Therapy as social construction. Newbury Park, CA: Sage.

Mc Name, S & Gergen, K. (1999). Relational responsibility. Resources for sustainable dialogue. Thousand Oaks, CA: Sage.

Miles, M. B. & Hubberman, A. M (1984). Qualitative data analysis: A sourcebook of new methods. Beverly Hills: Sage.

Miller, S. D. & Hubble, M. A & Duncan, B. L. (1995). Therapy under the glass: No more bells and whistles. Networker. March/April, pp. 53-63.

Miller, S. D., Duncan, B. L. & Hubble, M. A. (1997). Escaping from Babel. Toward a unifying language for psychotherapy practice. New York: Norton.

Minuchin, S. (1974). Families and family therapy. Cambridge, MA: Harvard University Press.

Minuchin, S. (1991). The seduction of constructivism, Networker. September/October, pp. 47-52.

Mishler, E. G. (1991) Representing discourse. The rhetoric of transcription. Journal of Narrative and Life History. Vol. 1, pp. 255-280.

Moon, S. M., Dillon, D. R. & Sprenkle, D. H. (1990). Family therapy and qualitative research. Journal of Marital and Family Therapy. Vol. 16, no 4, pp. 357-373.

Moon, S. M., Dillon, D. R. & Sprenkle, D. H. (1991). On balance and synergy: Family therapy and qualitative research revisited. Journal of Marital and Family Therapy. Vol. 17, no 2, pp. 187-192.

Morse, J. M. (1994). Qualitative research: Fact or fantasy? In Morse, J. M. (Ed.) Issues in Qualitative Research Methods. Thousand Oaks, CA: Sage, pp. 1-9.

Neimeyer, G. J. (Ed.) (1993). Constructivist assessment: a casebook. Counseling Psychologist Casebook Series. Vol. 2. Thousand Oaks, CA: Sage.

Neimeyer, R. A. & Feixas, G. (1990). Constructivist contributions to psychotherapy integration. Journal of Integrative and Eclectic Psychotherapy. Vol. 9, no 1.

Neimeyer, G. J. (1982). Qualitative strategies in counseling research. The Counseling Psychologist. Vol. 10, no 4, pp. 75-85.

Nystrom, D. & Pucket, K. (1998). Against bosses, against oligarchies: A conversation with Richard Rorty. Prickly Pear Pamphlets. Number Eleven.

O'Loughlin, S. (2003). Attending to the patient within us. Clinical Psychology. Vol. 27, July, pp. 24-26.

Odell, M. & Quinn, W. H. (1998). Therapist and client behaviors in the first interview: Effects on session impact and treatment duration. Journal of Marital and Family Therapy. Vol. 24, no 3, pp. 369-388.

Ogles, B. M., Lambert, M. J. & Fields, S. A. (2002). Essentials of outcome assessment. Wiley and Sons.

Orlinsky, D. E. & Howard, K. I. (1986). The psychological interior of psychotherapy: explorations with the therapy session's reports. In Greenberg, L. S. & Pinsof, W. M (Eds.) The Psychotherapeutic process: A research handbook. New York: Guilford, pp. 477-501.

Orlinsky, D. E. (1999). Ideal character or clinical fiction? Comments and questions on Jennings & Skovholt's "The cognitive, emotional, and relational characteristics of master therapists". Journal of Counseling Psychology. Vol. 46, no 1 pp. 12-16.

Papp, P. (1980). The Greek chorus and other techniques of Family therapy. Family Process. Vol. 19, no 1, pp. 45-58.

Paré, D. A. (1995). Of families and other cultures. The shifting paradigm of family therapy. Family Process. Vol. 34, no 1, pp. 1-19.

Paré, D. A. (1996). Culture and meaning: Expanding the metaphorical repertoire of family therapy. Family Process. Vol. 35, no 1, pp. 21-42.

Parlett, M. (1981). Illuminative evaluation. In Reason, P. & Rowan, J. (Eds.) Human inquiry. A sourcebook of new paradigm research. New York: Wiley & Sons, pp. 219-226.

Parry, A. (1991). A Universe of Stories. Family Process. Vol. 30, no 1, pp. 37-54.

Paula, C. (2003). Bubbles in a pound. Reflections in clinical practices. Clinical Psychology. Vol. 27, July, pp. 27-29.

Penn, P. & Frankfurt, M. (1994). Creating a participant text. Writing multiple voices, narrative multiplicity. Family Process. Vol. 33, no 2, pp. 217-231.

Piaget J. (1950). La construction du réel chez l'enfant. Neuchatel: Delachaux et Niestlé, Actualités Pédagogiques et Psychologiques.

Piaget J. (1956). Le langage et la pensée chez l'enfant. Préface de E. Claparède. Delachaux et Niestlé, Actualités Pédagogiques et Psychologiques.

Piaget, J. (1970). L'épistémologie Génétique. Paris: Presses Universitaires de France. Série: " Que sais-je", No. 1399.

Piaget J. (1974). La prise de conscience. Avec la collaboration de A. Blanchet. Paris: Presses Universitaires de France. Séries: Psychologie d'aujourd'hui.

Pinsof, W. M. & Wynne, L. C. (2000). Toward progress research: closing the gap between family therapy practice and research. Journal of Marital and Family Therapy. Vol. 26, no 1, pp. 1-8.

Pinsof, W. M. (1981). Family Therapy Process research. In Gurman A, & Kniskern, D. (Eds.) Handbook of Family Therapy. New York: Bruno Mazel, pp. 699-741.

Pinsof, W. M. (1989). A conceptual framework and methodological criteria for family therapy process research. Journal of Consulting and Clinical Psychology. Vol. 57, no 1, pp. 53-59.

Pinsof, W. M. (1995). The efficacy of marital and family therapy: an empirical overview, conclusions, and recommendations. Journal of Marital and Family Therapy. Vol. 21, no 4, pp. 586-613.

Polanyi, M. (1966). The Tacit dimension. New York: Doubleday.

Polkinghorne, D. E. (1984). Further extensions of methodological diversity for counseling psychology. Journal of Counseling Psychology. Vol. 31, no 4, pp. 416-429.

Polkinghorne, D. E. (1988). Narrative knowing and the human sciences. New York: Albany.

Polkinghorne, D. E. (1989). Phenomenological research methods. In Valle, R. S. & Halling, S. (Eds.) Existential-phenomenological perspectives in psychology. New York: Plenum, pp. 41-60.

Polkinghorne, D. E. (1991a). Qualitative Procedures for Counseling Research. In: Warkins, C. E. & Schneider, L. J. (Eds.) Research in Counseling. Hillsdale, NJ: Erlbaum, pp. 163-204.

Polkinghorne, D. E. (1991b). Postmodern epistemology of practice. In Kvale, S. (Ed.) Psychology and Postmodernism. pp. 146-165.

Polkinghorne, D. E. (1991c). Two Conflicting Calls for Methodological Reforms. The Counseling Psychologist. Vol. 19, no 1, pp. 103-114.

Polkinghorne, D. E. (1994). Reaction to a special section on qualitative research in counseling process and outcome. Journal of Counseling Psychology. Vol. 41, no 4, pp. 510-512.

Pope, K. S. & Tabachnick, B. G (1994). Therapists as patients: A national survey of psychologists' experiences problems and beliefs. professional psychology: Research and practice. Vol. 25, no 3, pp. 247-258.

Prigogène, I & Stengers, I. (1984). Order out of chaos: Man's new dialogue with nature. New York: Bantam Books.

Ramhoj, P. & Oliveira E. (1991). A phenomenological hermeneutic access to research of the old age area. Scandinavian Journal of Caring Science. Vol. 5, no 3, pp. 121-127.

Raskin, J. D. (1999a). Constructivism and the creative psychotherapist: a special issue of the Journal of Constructivist Psychology. Journal of Constructivist Psychology. Vol. 12, pp. 271-272.

Raskin, J. D. (1999b). Metaphors and meaning: Constructing the creative psychotherapist. Journal of Constructivist Psychology. Vol. 12, pp. 331-347.

Ray, M. A. (1994). The richness of phenomenology: Philosophic, theoretic, and methodological concerns. In Morse, J. M. (Ed.) Issues in qualitative research methods. Thousand Oaks, CA: Sage, pp. 117-135.

Real, T. (1990). The Therapeutic use of the self in constructionist, and systemic Therapy. Family Process. Vol. 29, no 3, pp. 255-272.

Reason, P. & Rowan, J. (Eds.) (1981). Human inquiry. A sourcebook of new paradigm research. New York: Wiley & Sons.

Reason, P. (1981). Issues of validity in new paradigm research. In Reason, P. & Rowan, J. (Eds.). Human inquiry. A sourcebook of new paradigm research. New York: John Wiley & Sons, pp. 239-250.

Reason, P. (1981). Methodological approaches to social science by Ian Mitroff and Ralph Killman: an appreciation. In Reason, P. & Rowan, J. (Eds.) Human inquiry. A sourcebook of new paradigm research. New York: Wiley & Sons, pp. 43-51.

Reason, P. (1981). On making sense. In Reason, P. & Rowan, J. (Eds.) Human inquiry. A sourcebook of new paradigm research. New York: Wiley & Sons, pp. 113-137.

Rennie, D. & Toukmanian, S. G. (1992). Explanation in psychotherapy process research. In Toukmananian, S. G. (Ed.) Explanation in psychotherapy process research. Paradigmatic and narrative approaches. Thousand Oaks, CA: Sage, pp. 235-251.

Rennie, D. (1992). Qualitative analysis of the client's experience of psychotherapy. The unfolding of reflexivity. In Toukmananian, S. G. & Rennie D. (Eds.) Psychotherapy process research. Paradigmatic and narrative approaches. Vol. 143, pp. 211-233. Thousand Oaks, CA: Sage.

Rennie, D. (1994). Human science and counseling: Closing the gap between research and practice. Counseling Psychology Quarterly. Vol. 7, pp. 235-250.

Rennie, D. (1996). Fifteen years of doing qualitative research in psychotherapy. British Journal of Guidance and Counseling, Vol. 24, no 3, pp. 317-327.

Resnick, R. (1999). Gestalt therapy and contact. Lecture at the GATLA. (Unpublished paper.)

Rice, L. M. & Greenberg, L. S. (1984). The new research paradigm. In Rice, L. M. & Greenberg, L. S. (Eds.) Patterns of change: Intensive analysis of psychotherapy process. New York: Guilford, pp. 7-25.

Ricoeur, P. (1983). Temps et récit. Paris: Seuil.

Rist, R. (1977). On the relationship among educational research paradigms: from disdain to "détente". Anthropology and Educational Quarterly. Vol. 8, pp. 42-49.

Rober, P. (1997). Nouvelles métaphores en thérapie familiale: de la cybernétique au paradigme narratif. Cahiers critiques de thérapies et de pratiques de réseaux. Constructivisme et constructionisme social. Vol. 19, pp. 27-55.

Rober, P. (1999). The therapist's inner conversation in family therapy practice: Some ideas about the self of the therapist, therapeutic impasse, and the process of reflection. Family Process. Vol. 38, no 2, pp. 209-229.

Rogers, C. R. (1942). Counseling and psychotherapy. Newer concepts in practice. By Carl Rogers. Boston: Houghton Mifflin Company.

Rorty, R. (1979). Philosophy and the mirror of nature. Princeton, NJ: Princeton University Press.

Rorty, R. (1989). Contingency, irony and solidarity. Cambridge, MA: Cambridge University Press.

Rorty, R. (1998). Truth and progress. Cambridge, MA: University Press.

Rosen, S. (1982). My voice will go with you. The teaching tales of Milton H. Erickson. New York: Norton.

Rowan, J. (1981). Illuminative evaluation. In Reason, P. & Rowan, J. (Eds.) Human inquiry. A sourcebook of new paradigm research. New York: Wiley & Sons, pp. 113-137.

Sandelowsky, M. (1994). The proof is in the pottery: Toward a poetic for qualitative inquiry. In Morse, J. M. (Ed.) Issues in qualitative research methods. Thousand Oaks, CA: Sage, pp. 47-65.

Satir, V. (1983). Conjoint family therapy. Palo Alto, CA: Science and Behavior Books.

Schachter, D. L. & Scarry, E. (Eds.) (2000). Memory, brain and belief. Cambridge, MA: First Harvard University Press.

Schacter, D. L. (1987) Implicit Memory: History and current status. Journal of Experimental Psychology: Learning Memory and Cognition. Vol. 13, no 3, pp. 501-518.

Schacter, D. L. (1994). Memory Systems. Boston: Bradford Book.

Schacter, D. L. (1996). Searching for memory. The brain the mind and the past. New York: Basic Books.

Schacter, D. L. (2001a). The seven sins of memory: How the mind forgets and remembers. Boston: Houghton Mifflin Books.

Schacter, D. L. (2001b). Forgotten ideas, neglected pioneers: Richard Semon and the story of memory. Harvard: Psychology Press.

Schön, D. A. (1983). The reflective practitioner: How professionals think in action? Basic Books.

Schön, D. A. (1987). Educating the reflective practitioner. Oxford: Jossey Bass.

Schutz, A. (1964). Collected papers. Studies in social theories. The Hague, IL: Martinus Nijhoff.

Schutz, A. (1967). The phenomenology of the social world. (Walsh, G. & Lehnert, F. Trans.) The Hague, Il: Northwestern University Press.

Schwartz, R. C. & Breulin, D. (1983). Research: Why clinicians should bother with it. Networker, pp. 23-27 & 57-59.

Schwartzman, J. (1984). Family theory and the scientific method. Family Process. Vol. 2, no 2, pp. 223-236.

Seidman, I.E. (1991). Interviewing as qualitative research. A guide for researchers in education and the social sciences. New York: Columbia University: Teachers College Press.

Selekman, M. D. (1997). Solution-Focused therapy with Children: Harnessing family strengths for systemic change. New York: Guilford.

Selvini-Palazzoli, M., Boscolo, L., Cecchin, G. et al. (1978). Paradox and counterparadox. New York: Jason Aronson.

Selvini-Palazzoli, M., Boscolo, L., Cecchin, G. et al. (1980a). Hypothesizing-circularity-neutrality: three guidelines for the conductor of the session. Family Process, Vol.19, pp. 3-12.

Selvini-Palazzoli, M., Boscolo, L., Cecchin, G., et al. (1980b). The problem of the referring person. Journal of Marital and family Therapy. Vol. 6, pp. 3-9.

Shadish, W. R., Ragsdale, K., Glaser, R. R et al. (1995). The efficacy of effectiveness of marital and family therapy: A perspective from meta-analysis. Journal of Marital and Family Therapy. Vol. 21, no 4, pp. 345-360.

Sherry, D. F. & Schachter D. L. (1987). The evolution of multiple memory systems. Psychological Review. Vol. 94, pp. 439-454.

Shoham, Salomon, V. (1990). Interrelating research process of process research. Journal of Consulting and Clinical Psychology. Vol. 58, no 3, pp. 295-303.

Shotter, J & Gergen, K. J. (1989). Texts of identity. London: Sage.

Shotter, J. (1993). Conversational realities. constructing life through language. Thousand Oaks, CA: Sage.

Siegel, D. J. (1999). The developing mind: how relationships and the brain interact to shape who we are. New York: Guilford.

Siegel, D. J. (2001). Toward an interpersonal neurobiology of the developing mind: attachment, "mindsight" and neural integration. Infant Mental Health Journal. Vol. 22, pp. 67-96.

Siegel, D. J. (2003). Attachment and self-understanding: Parenting with the brain in mind. Unpublished Paper. UCLA, School of Medicine Foundation for the Psycho-cultural Research, Los Angeles

Siegel, D. J. and Hartzell, M. (2003). Parenting from the inside out: How a deeper self-understanding can help you raise children who thrive. New York: Penguin Putnam.

Simon, R. (1985). A frog's eye view of the world. An interview with Humberto Maturana. Networker. May/June, pp. 32-43.

Sluzki, C. E. (1985). A minimal map of cybernetics. Networker. May/June, p. 26.

Sluzki, C. E. (1987). Bird talk sacred talk criminal talk: On jargon. Family Process. Vol. 26, no 3, p. 395.

Smith, J. K. & Heshusius, L. (1986). Closing down the conversation: The end of the quantitative qualitative debate among educational inquirers. Educational Researcher, Vol. 15, pp. 4-12.

Solomon, M. F., Neborsky, R. J. et al. (2001). Short-term therapy for long term change. New York: Norton.

Speed, B. (1984). How really real is real? Family Process. Vol. 23, no 4, pp. 511-517.

Speed, B. (1987). Over the top in the theory and practice of Family Therapy. Journal of Family Therapy. Vol. 9, no 4, pp. 231-240.

Speed, B. (1991). "Reality exists, OK". Journal of Family Therapy. Vol. 13, pp. 395-409.

Speed, B. (1999). Individuals in Context and Contexts in Individuals. A. N. Z. Family Therapy. Vol. 20, no 3, pp. 131-138.

Spradley, J. (1979). The ethnographic interview. New York: Holt Rinehard & Winston.

Sprenkle, D. H. (1991). Editor's introduction. Journal of Marital and Family Therapy. Vol. 17, no 2, pp. 173-174.

Sprenkle, D. H. (1994). Editorial: The role of qualitative research and a few suggestions for aspiring authors. Journal of Marital and Family Therapy. Vol. 20, no 3, pp. 227-229.

Squire, L. R. & Zola-Morgan, S. (1991). The medial temporal lobe memory system. Science. Vol. 253, pp. 2380-2386.

Squire, L. R. (1987). Memory and Brain. Oxford, UK: Oxford University Press.

Squire, L. R. (1994). Declarative and non-declarative memory. Multiple brain systems supporting learning and memory. In Schacter, D. L. & Tulving, E. (Eds.) Memory systems. Cambridge, MA: MIT Press.

Stanton, D. (1984). Fusion, compression, diversion and the workings of paradox: A theory of therapeutic/systemic change. Family Process. Vol. 23, no 2, pp. 135-168.

Stedmon, J., Mitchell, A., Johnstone, L., et al. (2003). Making reflective practice real: Problems and solutions in the South West. Clinical Psychology. Vol. 27, July, pp. 30-33.

Steier, F. (1985). Toward a cybernetic methodology of family therapy research: Fitting research methods to family practice. In Andreozzi, L. L. (Ed.) Integrating Research and clinical practice. Rockville, MD: Aspen, pp. 27-36.

Sterlin, R. C. (1987). Hypothesis, Testing, Theory building, and the philosophy of science. Journal of Counseling Psychology. Vol. 34, pp. 365-371.

Stern, D. N. (1995). The motherhood constellation. New York: Basic Books.

Stiles, W. B. & Honos-Webb, L. & Surko, M. (1998). Responsiveness in psychotherapy. Clinical Psychology: Science and Practice. American Psychological Association. Vol. 5, no 4, pp. 439-458.

Strauss, A & Corbin, J. (1990). Basics of qualitative research: Grounded theory procedures and techniques. Newbury Park, CA: Sage.

Strupp, H. H. , Horowitz, L. M. & Lambert, M. J. (1997a). Measuring patient changes: In Mood, anxiety and personality disorders. American Psychological Association Press.

Strupp, H. H. & Anderson, T. (1997b). On the limitations of Therapy manuals. Clinical Psychology, Science and Practice. (American Psychological Association). Vol. 4, no 1, pp. 76-82.

Strupp, H. H. (1981). Clinical research, practice and the crisis of confidence. Journal of Consulting and Clinical Psychology. Vol. 49, no 2, pp. 216-219.

Strupp, H. H. (1993). The Vanderbilt psychotherapy studies: Synopsis. Journal of Consulting and Clinical Psychology. Vol. 61, no 3, pp. 431-433.

Szasz, T. (1970). Ideology and Insanity. New York: Anchor.

Taggart, M. (1985). The Feminist critique in epistemological perspective: Questions of context in family therapy. Journal of Marital and Family Therapy. Vol. 11, no 2, pp. 133-126.

Tomm, K. (1983). The old hat doesn't fit. Networker. July-August, pp. 39-42.

Tomm, K. (1987). Interventive interviewing: part II. Reflexive questioning as a mean to enable self-healing. Family Process. Vol. 26, no 2, pp. 167-183.

Tomm, K. (1988). Interventive interviewing: part III. Intending to ask linear, circular, strategic or reflexive questioning? Family Process. Vol. 27, no1, pp. 1-15.

Tomm, K. (1991). Ethical postures that orient one's clinical decision making (reported by Bernstein, A.) Newsletter of the American family therapy association. Vol. 41, pp. 13-15.

Toukmananian, S. G. & Rennie, D. L. (1992). Psychotherapy, Process, Research, Paradigmatic and Narrative Approaches. Newbury: Sage.

Tripp-Reimer, T. (1983). Retention of a folk healing practice (matiasma) among four generations of urban Greek immigrants. Nursing Research. Vol. 32, no 1, pp. 97-101.

Tripp-Reiner, T., Sorofman, B.,Peters, J. et al. (1994). Research teams: Possibilities and pitfalls in collaborative qualitative research. In Morse, J. M. (Ed.) Issues in Qualitative Research Methods. Thousand Oaks, CA: Sage, pp. 319-331.

Tulving, E. (1999). Memory, consciousness and the brain: The Tallinn Conference. In Tulving E. (Ed.) Portland, Or: Taylor and Francis, Book News.

Tulving, E. (2000). The Oxford handbook of memory. In Tulving E. and Craik. F. (Eds.) Oxford University Press.

Varela, F. J. (1989). Reflections on the circulation of concepts between biology of cognition and systemic family therapy. Family Process. Vol. 28, no 1, pp. 15-24.

Von Foerster, H. (1984). On constructing a reality. In Watzlawick, P. (Ed.) The invented reality. New York: Norton.

Von Glaserfeld. (1984). An introduction to radical constructivism. In Watzlawick, P. (Ed.) The invented reality. New York: Norton.

Vygotsky, L. S. (1962). Thought and language. (Hanfman, E & Vakar, G. Trans.) Cambridge, MA: MIT Press. (Original work published in 1934).

Vygotsky, L. S. (1966). Development of the higher mental functions. In Leont'ev, A. N, Luria, A. R. & Smirnov, A (Eds.) Psychological research in the USSR. Moscow: Progress Publishers.

Vygotsky, L. S. (1986). Thought and language. (Rev. Ed.) (Kozulin, A. Trans.) Cambridge, MA: MIT Press. (Original work published in 1934, Norton)

Wacherhauser, B. R. (1986). Hermeneutics and modern philosophy. New York: University of New York Press.

Wangberg, F. (1991). Self-reflection: Turning the mirror inward. Journal of Strategic and Systemic Therapies. Vol. 10, no 3-4, pp. 18-29.

Warkins, C. E. & Schneider, L. J. (Eds.) Research in Counseling. Hillsdale, NJ: Erlbaum.

Watson, J. B. (1920). Is thinking merely the action of language mechanisms? British Journal of Psychology. Vol. 11, pp. 87-104.

Watson, W. H. (1991). The generic recursive epistobabble generator (G.R.E.G.). Journal of Marital and Family Therapy. Vol. 17, no 2, pp. 201-202.

Watzlawick, P., Beavin Bavelas, J. & Jackson, D. D. (1967). Pragmatic of human communication. New York: Norton.

Watzlawick, P. (1984). The invented reality. New York: Norton.

Watzlawick, P., Weakland, J. & Fisch, R. (1974). Change. Principles of problem formation and problem resolution. New York: Norton.

Webb, R. E. & Restucca, K. A. (1998). Truth, lies and wondering. Journal of Constructivist Psychology. Vol. 11, pp. 117-132.

Weiner, N. (1948). Cybernetics or control and communication in the animal and the machines. New York: Wiley.

Weingarten, K. (1991). The discourse of intimacy: adding a social constructionist and feminist view. Family Process. Vol. 30, no 2, pp. 285-305.

Weingarten, K. (1995). Cultural resistance: Challenging beliefs about men, woman and therapy. New York: Harrington Park Press.

White M. (1986). Negative explanation, restraint and double description: a template for family therapy. Family Process. Vol. 25, no 2, pp. 169-184.

White, M. & Epston, D. (1990). Narrative means to therapeutic ends. New York: Norton.

White, M. (1987). Family therapy and schizophrenia: addressing the in-the-corner lifestyle. Dulwich Centre Newsletter, Vol. 16, pp. 14-21.

White, M. (1988a). Anorexia nervosa: a cybernetic perspective. In Harkaway, J. E. (Ed.) Eating disorders. pp. 117-129.

White, M. (1988b). The process of questioning A therapy of literary merit? Dulwich Centre Newsletter, no 1, pp. 8-14.

White, M. (1989). Selected papers. Adelaide: Dulwich Centre Publications.

White, M. (1991). Deconstruction and therapy. Dulwich Centre Newsletter. No.3. Adelaide: Dulwich Centre Publications.

White, M. (1995). Re-authoring lives: interviews & essays. Adelaide: Dulwich Centre publications.

Wilder, C. (1982) Muddles & metaphors: a response to Keeney and Sprenkle. Family Process. Vol. 21, pp. 397-400.

Winslade, J & Monk, G. (1999). Narrative counseling in schools. Sage, Corwin Press.

Winslade, J. (1997). The archeology of hope. Thousand Oaks, CA: Sage.

Wittgenstein, L. (1969). On certainty. Anscombe, G. E. M. & von Wright, G. H. (Ed.) New York: Harper Torchbooks.

Wolcott, H.F. (1990). Writing up qualitative research. London: Sage.

Wolcott, H.F. (1994). Transforming qualitative data. Description, analysis and interpretation. Thousand Oaks, CA: Sage.

Worthen, V. & McNeill, B. W. (1996). A phenomenological investigation of "good" supervision events. Journal of Counseling Psychology. Vol. 43, no 1, pp. 25-34.

Wundt, W.M. (1832-1920). Elements of folk psychology, outlines and a psychological history of the development of mankind. (By Wilhelm Wundt. Authorized trans. E. L. Schaub. London: Allen & Unwin). New York: Mac Millan compagny (1916).

Wynne, L. C. (1983). Family research and family therapy: A reunion? Journal of Marital and Family Therapy. Vol. 9, no 2, pp. 113-117.

Wynne, L. C. (1984). The epigenesis of relational systems: A model for understanding family development. Family Process. Vol. 23, no 3 pp. 297-318.

Wynne, L. C., Mc Daniel, S. H. Weber, T. T. (1987). Professional politics and the concepts of family therapy, family consultation, and systems consultation. Family Process. Vol. 26, no 2 pp. 153-166.

Yalom, I. D. (1974). Ever day gets a little closer. A twice told therapy. New York: Basic Books.

Yalom, I. D. (1989). Love's executioner and other tales of psychotherapy. New York: Basic Books.

Yalom, I. D. (1992). When Nietsche wept. New York: Basic Books.

Yalom, I. D. (2000). Momma and the meaning of life. Tales of psychotherapy. New York: Harper Collins.

Yalom, I. D. (2002). The gift of therapy. An open letter to a new generation of therapists and their patients. New York: Harper Collins.

Yin, R. K. (1989) Case study research design and methods. (Second edition). Newbury Park, CA: Sage.

Zichi-Cohen, M. & Omery, A. (1994). Schools of phenomenology: implications for research. In Morse, J. M. (Ed.) Issues in qualitative research methods. Thousand Oaks, CA: Sage, pp. 136-156.

Zinberg, N. (1987). Elements of the private therapeutic interview. American Journal of Psychiatry. Vol. 144, no 12, pp. 1527-1533.

## Other sources of reference

Berg, I. K. (1994a). From problem solving to solution building. Garden Grove, CA: Infomedix. (Audiocassette).

Berg, I. K. (1994b). Supervision. Garden Grove, CA: Infomedix. (Audiocassette).

De Shazer, S. (1994a). Numbers are magic. Garden Grove, CA: Infomedix. (Audiocassette).

Gergen, K. J. (1993a). Social constructivism and postmodern possibilities. Boulder, Co: Perpetual motion unlimited. (Audiocassette).

Gergen, K. J. (1993b). Conflict and change in a pluralistic world. Boulder, CO: Perpetual Motion Unlimited. (Audiocassette).

Gergen, K. J. (1994a). Between alienation and deconstruction: revisioning therapeutic communication. Garden Grove, Ca: Infomedix. (Audiocassette).

O'Hanlon, W. H. (1994a). Brief solution & narrative therapies: a primer on the post-modern view of psychotherapy. Garden Grove, CA: Infomedix. (Audiocassette).

O'Hanlon, W. H. (1994a). Brief solution & narrative therapies: a primer on the post-modern view of psychotherapy. Garden Grove, CA: Infomedix. (Audiocassette).

O'Hanlon, W. H. (1994b). No guru, no teacher, no method, if you meet Erikson on the road kill him. Garden Grove, CA: Infomedix. (Audiocassette).

Evolution of Psychotherapy. A conference. Milton Erickson Foundation. May 1995, Las Vegas, Nevada, USA.

Evolution of Psychotherapy: A Conference. Milton Erickson Foundation. May 2000, Anaheim, USA.

# Index